#LANGUAGE HACKING

A CONVERSATION COURSE
FOR BEGINNERS

GERMAN

> *Learn how to speak German*
> *– with actual people –*
> *right from the start!*

BENNY LEWIS
THE IRISH POLYGLOT

First published in Great Britain in 2016 by Hodder and Stoughton. An Hachette UK company.
First published in US 2016 by Quercus.
This edition published in 2016 by John Murray Learning
Copyright © Brendan Lewis 2016
The right of Brendan (Benny) Lewis to be identified as the Author of the Work has been
asserted by her in accordance with the Copyright, Designs and Patents Act 1988.
Database right Hodder & Stoughton (makers)
The Teach Yourself name is a registered trademark of Hachette UK.

British Library Cataloguing in Publication Data: a catalogue record for this title is available
from the British Library.

Library of Congress Catalog Card Number: on file.

9781473633155
3

The publisher has used its best endeavours to ensure that any website addresses referred to
in this book are correct and active at the time of going to press. However, the publisher and
the author have no responsibility for the websites and can make no guarantee that a site
will remain live or that the content will remain relevant, decent or appropriate.

The publisher has made every effort to mark as such all words which it believes to be
trademarks. The publisher should also like to make it clear that the presence of a word in
the book, whether marked or unmarked, in no way affects its legal status as a trademark.

Every reasonable effort has been made by the publisher to trace the copyright holders
of material in this book. Any errors or omissions should be notified in writing to the
publisher, who will endeavour to rectify the situation for any reprints and future editions.

Cover image © Allison Hooban
Illustrations © Will McPhail
Typeset by Integra
Printed and bound by Clays Ltd, St Ives plc

John Murray Learning policy is to use papers that are natural, renewable and recyclable
products and made from wood grown in sustainable forests. The logging and
manufacturing processes are expected to conform to the environmental regulations of the
country of origin.

Carmelite House
50 Victoria Embankment
London EC4Y 0DZ
www.hodder.co.uk

YOUR MISSIONS

A NOTE FROM BENNY

It's true that some people spend years studying German before they finally get around to speaking the language.

But I have a better idea.

Let's skip the years of studying and jump right to the speaking part.

Sound crazy? No, it's language hacking.

#LanguageHacking is a completely different approach to learning a new language.

It's not magic. It's not something only 'other people' can do. It's simply about being smart with *how* you learn: learning what's indispensable, skipping what's not, and using what you've learned to have real conversations in German right away.

As a language hacker, I find shortcuts to learning new languages – tricks and techniques to crack the language code and make learning simple so I can get fluent faster. When it comes to learning new languages, I focus on getting the biggest bang for my buck.

There's no need to learn every word and grammar rule before you start using the language. You just need to know *the most common* and *the most versatile* phrases you'll need in most situations, and how to 'speak around' the problem when there's something you don't understand or know how to say yet.

#LanguageHacking isn't just a course. It's a new way of thinking about language learning. It shows you how to learn a language as well as gives you all the language you need – and none of what you don't. You can use it on your own or with any other book to start speaking languages faster.

I'd like to show you how it's done. See you on the inside.

Benny

Benny Lewis, Language Hacker

HOW TO USE THIS COURSE

The most common complaint I hear from learners of German is:

'I studied German for years in school. I can understand a few words when I see them, and even sometimes when I hear them, but I still can't speak the language.'

#LanguageHacking isn't like traditional grammar-based courses. It's a *conversation* course, which means you will focus on building the language skills you need to have meaningful, real-life conversations with other people in German – right away.

By the end of this course, you'll be able to introduce yourself and ask and answer hundreds of typical questions in German. You'll know how to find and connect with other German speakers no matter where you live. And you'll gain the skills and strategies to have countless conversations entirely in German – as well as the confidence to keep them going.

#LanguageHacking can be used either on its own or alongside any other language course, whether written, online, or in the classroom.

WHAT YOU'LL FIND INSIDE

This course will challenge you to *speak from day one* by completing ten missions, which will grow your conversational abilities in German. To keep that promise, I invite you to become a part of the language hacking community, built with this course in mind, that gives you a safe and fun place to communicate with other like-minded and determined learners. You can complete the missions on your own, but you'll progress much faster if you use the language with real people, so I encourage you to submit your missions to the *#LanguageHacking* online community www.teachyourself.com/languagehacking for feedback (and secret mini-missions).

SPEAKING FROM DAY 1

You can't learn to play the piano until you sit down and put your fingers on the keys. You can't play tennis until you pick up the racquet. And you can't learn a language if you don't speak it. By speaking from day one, you will:

- pick up expressions and language from others
- notice the expression gaps in your language you need to fill
- become aware of how other people say things
- get feedback from others
- improve your pronunciation and fluency
- conquer the fear of speaking a new language
- feel motivated by hearing your own progress.

BUILD YOUR LANGUAGE SKILLS

Build language through typical conversations

Each unit takes you through three *conversations* in German that show you how the language is used in common, everyday contexts. The conversations build on each other to grow your vocab and prepare you for your mission. Treat each conversation like a lesson, and make sure you understand everything before you move on to the next conversation.

Figure it out exercises

You'll read each conversation and listen to the audio, then I'll help you *figure it out*. These exercises train you to start understanding German on your own – through context, recognizing patterns, and applying other language learning strategies – without relying on translations. By figuring out language for yourself, you'll internalize it better and recall it faster when you need it.

Notice exercises

Every conversation is followed by a *phrase list* with the key phrases, expressions, and vocab to know from that conversation, with English translations and pronunciation to help you. *Notice* exercises get you thinking about the new language and noticing how the language works, so you're gaining an intuitive understanding of German.

Practice exercises

Practice exercises reinforce what you learn. You'll piece together different parts of what you know to figure out how to create new German phrases on your own.

Put it together

Finally, you'll take everything you've learned and *put it together* to create your own repertoire in German. I'll help you prepare 'me-specific' language you can use in real life conversations – language that's actually relevant to you.

SUPPORT, TECHNIQUES AND STRATEGIES

In language hacking, your ability to have conversations in German is not limited by the number of words you know.

#languagehacks

You'll *learn unconventional shortcuts* to boost your language abilities exponentially. I reveal the different patterns, rules and tools to help you *crack the code and get fluent faster.* Each of the ten hacks equips you with techniques you can use in this course and throughout the rest of your learning journey.

Conversation strategies

You'll learn essential conversation strategies, like *conversation connectors, filler words, and survival phrases* to strike up conversations and keep them flowing.

Grammar and pronunciation

We'll cover the foundation of the *grammar you need to know*, but I won't overload you with what's not essential to communication. I'll help you understand the important parts of German *pronunciation* and share techniques to help you get them right.

Side notes

I'll share more insights as we go along – like culture tips about German speakers and German-speaking countries, vocab tips on how to get creative with new phrases, and mini-hacks for better learning.

Progress you can see

You will see your progress build steadily throughout this course. Before you finish each unit, you'll *check your understanding* with audio practice that acts as a 'virtual conversation partner'. This practice gives you time to collect your thoughts and speak at your own pace.

Before you move on to your mission, you'll do a *self assessment checklist* to make sure you're prepared and to keep a visual record of the progress you're making.

MISSIONS

Each unit ends with *three tasks* that you'll complete as your final mission.

STEP 1: build your script

To get ready for spoken practice with other people, you'll build 'me-specific' scripts with the language you need to talk about your life. These scripts make sure you're learning useful German phrases that are truly relevant to you.

As you go along, you may develop your own shortcuts for making learning simple. If you do, share them with others and me, and use the hashtag #languagehacking.

You don't need to learn all the grammar. A lot of the time you can learn language in 'chunks' – the same way you learned your native language. You learned to say 'there it is' before you ever understood what each individual word meant on its own ... and you still got your point across.

STEP 2: speak German with other people ... *online*

Speaking from day one is the best way I've found to quickly reach fluency. I'll help you implement this strategy, no matter where you live, with the missions you'll complete as part of the language hacking community.

You'll record yourself speaking your scripts aloud in German and upload them to the community where you'll get feedback from other learners and keep the conversation going. This is the best practice you can get – aside from one-to-one conversations with a native speaker. By speaking in front of others you'll become more confident using German in the real world.

STEP 3: learn from other learners

When you share your missions with other learners, you'll get more comfortable speaking German – and more importantly, you'll get comfortable speaking the imperfect beginner's German that everyone must use on the road to fluency. You'll gain insight into how conversations flow in German, and you'll learn where the 'expression gaps' are in your scripts that you need to fill to expand your conversation skills.

In other words, you'll have everything you need to genuinely start having conversations with other people in German. After all, isn't that the point?

Let's get started.

WHAT YOU'LL FIND ONLINE

Go to www.teachyourself.com/languagehacking to:

···⫶ Submit your missions
···⫶ Download the course audio
···⫶ Find an up-to-date list of the best free online resources to support your learning
···⫶ Review the transcripts for the audio
···⫶ Discover additional materials to help you on your learning journey
···⫶ Find out more about #LanguageHacking and Benny Lewis

Check back frequently as we add new cool language hacking features.

THE LANGUAGE HACKER CONTRACT

In this course you will:

···⋮ **get shortcuts (#languagehacks)** to learn a new *Sprache* fast
···⋮ **learn the words and phrases you need** to have real conversations immediately
···⋮ **gain the confidence** to start speaking *Deutsch* from day one
···⋮ **have access** to a *Gruppe* of like-minded language learners

That's my side of the bargain. It's what I'm giving you.

Now here's your side of the contract. I recommend you read it every day so it embeds in your memory and becomes part of who you are.

I will speak German today and every day – if only a little. It will feel awkward and uncomfortable at times. And that's okay.

I will accept that the only way to speak perfectly is to first make mistakes. The only way to overcome my fear is to face it. The only thing preventing me from speaking German is ... speaking German.

I will embrace my inner Tarzan. I will say things in German like 'I Benny. Me writer. I Ireland.' I'll do this because I'm still learning, and because I don't take myself too seriously. I will communicate effectively instead of perfectly. Over time, I will make massive leaps.

I will build 'me-specific' scripts – mini monologues about myself. I will memorize these scripts and rely on them whenever I'm asked questions. I will discover time and time again that I can manage the most common situations I come across in a new language. I will quickly feel my confidence build as I equip myself with the language I need.

I will speak at every opportunity and be an active participant in the language hacking community. I will learn from giving and getting feedback.

I will build my skills, day by day, piece by piece.

I will learn smarter. I will be self-sufficient. I will make learning German part of my daily routine. I will become fluent faster than I ever imagined possible.

I am a language hacker.

Sign here: _____   *Date:* _____

PRONUNCIATION GUIDE

German is a phonetic language, which means that each letter, or letter combination follows the same rule all the time.

Most letters are pronounced as you'd expect, but here's a quick overview of some key rules to keep in mind. Use the native recordings provided to train your ear and tongue to the sounds!

CONSONANTS

◀)) 00.01 Most consonants in German are similar to those in English, but here are the noteworthy exceptions.

Seen in	Sounds like	Examples
j	'y'	ja
ch (after 'a', 'o', 'u')	Guttural sound like the 'ch' in the Scottish loch	Buch
ch (otherwise)	Like the 'h' in the name 'Hugh'	ich
r	Sound from the back of the throat. Can be similar to guttural 'ch'.	Reise
s (start of word)	'z'	sehen
s (end of word)	's'	Haus
ß	's'	heiße
z	'ts' (like in 'tsunami' or 'cats')	Zeit
v	'f'	Vater
w	'v'	weil

VOWELS

◀)) 00.02 Here are some important rules and new letters to keep in mind.

Seen in	Explanation	Examples
ä	'eh'	nächste
ö	'er'	schön
ü	Purse your lips, as if to say 'oo', and try to say 'ee' instead	für
au	Like the 'ou' sound in 'loud'	aus
ei	same sound as the word 'eye'	leider
ie	'ee'	Familie

1 TALKING ABOUT ME

Your mission

Imagine this – you've just arrived in Germany. You step up to get your passport checked, and the agent asks you about yourself.

Your mission is to convince the agent to let you through. Be brave and say *hallo* in German. Then have a basic exchange – entirely in German – for 30 seconds. Be prepared to **say your name**, **where you're from**, **where you live**, **why you're coming to Germany**, and especially **why you're learning German**.

This mission will prepare you for the inevitable questions you'll be asked in any first conversation you have in German.

Mission prep

⋯⟩ Learn basic phrases for talking about yourself: *ich bin …*
⋯⟩ Develop a conversation strategy: turn the tables and ask questions with: *Und du?*
⋯⟩ Learn the words for countries, professions and interests.
⋯⟩ Create simple sentences to talk about your likes and wants, using *ich möchte*, *gern*.
⋯⟩ Learn the connector words *und*, *aber*, *weil*, *oder*.

BUILDING SCRIPTS

Most first conversations in a new language are predictable. As a beginner, this is great news for you. We're going to start by building your first 'script' to help you prepare for what you'll need to say most, right away. We'll start slow and build as we move on.

If you've studied German before, some of the words in this unit may be familiar to you. But we'll be doing much more than just learning words in each unit: we're going to start building scripts. Once you learn a script, you can customize it to your needs. This will help you build your language so you can use it from the start.

#LANGUAGEHACK
get a head start with words you already know

CONVERSATION 1

The first words you'll use in every conversation

PRONUNCIATION: *ch*
The German *ch* is a new sound we don't use in English. You can get quite close to it with the starting sound of the name 'Hugh'. Or you can start by pronouncing it as a soft 'sh' for now.

Let's follow the story of Ellen, a German learner who has just arrived in Berlin to spend the summer immersing herself in German while working as a designer. She signs up for an in-person German class, and today she's meeting her teacher, Peter, for the first time.

◀)) 01.01 This is a typical introductory conversation – one you'll have yourself over and over. Listen to the way Ellen asks *Und du?*

> **Ellen:** Hallo! Ich bin Ellen. Und du?
>
> **Peter:** Hallo! Ich bin Peter. Also, ich komme aus Deutschland. Ich bin Lehrer und wohne in Berlin. Und du?
>
> **Ellen:** Ich komme aus England. Aber ich wohne hier in Berlin. Und ich bin Designerin.
>
> **Peter:** Wie interessant!

CULTURE TIP:
how are you?
In keeping with their natural frankness, Germans don't always bother with small talk. If a German asks *Wie geht's?* (how are you?) it's because they genuinely want to know. And when you ask a German speaker *Wie geht's?* don't be surprised if they start describing any recent luck or misfortunes they've had!

When you see or hear new German words for the first time, they may seem like random noise. But if you train yourself to look and listen a little closer, you'll realize there's a lot you can figure out based on the context of the conversation and how the words relate to English. The key is to try to notice the language for yourself.

As a beginner, you need to build towards an introductory conversation as your first step. After an initial greeting, a conversation will usually be about what you do and where you live.

Time to think about the conversation you just heard! Notice how German sentence structure differs from English. The more you actively think about German word order and expressions, the faster you'll learn.

FIGURE IT OUT

1 Based on the context of the conversation, what does *ich bin* mean?

_____

2 What do you think *du* means? _____

3 Find the German word that answers each question, and write it out.

Example: **Where is Peter from?** Deutschland _____

a What's Ellen's job? _____

b Where is she from? _____

c Where does Ellen live? _____

4 What phrase do Peter and Ellen use to say 'I come from ...'?

a Highlight it, then write it here. _____
b Can you guess how to say 'I come from America'? (*Amerika*) or 'I come from Canada'? (*Kanada*). Write it here.

_____

5 What phrase does Ellen use to bounce the question back to Peter? Highlight it, then write it here. What do you think it means?

_____

NOTICE

🔊 **01.02** Listen to the audio and study the table.

Essential phrases for Conversation 1

German	Meaning
Hallo! Ich bin ...	Hello. I am ...
Und du?	And you?
Also, ...	So, ...
Ich komme aus ...	I come from ...
Deutschland	Germany
Aber ich wohne hier in ...	But I live here in ...
Ich bin Lehrer / Designerin.	I am a teacher / designer.
Wie interessant!	How interesting!

1 The German phrase for 'I am a teacher' doesn't translate word-for-word from English. Which English word does the German phrase omit? _____

While you may not be able to figure out what a word means in isolation, the words around it will help you deduce the meaning. So you can figure out the answers to all these questions thanks to context. Pretty cool, huh?

CULTURE TIP: *du* **or** *Sie*? German has two ways of saying 'you': *du* is informal, and *Sie* is formal. In this book, we'll mostly use *du*, because that's the form you'll use most when chatting with people your age.

PRONUNCIATION: w The letter *w* in German is pronounced just like a 'v' in English. There are a few more sounds that are spelled differently in German, but you'll get used to them quickly. German is very phonetic, which is great for learners.

2 Translate these phrases into German:

a I am _____

b I live in (city). _____

c I'm from Berlin. _____

d I'm from Germany. _____

CONVERSATION STRATEGY: *und du?*

If you're uncomfortable doing a lot of talking at first, a trick I like to use is to bounce the question back to the other person, so that I can listen for a while. In German, it's easy to do, with a simple *Und du?*

Und du? can also be used as a 'universal question' that saves you the burden of memorizing hundreds of questions. If you don't know the German translation of 'Where do you live?', 'What do you do for a living?' or 'Do you like The Beatles?' you could just answer and then ask *Und du?* to turn the question around to the other person.

PRACTICE

Though some of this language may be familiar, you should still practise pronouncing these words out loud now to start building muscle memory. This will help you develop your German accent right away. Make sure you understand the conversation before moving on.

Here's some new vocab to help you to build your language script.

🔊 **01.03** Listen to the audio and study the table.

Countries	die USA, Kanada, Italien, Deutschland, Spanien, China, Australien, Russland, Japan, Irland
Professions	Autor, Fotograf, Architekt, Professor, Programmierer, Elektriker, Rezeptionist, Agent, Tänzer, Blogger
Interests	der Sport, die Fotografie, die Musik / das Konzert, das Joggen, das Karate, der Film, das Tennis, das Yoga, das Shopping, Sprachen (languages)

If you don't already have one, find a good German dictionary. This will help you build vocab that's what I call 'me-specific'. As we go along, look up words that apply to your life to make your script more useful. Let's start now.

GRAMMAR EXPLANATION: *-in* female ending

You'll notice that sometimes, words are written differently depending on whether the speaker is male or female. In German, words describing people usually add *-in* to the end when referring to a woman, similar to the words 'actor' and 'actress' in English – but German applies this to almost all professions. This gives us:

Student (m)	*Musiker* (m)	*Lehrer* (m)
*Student**in*** (f)	*Musiker**in*** (f)	*Lehrer**in*** (f)

Like when Ellen says **Ich bin Designerin**, *whereas Peter says* **Ich bin Lehrer**.

1   What countries are the people in your life from? What are their professions? Interests? Add three new words to each category in the table using words specific to you or people close to you. (Be sure to add *-in* to the endings of professions that describe a female!)

I've listed some good free online dictionaries and apps in our Resources. You can also use a learner-friendly ink-and-paper dictionary.

2   Use a dictionary to create four phrases about yourself with *ich bin*.
Example: <u>Ich bin Benny.</u>   <u>Ich bin Vegetarier.</u>   <u>Ich bin Blogger.</u>

_____   _____

_____   _____

3   Practise using *Und du?* to ask questions.
   a   Find out someone's profession by saying 'I'm a teacher. And you?'

   _____

   b   Find out where they come from by saying 'I come from Canada. And you?' _____

   c   Find out where they live by saying 'I live in Berlin. And you?'

   _____

Cover up the translations in the phrase list and see if you can remember what the German expressions mean.

PUT IT TOGETHER

Let's keep building your script. Using the conversation as a model, as well as the 'me-specific' words you just looked up, say in German:

⋯⫶ your name

⋯⫶ where you're from

⋯⫶ where you live

⋯⫶ what you do for a living.

Throughout this book, I'll help you keep building this script. You'll draw on this again and again as you start having your first conversations in German with actual people.

CONVERSATION 2

Describing your interests

There's so much German you already know thanks to **cognates** – words that are the same, or nearly the same, in both English and German.

When you talk to someone for the first time, you'll often get a question like, 'So, what do you like to do?' In this conversation, Peter and Ellen talk about their interests.

🔊 01.04 Listen for familiar-sounding words to see if you can understand the gist of what the speakers are saying.

HACK IT:
language 'chunks'
Learn phrases in chunks rather than understanding each part of every phrase. *Was sind deine …?* is a great example. Learn this as a set phrase that means 'What are your …?'

Ellen:	Was sind deine Hobbys, Peter?
Peter:	Ich höre gern Pop oder klassische Musik und ich spiele Gitarre. Und du?
Ellen:	Ich höre nicht gern Pop, aber klassische Musik ist okay.
Peter:	Gymnastik ist mein Lieblingssport. Ich bin sehr aktiv. Und du?
Ellen:	Ich spiele Basketball, aber mein Lieblingssport ist … Schlafen.
Peter:	Ach so!
Ellen:	Und Pizza ist mein, ähm, Lieblingsessen! Ich singe gern und ich bin Beatles-Fan.
Peter:	Super! Das ist meine Lieblingsband!

Spezialität des Hauses: Spaghetti

FIGURE IT OUT

1   Use context and words you recognize to figure out the following:

   a   What phrase does Ellen use to ask Peter about his hobbies?

   _____

   b   What two types of music does Peter like?

   _____   _____

   c   Write out (in German or English) three of Peter and Ellen's interests.

   _____   _____   _____

2   Scan the conversation and find eight German words that are the same or very similar to English and highlight them.

3   Guess the meaning of: a *aber* _____   b *Lieblings-* _____

4   Find the German equivalent of the phrases and highlight them. Then write them here.

   a   I like listening to _____

   b   I don't like listening to _____

   c   I play _____

   d   I like to sing _____

5   Look at items a and b in Exercise 4. Which word means 'not'? _____

NOTICE

🔊 01.05 Listen to the audio and study the table.

Essential phrases for Conversation 2

German	Meaning
Was sind deine ...	What are your ...
Hobbys	hobbies
Ich höre gern ...	I like to listen to ... (I listen-to gladly)
Pop oder klassische Musik	pop or classical music
Ich höre nicht gern ...	I don't like to listen to ... (I listen-to not gladly)
... ist okay	... is OK
Ich bin sehr aktiv.	I am very active.
Ich spiele Gitarre.	I play the guitar.
Schlafen ist ...	Sleeping is ...
mein Lieblingssport	my favourite sport
mein Lieblingsessen	my favourite food
Das ist meine Lieblingsband.	That is my favourite band.
Ich bin Beatles-Fan.	I am a Beatles fan.

CULTURE TIP:

speaking with precision
Germans like to express themselves rather precisely. Unless they really hate or love something, you won't hear them saying *Ich hasse* (I hate) or *Ich liebe* (I love). Instead, they add the little word *gern* to a verb to express what they like or enjoy. (You can also use *gerne* – they're interchangeable) You're likely to hear *ich helfe gern* (I gladly help) or *ich gehe gern* (I gladly go) but *lieben* is reserved for deeper expressions of love: *Ich liebe Anna!*
As a side note, it should come as no surprise that one of the most commonly heard German words is *genau*, which means 'precisely'!

1   Notice how *Lieblings-* appears at the beginning of three words in the conversation. Figure out how you'd say in German:

   a   favourite book   (book = *Buch*)   _____

   b   favourite song   (song = *Song*)   _____

2   Look at the phrase list to find the German equivalents for these English words. Then write them here in German.

   a   is   _____   b   very   _____

3   Notice that German more commonly uses the word *gern* and a different sentence structure from English to describe likes and dislikes. Compare the sentences and write the missing literal translations.

Example: I like music. *Ich höre gern Musik.* ´I listen-to gladly music´

   a   I don't like pop.   *Ich höre nicht gern Pop.* _____

   b   I like basketball.   *Ich spiele gern Basketball.* _____

4 Match the German phrases with their correct English translations.

a *Ich höre*   1 I like to listen

b *Ich höre gern*   2 I listen

c *Ich höre nicht gern*   3 I like to play

d *Ich spiele*   4 I play

e *Ich spiele gern*   5 I don't like to play

f *Ich spiele nicht gern*   6 I don't like to listen

g *Ich singe*   7 I don't like to sing

h *Ich singe gern*   8 I sing

i *Ich singe nicht gern*   9 I like to sing

5 How do you think you would say the following in German?

a I like coffee. (*Kaffee*) (I drink = *ich trinke*) _____

b I like Bratwurst. (I eat = *ich esse*) _____

c I don't like photography. (I photograph = *ich fotografiere*)

_____

d I like tennis. _____

e I don't like bananas. (bananas = *Bananen*) _____

f I like German. (I speak = *ich spreche*) _____

6 Notice the phrase used to say, 'I am a Beatles fan'. Based on this, how would you say the following in German?

a I am a Tolkien fan. (*Tolkien*) _____

b I am a jazz fan. (*Jazz*) _____

c I am a volleyball fan. (*Volleyball*) _____

⚙️ #LANGUAGEHACK: get a head start with words you already know

I've already introduced you to a lot of familiar words (cognates) in this unit. Can you guess the English meaning of these German cognates (or near cognates)?

Englisch, Moment, Gras, negativ, Park, Sand, Brokkoli, modern, Adresse, Hotel

As an English speaker, you know more German words than you realize!

How to guess English–German cognates

There are distinct patterns that can give you a hint at which words may be similar in German and English. For instance, the less formal version of a word in English may be similar in German, so if you wanted to translate 'I consider' to German, it's actually easier to think of a less formal alternative, like 'I think' (*ich denke*).

Technology and trendy vocab

German has also more recently started to borrow a number of English words related to technology, American/British culture and products, some business terminology, and even some trendy words:

der Lifestyle, die Party, der Cocktail, das Date, sexy, das Fastfood, die Fitness, das Tattoo, das Piercing, der Trend, trendy, der Hipster, der Soundtrack, das T-Shirt, die Shorts, die Jeans, der Pullover, Basketball, fair, das Game, der Computer, der Laptop, die Happy Hour, die Cola, die E-Mail, cool

How to recognize cognates

Sometimes the spelling of these words is the same in both languages, and sometimes there are slight changes. Knowing these four simple patterns in spelling changes can help you work out the meaning of more words:

⤑ v/f in English sometimes changes to *b* in German
  (half → *halb*, seven → *sieben*, silver → *Silber*, over → *über*)
⤑ d in English sometimes changes to *t* in German
  (bread → *Brot*, old → *alt*, hundred → *hundert*, dream → *Traum*, good → *gut*)
⤑ k in English sometimes changes to *ch* in German
  (milk → *Milch*, book → *Buch*, week → *Woche*)
⤑ sh in English sometimes changes to *sch* in German (English → *Englisch*)

English and German are actually part of the same family (called 'Germanic'), and because of this many words that existed thousands of years ago are still similar today. This is the case with some body parts (like Arm, Finger, Nase, Lippe, Haar) or words for the weather/ environment (like Wind, Wetter, kalt, warm, Sturm).

These patterns are just a taste of what's to come – you'll start to recognize other ways words tend to be very familiar as you speak more of the language!

YOUR TURN: use the hack

You'll start to recognize other similarities as you speak more of the language! Let's get you using this hack right away to internalize it better.

1 ◄))) 01.06 Practise pronouncing the German cognates in the table, and notice how they sound different from the English version.

Cognates

Sport	perfekt	Garantie	Disziplin	ideal
Bett	Musik	Gott	original	hart
kalt	unter	Gruppe	breit	Sonntag
frisch	waschen	Methode	Fisch	Kirche

PRONUNCIATION:
German is a phonetic language!
German letters tend to have very predictable pronunciations. While English has inconsistent spelling to pronunciation associations (it can be learned 'through tough thorough thought, though ...'), every single letter in German has a consistent sound.

2 Look at the words and select the one in each list likely to be a cognate. Use a dictionary to check your answers.

a letter/e-mail/write/read
b computer/bedroom/chair/desk
c vest/knee/trousers/skirt

3 What English words can you think of that are likely to be German cognates? Guess four new cognates using the rules you've just learned, then use your German dictionary to check your answers. Write down new cognates you discover in the table!

Example: under → <u>unter</u>

GRAMMAR EXPLANATION: *ich* + verb + noun

The sentence structure introduced in this conversation is the verb + noun form. It uses action words (verbs) followed by a person, place or thing (noun) – the same way we do it in English. Because of this, this sentence structure will be simple for you to learn and use. You'll just need to decide which verb you want to use, followed by the thing you want to talk about. So, *Ich spiele Basketball* is 'I play basketball'.

GRAMMAR TIP:
understanding the terminology
In this book, I'll avoid using overly technical grammar terms, but there are a few worth knowing. Here, we talk about **verbs** – action words (like *wohne, komme, höre, spiele* that you've seen follow *ich*) and **nouns** – people, places and things (like *Journalist, Deutschland, Gitarre*). These are the building blocks of all sentences.

Example: *Ich spiele Basketball.*   *Ich höre Musik.*   *Ich spiele Gitarre.*
        verb + noun   verb + noun   verb + noun

PRACTICE

1 Cover up the English translations in the phrase list and see if you can remember what the German expressions mean.

2 What do you like or dislike? Rewrite these sentences with *gern* or *nicht gern* to make them true for you. (Be sure to use the correct word order!)

a *Ich spiele Tennis.*
_____

e *Ich trinke Kaffee.*
_____

b *Ich höre Radio.*
_____

f *Ich trinke Bier.*
_____

c *Ich esse Pizza.*
_____

g *Ich tanze Tango.*
_____

d *Ich esse Spaghetti.*
_____

h *Ich esse Brokkoli.*
_____

3 Use the vocab given in the box to ask three questions in German about someone's favourite thing.

		Interessen (interests)?
Was sind deine …	Lieblings-	Alben (albums)? Autoren (authors)? Filme (films)? Songs (songs)?

_____

_____

_____

4 Now adapt some of the phrases from this conversation with new vocab.

a Use *Ich + (verb) + nicht gern … aber … ist okay.*
to say something you don't like, then something you do like.

Example: Ich höre nicht gern Pop, aber klassische Musik ist okay.

_____

b Use *Ich bin ein …-Fan* to say two things you are a fan of! (It could be anything, from teams to brands to artists to people.)

_____

_____

PUT IT TOGETHER

It's time to use the new forms you've learned to talk about your own likes and dislikes!

1 Use your dictionary to look up new words in German that you'd use to describe yourself. Be sure to:

···⋗ combine verbs with places and things (nouns)
···⋗ use *gern* or *nicht gern* to talk about what you like and don't like
···⋗ include set phrases you learned (*Ich bin ein ...-Fan*).

_____

_____

_____

_____

2 Use the sentence structure you've learned in this conversation to create new sentences in German. Use your dictionary to find new 'me-specific' words to create sentences that are true about you.

a Say something you like to play, using *Ich spiele.*

_____

b Say something you like to eat, using *Ich esse.*

_____

c Say something you like to drink, using *Ich trinke.*

_____

d Say two things you don't like doing using *nicht gern.*

_____

_____

Now read your script over and over again until you feel comfortable saying it. Try to memorize it too!

CONVERSATION 3

Why are you learning German?

One question you'll almost certainly get when you have your first conversation in German is simply, 'Why are you learning German?' so let's prepare your answer now.

🔊 01.07 Peter wants to know why Ellen is learning German. Pay attention to the way Ellen forms her answer. How does she say 'because'?

One way that German is simpler than English is that there's no difference between 'I learn' and 'I am learning'. In German, both are said the same way – *ich lerne*.

> **Peter:** Ich lerne gern Sprachen. Und du? Warum lernst du Deutsch?
>
> **Ellen:** Ich lerne Deutsch, weil .... na ja, ich habe Familie hier in Deutschland und ich möchte hier wohnen. Und ich finde die Sprache faszinierend! Ich möchte Land und Leute kennenlernen und vielleicht einen Job finden.
>
> **Peter:** Dein Plan ist toll! Und dein Deutsch ist sehr gut. Bravo!
>
> **Ellen:** Danke schön!

CULTURE TIP:

being complimented!
Germans are unlikely to give compliments just for the sake of being nice. In fact, if you compliment them, they are likely to carry on the conversation without remarking on it or saying 'thank you', as compliments are seen more as statements of fact than flattery. So, when a German tells you they like something, you can trust that they really do like it! They would have no trouble telling you if they didn't. In fact, if they don't say they dislike something, you can assume they like it!

FIGURE IT OUT

1   Use context to find the following information in the conversation. Highlight the phrases.

   a   Two reasons Ellen gives for learning German.
   b   Peter says what he thinks of Ellen's plan.
   c   Peter compliments Ellen.

2   Can you guess the meaning of these phrases?

   a   *ich habe Familie hier* _____

   b   *Dein Plan ist toll!* _____

   c   *vielleicht einen Job finden* _____

   d   *ich finde die Sprache faszinierend*

   _____

3 What words do the speakers use to ask a question (why?) and give an answer (because)? Highlight them, then write them out here.

_____ _____

4 Find at least three cognates in the dialogue and write them here.

_____ _____ _____

NOTICE

🔊 01.08 Listen to the audio and study the table.

Ich möchte can be used to express both 'I would like' and 'I want'. You can pronounce this as 'mukte' for now, and we'll brush up your pronunciation in Unit 3!

Essential phrases for Conversation 3

German	Meaning
Ich lerne gern Sprachen.	I like learning languages.
Warum lernst du Deutsch?	Why are you learning German? (Why learn you German?)
Ich lerne Deutsch, weil …	I'm learning German because … (I learn German because)
na ja …	well …
Ich habe Familie hier in Deutschland.	I have family here in Germany.
Ich möchte …	I want … (I would-like)
… hier wohnen	… to live here (here to-live)
… Land und Leute kennenlernen	… to get to know the country and the people (land and people get-to-know)
… und vielleicht einen Job finden	… and maybe find a job (and maybe a job to-find)
Ich finde die Sprache faszinierend.	I find the language fascinating.
Dein Deutsch ist sehr gut.	Your German is very good.
Dein Plan ist toll!	Your plan is cool!
Danke schön!	Thank you very much! (Thank-you beautifully.)

1 Notice how German uses different word order to English. How do you say these sentences in German?

a Why are you learning German? _____

b I want to get to know the country and people.

_____

c I would like to live here. _____

The word Leute (pronounced loy-teh) meaning 'people' may be tricky to remember – imagine saying to a group of dawdling people, 'Don't loiter, people!' to help the new vocab stick in your memory.

2 How can you say 'thank you very much' in German?_____

3 Look at the phrase list again. Which three verbs follow the expression *ich möchte*? Write them out here in German.

    a to live _____   c to find _____

    b to get to know _____

4 Match the verbs from the conversation with their English equivalents.

    a *Ich lerne*   1 I have

    b *Ich habe*   2 I'm learning

    c *Ich möchte*   3 I find

    d *Ich finde*   4 I would like

CONVERSATION STRATEGY: smooth out your sentences with connector words

When you're a beginner in German, speaking in short, simple sentences is all you need to get the job done, but sometimes it doesn't sound very natural. You can start smoothing out your sentences by adding in connector words. Words like 'because' (*weil* ...) and 'well' (*na ja* ...) help you connect your thoughts to sound more natural.

Hack it: use *weil ... na ja ...* to 'reset' a German sentence

German word order can be quite different to English at times. For instance, when you give a reason starting with *weil* (because), this usually requires a change in the word order. It really isn't that hard to learn, it just takes some getting used to. But until then, there's a #languagehack you can use to get around this!

You can 'reset' a German sentence to use the simpler sentence structure you already know by adding in a brief pause and a filler word like: *na ja*, as Ellen does in the conversation. (More on filler words in Unit 2!) This pause may sound like hesitation to the untrained eye, but it's a strategic technique that allows you to use two simple sentences instead of one complex one!

1 What words in German correspond to these English connector words?

    a and _____   c or _____

    b because, well ... _____   d but _____

2 Now practise using the connector words from Exercise 1 to join sentences together in German. Use each word once.

Example: *Ich trinke gern Kaffee. Ich trinke gern Tee.* →
Ich trinke gern Kaffee und Tee.

a   *Ich spiele gern Baskettball. Ich spiele gern Tennis.*

_____

b   *Ich schwimme gern. Ich jogge nicht gern.*

_____

c   *Ich möchte Salat essen. Ich möchte Bratwurst essen.*

_____

d   *Ich lerne Englisch. Ich möchte in Kanada wohnen.*

_____

GRAMMAR EXPLANATION: combining two verbs

In Conversation 3, you saw a new sentence structure that combines two forms of German verbs – the 'I form' and the 'dictionary form'. Use this set phrase, which combines these two verb types, to help you avoid using complicated phrases in German:

I would like + (to do something) = ***ich möchte*** + verb (dictionary form)

Examples: *Ich möchte ... lernen*   (I'd like to learn ...)
          Ich möchte ... gehen   (I'd like to go ...)

You can use this phrasing in almost endless ways, and it comes up in most German conversations.

There's just one peculiarity: whenever you're using more than one verb in German, the second verb (e.g. *lernen* and *gehen*) will usually come at the very end of the sentence. The result sounds a bit like how Yoda speaks: *Ich möchte Karate lernen.* I'd like karate to learn (rather than 'I'd like to learn karate').

We call this the 'dictionary form' because it's the way the verb looks when you find it in a dictionary. You can also think of it as the 'to form' (*lernen* is 'to learn'), and language teachers call it the 'infinitive'. This form will always end in -en, or -n in German.

Listen to the audio and study the table. Pay careful attention to the pronunciation of the words – especially their endings.

Common verbs

Dictionary form – *Ich* form		
wohnen – ich wohne (I live)	treffen – ich treffe (I meet)	gehen – ich gehe (I go)
finden – ich finde (I find)	verstehen – ich verstehe (I understand)	reisen – ich reise (I travel)
sprechen – ich spreche (I speak)	helfen – ich helfe (I help)	sehen – ich sehe (I see)
lernen – ich lerne (I learn)	essen – ich esse (I eat)	singen – ich singe (I sing)
spielen – ich spiele (I play)	trinken – ich trinke (I drink)	studieren – ich studiere (I study) [at university]

1 Practise German Yoda-speak! Use the verb list to complete the sentences.

Example: *Ich möchte ...* (to drink cola) → <u>*Ich möchte Cola trinken.*</u>

a *Ich möchte ...* (to eat pizza)

_____

b *Ich möchte ...* (to speak German)

_____

c *Ich möchte ...* (to help Ellen)

_____

d *Ich möchte ...* (to see Berlin)

_____

2 Use Conversation 3 and the verb list to figure out how to say these sentences in German.

a I want to live in Germany.

_____

b I like learning languages!

_____

c I like speaking German.

_____

d I want to drink coffee.

_____

e I want to sing.

_____

f I want to listen to classical music.

_____

g I like travelling.

_____

3 Practise using the new sentence structure and vocab you've seen. Use the prompts given to answer the questions in German.

Warum lernst du Deutsch?

a _____ _____ *die Sprache faszinierend.* (I find the language fascinating.)

b _____ _____ *in Deutschland* _____*!* (I would like to live in Germany!)

c _____ _____ _____ *Sprachen!* (I like learning languages!)

d _____ _____ *bald nach Deutschland.* (I'm travelling to Germany soon.)

Warum bist du in Deutschland?

e _____ _____ *Deutsche* _____*.* (I want to meet German people.)

f _____ _____ _____ *Bratwurst.* (I like eating Bratwurst!)

g _____ _____ *hier* _____*.* (I want to study here.)

h _____ _____ *die deutsche Kultur* _____*.*
(I want to understand the German culture.)

PUT IT TOGETHER

1 Now it's time for you to practise using the sentence structure yourself!

Create four sentences in German that combine *ich möchte* + dictionary form of verbs to say things that are true for you. Look up new words in your dictionary that let you form sentences you think you'll want to use early on. One of your sentences should say why you are learning German.

Example: Ich möchte Deutsch verstehen. (I'd like to understand German.)

As you're learning new phrases in German, always think about how you can adapt them for you! Then look up the 'me-specific' words you need to personalize them.

If you're planning to visit a German-speaking country, one of your sentences should **share why** you're **visiting** or what you like about the country!

COMPLETING UNIT 1

Check your understanding

◄)) 01.10 Go back and reread the conversations. Then when you're feeling confident:

···⟩ listen to the audio rehearsal, which will ask you questions in German
···⟩ pause or replay the audio as often as you need to understand the questions
···⟩ repeat after the speaker until the pronunciation feels and sounds natural to you
···⟩ answer the questions in German (in complete sentences).

Each unit will build on the previous one, helping you to review as you move ahead.

Show what you know ...

Here's what you've just learned. Write or say an example for each item in the list. Then tick off the ones you know.

☑ Introduce yourself.   *Ich bin Benny!*
☐ Say where you're from.
☐ Give the names of three countries.
☐ Say what you do.
☐ Give the names of three professions.
☐ Talk about something you like and something you don't like.
☐ Give three German–English cognates.
☐ Ask the question, 'Why are you learning German?'
☐ Give a reason why you are learning German, 'Because ... well ...'.
☐ Use each of the German connector words 'and', 'but' and 'or' in a sentence.
☐ Give a phrase you can use to bounce a question back to someone else.
☐ Describe your interests using different sentence structures:
    ☐ I like ...
    ☐ I want to ...
    ☐ I'm a ... fan!
    ☐ ... is my favourite!

COMPLETE YOUR MISSION

It's time to complete your mission: convince the airport agent to let you through, so your German-speaking adventure can begin! To do this, you'll need to prepare answers to the questions you'll most likely be asked.

STEP 1: build your script

Start your script with the phrases you've learned in this unit, combined with 'me-specific' vocab to answer common questions about yourself. Be sure to:

···⟩ say your name and occupation using *Ich bin*
···⟩ say where you're from and where you live, using *Ich komme aus … Ich wohne in …*
···⟩ say what you do and what you like using *Ich … gern …*
···⟩ say why you're learning German using *Ich lerne Deutsch, weil …. na ja, …*
···⟩ use connector words (*und, aber, oder*) along the way to help your sentences flow better!

Write down your script, then repeat it until you feel confident.

STEP 2: real language hackers speak from day one … *online*

If you're feeling good about your script, it's time to complete your mission and share a recording of you speaking your script with the community. So, go online, find the mission for Unit 1 and give it your best shot.

> You'll find some bonus missions, too for serious German hacking! Go to www.teachyourself.com/ languagehacking

STEP 3: learn from other learners

How well can you understand someone else's introduction? After you've uploaded your own clip, check out what the other people in the community have to say about themselves. Would you let them past the checkpoint? **Your task is to ask a follow-up question in German to at least three different people.**

STEP 4: reflect on what you've learned

What did you find easy or difficult about this unit? Did you learn any new words or phrases in the community space? After every script you write or conversation you have, you'll gain a lot of insight for what 'gaps' you need to fill in your script. Always write them down!

_____

_____

_____

_____

_____

HEY, LANGUAGE HACKER, LOOK AT YOU GO!

You've only just started on the path to language hacking, and you've already learned so much. You've taken the first crucial steps, and started to interact with others using German. This is something some students don't do even after years of study, so you should be truly proud.

Sehr gut!

2 ASKING ABOUT YOU

Your mission

Imagine this – your friend brings you to your first *Biergarten* in Germany. You want to blend in and not rely on English.

Your mission is to trick someone into thinking you're a high-level German speaker for 30 seconds. Be prepared to strike up a conversation and talk about **how long you've been** living in your current location, **what you like to do**, and the **languages you speak** or want to learn. After the 30 seconds have passed, reveal how long you've been learning German and dazzle them! To avoid arousing suspicion, keep the other person talking by asking casual questions to show your interest.

This mission will give you the confidence to initiate conversations with new people.

Mission prep

⋯⋙ Ask and respond to questions using the *du* form.
⋯⋙ Use the question words *wie viele*, *wie*, *seit wann* and the answer word *seit*.
⋯⋙ Negate sentences using *nicht*.
⋯⋙ Develop a conversation strategy: using filler words (*na ja …*) to create conversational flow.
⋯⋙ Pronounce the German sounds: *ä/ö/ü, ß, s/st/sp*, hard and soft *ch*.

BUILDING LANGUAGE FOR ASKING QUESTIONS

Let's build on the simple (but effective!) technique of bouncing back a question with *Und du?* and learn to form more specific questions using several new question words.

#LANGUAGEHACK
learn vocab faster with memory hooks

CONVERSATION 1

Words you need to ask questions

A week into her stay in Berlin, Ellen attends a language learners' meet-up near her house. There, she meets Jakob, a Berliner. After the initial introductions, they start to talk about their language skills.

🔊 02.01 Pay attention to the differences between the way Jakob asks questions and how Ellen answers them.

> **Jakob:** Na, Ellen, wie findest du Berlin?
>
> **Ellen:** Ich liebe Berlin! Ich lerne viel Deutsch hier.
>
> **Jakob:** Sehr gut! Lernst du auch andere Sprachen?
>
> **Ellen:** Nein, ich lerne nur Deutsch. Und du?
>
> **Jakob:** Ich spreche ziemlich gut Italienisch und ich spreche ein bisschen Russisch.
>
> **Ellen:** Echt?
>
> **Jakob:** Ja, echt!
>
> **Ellen:** Sag mal, sprichst du auch Englisch?
>
> **Jakob:** Noch nicht. Vielleicht kann ich heute ein bisschen Englisch üben.

CONVERSATION STRATEGY: *anticipate common questions*
When you start speaking German, a common conversation topic is language learning itself. It makes sense – if you're learning German, people will ask if you speak other languages. Have your answer prepared!

CULTURE TIP:

bragging rights
Germans aren't ones to brag about their achievements – it's one of the authentic parts of the culture I love so much! To blend in, make sure to give humble statements of your abilities. It's better to say that you can do something *ziemlich gut*, rather than the slightly overconfident *(sehr) gut*.

FIGURE IT OUT

1 Use context to figure out:

   a How many languages does Ellen speak?   two / three
   b Does Ellen like living in Berlin?   *ja* (yes) / *nein* (no)
   c How many languages does Jakob speak?   two / three

2 Are these statements about the conversation true (*richtig*) or false (*falsch*)?

   a Ellen is not learning German.   *richtig / falsch*
   b Jakob speaks Italian.   *richtig / falsch*
   c Jakob speaks English.   *richtig / falsch*
   d Ellen speaks Russian.   *richtig / falsch*

3 What word does Ellen use to express surprise? _____

NOTICE

🔊 02.02 Listen to the audio and study the table.

Essential phrases for Conversation 1

German	Meaning
Na ...	So ...
Wie findest du Berlin?	How do you like Berlin? (How find you Berlin?)
Lernst du ...	Are you learning ... (Learn you)
auch andere Sprachen?	any other languages? (also other languages?)
nein	no
Ich lerne ...	I'm learning ...
... nur Deutsch	... only German
... viel Deutsch	... a lot of German
Ich spreche ...	I speak ...
... ziemlich gut Italienisch	... Italian quite well
... ein bisschen Russisch	... a little bit of Russian
Echt?	Really?
ja	yes
Sag mal ...	Tell me ...
Sprichst du ...?	Do you speak ...?
auch	also
Noch nicht.	Not yet.
Vielleicht kann ich ...	Maybe I can ... (Maybe can I)
heute ein bisschen Englisch üben	practise a little bit of English today (today a bit English to-practise)

To remember that the word *vielleicht* (pronounced ´feel-eye-CHt´) means ´maybe´, think to yourself: Maybe, if I ´feel like it´!

LEARNING STRATEGY:
Yoda-speak
Remember Yoda-speak from Unit 1? Whenever there's more than one verb in a sentence in German, the second verb goes all the way to the end. Though German word order can be different from what you're used to, don't worry! If you use incorrect word order, people can usually still understand you. As you read through this book, notice the word-for-word translations in brackets, and you'll start to get a feel for how the language works.

1 Reread the conversation, then write out in German:

a the two phrases Jakob uses to describe how well he speaks Russian and Italian:

_____   _____

b the phrase Ellen uses to say which language she's 'only' learning:

_____

2 Highlight the German phrases meaning:

   a Really?   b Not yet   c Maybe

3 Compare the sentences: *Ich spreche gut Italienisch.* and 'I speak Italian well'. How does the word *gut* work differently in terms of word order? Fill in the gaps in German:

   a *Ich spreche* ＿＿＿＿＿ ＿＿＿＿＿. (I speak **English well**.)

   b *Ich möchte* ＿＿＿＿＿ ＿＿＿＿＿ *sprechen.* (I want to speak **German well**.)

4 Use the phrase list to fill in the sequence in German:

   a ＿＿＿＿＿ I speak → ＿＿＿＿＿ you speak

   b ＿＿＿＿＿ I'm learning → ＿＿＿＿＿ you're learning

   c ＿＿＿＿＿ I find → ＿＿＿＿＿ you find

5 Match the words from the phrase list with their equivalents in English.

   a *nur*   e *andere*   1 so   5 other
   b *viel*   f *noch*   2 any other   6 yet
   c *auch*   g *auch andere*   3 a lot of   7 only
   d *na*   4 also

GRAMMAR EXPLANATION: asking questions

Asking yes or no questions in German is very easy. Just change the word order of a statement (by putting the verb first):

   Du bist Lehrer. → *Bist du Lehrer?* (You are a teacher. → Are you a teacher?)

One important difference in German (which is simpler than in English!) is that there's no need to translate the word 'Do' at the start of many questions. The verb still comes first to show that it's a question:

   Du sprichst Deutsch. → *Sprichst du Deutsch?*
   (You speak German. → Do you speak German? lit. 'Speak you German?')

We do this in English too with certain words ('Are you ...?', 'Am I ...?', 'Can you ...?'). German keeps it simple and does this with all words!

1 How does Ellen ask the question, 'Do you speak …?' Highlight it in the phrase list. Then, put the words in the correct order to make sentences.

   a *Deutsch/du/sprichst?* _____

   b *viel/du/Deutsch/lernst?* _____

   c *Sprachen/auch/du/sprichst/andere?* _____

2 Complete the questions in German by filling in the missing words.

   a _____ _____ *auch Russisch?* (**Are you learning** Russian too?)

   b _____ _____ _____ *Berlin?* (**How do you like (find)** Berlin?)

3 How would you ask the following questions in German?

   a Do you live in New York? (*wohnst*)? _____

   b Do you like learning English? _____

   c Are you a designer? _____

PRACTICE

1 Practise using the vocab you've learned! Fill in the missing word(s) in German.

   a *Ich spreche* _____ *Englisch.* (I speak **only** English.)

   b _____ _____ _____ _____ *Russisch.* (**I'm learning a bit of** Russian.)

   c _____*! Ich spreche* _____ _____ _____*!* (**Really! I speak a bit of Italian!**)

   d _____ _____ _____ *Spanisch?* (**Do you speak** Spanish **well?**)

   e *Ich möchte* _____ *Deutsch* _____. (I would like to **speak a lot of** German.)

2 ◀» 02.03 Practise recognizing the difference in intonation between questions and statements in German. Listen to the audio, and select *F* if you hear a *Frage* (question), and *A* if you hear an *Antwort* (answer) or general statement.

   a F/A   b F/A   c F/A   d F/A   e F/A   f F/A

3 Change these statements to questions. Then say them out loud.

    a *Alex wohnt in Berlin.* b *Du sprichst Italienisch.* c *Mark lernt Deutsch.*

    _____   _____   _____

PUT IT TOGETHER

1 You should always be learning new German vocab of your own! **Use a dictionary to look up the German translations for the languages given.** Then add two more languages in German that you would like to learn.

    a Japanese _____   c Chinese _____   d _____

    b French _____   e _____

2 If you speak other languages, say whether you speak them 'well' or only 'a little bit', and if you want to learn other languages, say which ones. Write out your answers here in German. Then repeat them out loud.

    a *Sprichst du andere Sprachen?*

       Ja/Nein, ich spreche (nur) _____

       _____

    b *Möchtest du andere Sprachen lernen?*

       Ja/Nein, ich möchte (nur) _____

       _____

PRONUNCIATION: *a* sounds like 'ah'
German has a different pronunciation on some vowels. In many cases, for instance, *a* is pronounced as 'ah' (like in 'cat'), not as 'aw' (like in all). This is the case for the phrase *Sag mal* (pronounced 'sahg mahl').

#LANGUAGEHACK:
learn vocab faster with memory hooks

You may think you don't have the memory to learn lots of new words. But you absolutely can! The trick I use for remembering new vocab is **mnemonics**, or memory hooks.

A mnemonic is a learning tool that helps you remember a lot more words and phrases. I've already given you some mnemonics. Remember:

die Leute (people) – 'Don't loiter, people!' *vielleicht* (maybe) – 'if you 'feel like it!'

These associations act like glue for your memory. The key to a good mnemonic is to think about an image or sound that connects the word to its meaning, then try to make it silly, dramatic, or shocking – make it memorable! Simply say the German word out loud until you can think of an English word that sounds like it. (It may even be similar in meaning.) Then you can attach a powerful (silly, weird or funny) image to it – anything that helps.

Examples:
···} the word *schreiben* is pronounced like [shry-ben] and means 'to write'. Imagine a boy called Ben, who is shy, sitting to write a novel. Shy Ben likes *schreiben*.
···} to remember that the word *reisen* means 'to travel', think of rising early to go on a journey.

YOUR TURN: use the hack

1 🔊 02.04 Listen to the audio to hear the pronunciation of each word. Repeat the words **and then** use sound or image association to create your own mnemonics.

    a *die Straße*, 'street'   c *der Mond*, 'moon'   e *teuer*, 'expensive'
    b *das Ding*, 'thing'   d *lustig*, 'funny'

> I'll occasionally hint at tricks you can use to remember new vocab. For now, you should get used to creating new mnemonics yourself!

_____

_____

CONVERSATION 2

How long have you been learning German?

VOCAB: *lernen* and *studieren*
The meaning of *lernen* (to learn) and *studieren* (to study) isn't quite the same as in English. The sense of having your head in the books and purposefully learning something specific would be 'I study …' in English, but *ich lerne* … in German. *Studieren* is used specifically for studying at university. Similarly, *Student* refers to a university student. Primary and secondary school students would be called *Schüler*.

Another 'first question' you can expect when you speak German with someone new is 'How long have you been learning German?'

🔊 02.05 Let's prepare your response to that question now. Can you identify how Jakob asks Ellen, 'How long … '?

> **Jakob:** Seit wann lernst du Deutsch?
>
> **Ellen:** Ich lerne seit zwei Wochen Deutsch.
>
> **Jakob:** Nur zwei Wochen? Du sprichst schon sehr gut Deutsch!
>
> **Ellen:** Nein, das stimmt nicht, aber es ist nett. Danke!
>
> **Jakob:** Bitte!
>
> **Ellen:** Sag mal, wie viele Sprachen möchtest du noch lernen, Jakob?
>
> **Jakob:** Vielleicht noch zwei oder drei Sprachen: Japanisch, Arabisch und Englisch. Besonders Japanisch! Ich finde die Sprache exotisch und die Kultur ist so faszinierend.

VOCAB: *seit*
'since' or 'for'
English uses the phrase 'have been' in statements such as 'I have been learning German for two weeks' whereas Germans would say 'I learn German *since* two weeks'. You'll use the word *seit* in situations like this. In questions, *Seit wann?* can mean 'Since when?' or 'For how long?' In answers, *seit* can mean both 'since' and 'for'.

FIGURE IT OUT

1 Use context along with what you learned in Unit 1 to figure out:

   a How long has Ellen been learning German? Select the correct answer, then write it out here in German. _____ long time/one day/two weeks

   b Which language does Jakob most want to learn and why? Highlight the relevant statements in the conversation.

2 Highlight the German forms of the following words and phrases.

   a only _____   b very well _____   c languages _____

   d You already speak German very well! _____

   e but _____

   f … do you want to learn …? _____

3 Write out the German phrases that are used in Conversation 2 to ...

a ... say 'you're welcome' _____

b ... ask 'how many' _____

c ... ask 'how long' or 'since when' _____

4 Find five cognates in the conversation and highlight them.

NOTICE

◄ѹ 02.06 Listen to the audio and study the table.

Essential phrases for Conversation 2

German	Meaning
Seit wann ...?	How long ...? (Since when ...?)
... lernst du Deutsch?	... have you been learning German? (learn you German?)
Ich lerne ... Deutsch	I've been learning German ...
seit zwei Wochen	for two weeks (since two weeks)
Du sprichst schon sehr gut Deutsch!	You already speak German very well! (You speak already very good German.)
Nein, das stimmt nicht ...	No, that's not true ...
... aber es ist nett	... but that's nice
Bitte.	You're welcome.
Sag mal!	Tell me!
Wie viele ...?	How many ... ?
... Sprachen möchtest du noch lernen?	... more languages do you want to learn? (languages would-like you still to-learn)
Ich möchte drei Sprachen lernen.	I want to learn three languages.
Besonders Japanisch!	Especially Japanese!

VOCAB: *sehr gut!* *'very good', / 'very well'* One handy trick in German is that you often get two words for the price of one. Words like *gut* can be used to say something is 'good', as in *Der Film ist gut*, or to say someone does 'well', as in *Du sprichst gut Deutsch* (You speak German well).

You'll see this work for words ending in '-ly' in English: *Du singst schön.* (You sing beautifully.) / *Die Stadt ist schön.* (The city is beautiful.) *Du gehst sehr langsam.* (You walk very slowly.)/ *Der Zug ist sehr langsam.* (The train is very slow.)

VOCAB: *noch* *Noch* is an extremely versatile word. Though it's often used to mean 'yet', you'll see it used to mean 'still' as in *Wie viele Sprachen möchtest du noch lernen?* It can also mean 'nor' as in *Ich spreche weder Japanisch noch Koreanisch.* When you're out out and about in Germany, you'll hear broad uses of *noch*, such as being asked *Sonst noch etwas?* (Anything else?) at the bakery.

PRONUNCIATION: s, st, sp

Notice how the pronunciation of the letter *s* works a little differently in German depending on the letters around it.

···⟩ When you see an 's' before a vowel, pronounce it like a 'z'.

   Example: *seit* is pronounced as [zait]

···⟩ Before a *t* or *p* at the start of a word, it gets a distinctive 'sh' sound.

   Example: *stimmt* is said as [shtimt]; *Sport* is said as [shport]

···⟩ At the end of words or when doubled, it's like an English 's'.

   Example: *Reis* (rice) is pronounced as [R-ice]

1 ◀)) 02.07 Read the following words out loud to practise your pronunciation of the German *s*, keeping these rules in mind. Then listen to the native pronunciation to see if you got it right.

   a *studieren, Straße, besonders*   c *spielen, singen, verstehen*
   b *Sprache, es, sehr*   d *super, essen, sagen*

2 Highlight the phrase that means 'for how long' in the phrase list. What does the word *wann* mean on its own? _____

3 How do you say the following in German?

   a Tell me! _____   b already _____   c especially _____

4 Use the words and phrases from Exercise 3 to complete the sentences.

   a *Sprichst du* _____ *Italienisch?*

   b *Ich spreche gern viele Sprachen.* _____ *Russisch!*

   c _____, *hörst du gern klassische Musik?*

5 Notice how the speakers ask and answer questions starting with *Wie viele* and *Seit wann*. Fill in the gaps with the correct words.

   a _____ _____ *Sprachen sprichst du? – Ich spreche zwei Sprachen.*

   b *Seit wann lernst du Esperanto? – Ich lerne* _____ _____ _____ *Esperanto.* (for two weeks).

c   *Wie viele Sprachen lernst du?* – _____ _____ *drei* _____.

d   _____ _____ *sprichst du die Sprache?* – _____ _____ *die Sprache*
    _____ *zwei Tagen.*

6 Notice the use of the word *noch* in Conversations 1 and 2. How is it different? Give the meaning
of the phrases:

a   *noch nicht*   Meaning: _____

b   *... Sprachen möchtest du noch lernen?*   Meaning: _____

7 🔊 02.08 Listen to the audio and study the Numbers and Time periods tables.

Numbers (0–10)

German	ein (Jahr)	zwei (Wochen)	drei	vier	fünf	sechs	sieben	acht	neun	zehn	null
Meaning	one (year)	two (weeks)	three	four	five	six	seven	eight	nine	ten	zero

Time periods

German			Meaning		
seit	einem Tag		for	a day	
	einem Monat			a month	
	einem Jahr			a year	
	einer Woche			a week	
	zwei	Tagen		two	days
	drei	Monaten		three	months
	vier	Jahren		four	years
	fünf	Wochen		five	weeks

GRAMMAR TIP: *plurals*
Just like in English, there are many different spellings for plurals in German. You'll notice that the word 'language' in the singular is *Sprache*, but in the plural is *Sprachen*. Many German plurals end in *-en*. It doesn't always work like this ... but we'll get to that later.

PRONUNCIATION EXPLANATION: the 'hard *ch*' and 'soft *ch*' sounds in German

One way to think of this is as the 'auch-noch' rule, since all of the vowels that lead to a hard 'ch' are in those two words.

As you hear German, you'll notice the 'hard *ch*', or guttural sound. Think of it as a forced aspirated 'h', or like the 'ch' in the Scottish 'loch'. You hear this sound whenever you see the combinations *ach, uch, auch,* or *och,* like in the words *Wochen, Sprachen* or *auch.* The rest of the time, you would hear it pronounced as a 'soft *ch*' that you've seen in words like *ich* (with a sound like the start of 'Hugh').

1 🔊 02.09 Listen to the audio and repeat the words in the box. Can you hear the difference? After you say each word, write it out in the table based on whether it has a hard or soft '*ch*' sound.

> *ich   auch   noch   nicht   Sprache   sprechen   sprichst   vielleicht   Wochen   leicht*

Soft *ch*						
Hard *ch*						

2 Translate the following phrases into German. Use the tables to help you.

a For five days. _____

b For three years. _____

c For eight months. _____

d For four weeks. _____

PRACTICE

1 Translate the following sentences into German. Use the tables to help you.

a I have been living in Germany since September. (*September*)

_____

b I have been learning German for nine weeks.

_____

c Since October I have been learning two languages, German and Italian. (*Oktober*)

_____

2 Can you think of some interesting mnemonics for the following words?
(Focus on the pronunciation, rather than the spelling.)

a *drei*   b *vier*   c *fünf*

Let's use what you've learned to prepare a cheat sheet with the numbers and times of the year you're likely to use when talking about yourself. Keep coming back to the cheat sheet to add information as you go along.

HACK IT: *learn vocab strategically* Remember, you don't need to memorize all of the numbers or other types of vocab in German right away. Start by thinking about what you'll need to say most often, and learn that first. The rest will come with time, and conversation!

Numbers and times of year cheat sheet

	Useful phrases	My info
Phone number	Meine Telefonnummer ist ...	
Age		
Month I started learning German		

3 How do you say your phone number? Write the numbers out in words in the cheat sheet.

4 Look up the number that corresponds to your age, and add it to the cheat sheet. How old are you in German?

You can find a list of German numbers from 1–110, and other additional vocab, in our Resources online!

Example: *Ich bin siebenundzwanzig Jahre alt.* (I'm 27 years old).

Ich bin _____ Jahre alt.

If someone asks you in, say, August when you started learning German, you can use *seit* to say either **seit Mai** (since May), or **seit drei Monaten** (for three months) ... whichever is easiest for you to remember!

PUT IT TOGETHER

1   Use your German dictionary to look up the month (or year!) you started learning German. Add it to your cheat sheet. Then, use *seit* to answer the question: *Seit wann lernst du Deutsch?*

Example: Ich lerne <u>seit Januar</u> Deutsch.

Ich lerne _____ _____ Deutsch.

2   Look up other important numbers in your life and add them to your cheat sheet! For instance, you might add:

···❖ how many children/cats you have
···❖ how many languages you speak.

3   Use the phrases you've learned to figure out how to ask in German:

a   How long have you been living in Germany? (*du wohnst*)

_____

b   How long have you been teaching German? (*du unterrichtest*)

_____

4   Now create an entire sentence that's true for you. Respond to the question by saying how many days, weeks, months or years you've been learning German.

Seit wann lernst du Deutsch? _____

CONVERSATION 3

Sharing your opinions

Ellen and Jakob start to have a light debate about how to learn a new language.

🔊 02.10 Can you understand Ellen's method of learning German?

> **Jakob:** Ellen, wie lernst du Deutsch?
>
> **Ellen:** Na ja … ich lerne Vokabeln und ich gehe jeden Montag zum Deutschkurs.
>
> **Jakob:** Nun … Ich finde das nicht effektiv.
>
> **Ellen:** Echt?
>
> **Jakob:** Ja. Ich gehe lieber jeden Tag zum Italienischkurs.
>
> **Ellen:** Wirklich? Jeden Tag? Wie geht das denn?
>
> **Jakob:** Das heißt … ähm … ich habe Unterricht online. Das Internet ist so praktisch!
>
> **Ellen:** Gute Idee! Das sollte ich machen!
>
> **Jakob:** Du liest gern Bücher, oder? Das ist auch sehr effektiv!
>
> **Ellen:** Ja, das stimmt. Ich denke, du hast Recht.
>
> **Jakob:** Du solltest jeden Tag ein bisschen Deutsch lernen. Das ist ganz leicht, weißt du?

CULTURE TIP:

constructive criticism
My friend Bálint once told me that when he's speaking Spanish, he could go years using a word incorrectly, and no one would ever tell him. German speakers on the other hand will be more likely to point out a mistake when they see it. I really appreciate this directness when in Germany. It's all out of a desire to be truly helpful!

The word **lieber** works similarly to gern, and means that you prefer to do something (rather than something else). Ich esse gern Nudeln, aber ich esse lieber Pizza. (I like to eat pasta, but I prefer to eat pizza.)

FIGURE IT OUT

1 Answer (briefly) these two questions in German.

    a How often does Ellen have a German class? _____

    b How often does Jakob have an Italian class? _____

2 *Richtig oder falsch?* Select the correct answer.

    a Jakob prefers to have Italian classes at home, on the internet. *richtig / falsch*
    b Ellen doesn't think she should have online classes too.   *richtig / falsch*
    c Ellen agrees that reading books helps learn a language.   *richtig / falsch*
    d Jakob suggests studying a little bit every week.   *richtig / falsch*

3 Can you figure out how to say 'you learn'/'you're learning' in German?

    *lernen/ich lerne/*_____ *(to learn/I'm learning/you're learning)*

4 Can you guess the meaning of the phrases?

    a *Das ist auch sehr effektiv!* _____
    b *Wie lernst du Deutsch?* _____

5 Highlight the cognates or near cognates in the conversation.

NOTICE

🔊 02.11 Listen to the audio and study the table.

Essential phrases for Conversation 3

German	Meaning
Wie lernst du ...?	How are you learning ...?
Ich lerne Vokabeln.	I'm learning vocabulary
ich gehe ...	I go ...
... jeden Montag zum Deutschkurs	... to a German class every Monday (every Monday to-the German-course)
Das ist ganz leicht, weißt du?	It's totally easy, you know?

PRONUNCIATION: ß – the 'double s' This is an easy one. It looks like a 'b', but sounds like an 's'. That's it!

Nun …	Well …
Ich finde das nicht effektiv.	I don't find that effective. (I find that not effective.)
Ich gehe lieber …	I prefer to go … (I go rather)
jeden Tag zum Italienischkurs	to Italian classes every day (each day to-the Italian-course)
Wie geht das denn?	How does that work then? (How goes that then?)
Das heißt …	That means …
Ich habe Unterricht online.	I have classes online.
Das sollte ich machen!	I should do that! (That should I do.)
Du liest gern Bücher, oder?	You like to read books, right?
Das ist auch sehr effektiv!	That's also very effective!
Das stimmt.	That's true.
Ich denke, …	I think …
… du hast Recht	… you're right (you have right)

HACK IT: double your vocab with nicht
Since you know the word *nicht*, you've practically doubled your vocab with a shortcut to saying opposites. Imagine you want to tell your German friend, 'this is hard', but you haven't learned the word 'hard' yet. You can simply say it's 'not easy'. *Das ist nicht leicht.*

CULTURE TIP: typing German letters
If you can't type ä, ö, ü or ß, substitute ä with ae, ö with oe, ü with ue and ß with ss. Germans do it, too!

1 There are several phrases the speakers use to give their opinions in the vocab list. Find them and write them here.

a I find … _____

b I prefer to go … _____

c It's totally easy. _____

d Good idea! _____

e That's true. _____

f You're right. _____

2 How do you think you'd say 'I don't learn' and 'I don't play' in German?

a *Ich lerne* (I learn) → _____ (I don't learn)

b *Ich spiele* (I play) → _____ (I don't play)

3 Go through the phrase list and identify all *ich* and *du* verb forms. Arrange them in the table.

ich	lerne						
du	lernst						

You can also use the word **oder** (or) at the end of a statement to turn it into a question in order to confirm something you're saying. It translates as 'Isn't it so?', 'Isn't it true?' or in this example as 'don't you?' or simply 'right?' It's a useful little trick. Deutsch ist leicht, oder?

PRONUNCIATION: the umlaut – *ä*, *ö* and *ü*

The dots on the *ä* are called an **umlaut**. Without the dots, the German *a* is pronounced as in 'father'. But with the dots, *ä* is pronounced roughly like the 'a' sound in 'bad', the 'eh' sound in 'bed', or the 'ay' sound in 'say'.

You'll have heard the *ö* sound in the word *möchte*. We don't really have this sound in English, so it does take a bit of practice. The sound it makes is similar to the vowel in the word 'her'. Top tip: to pronounce *ö*, say 'ay', as in the word 'day', and then pucker up your lips as if you're about to kiss someone! The resulting sound is *ö*.

The pursed lips trick works well for the *ü* sound too. Start by saying 'ee' as in 'bee' and then tightly purse your lips as you do so.

◀)) 02.12 Read the following words out loud to practise your pronunciation of German umlauts. Then listen to the native pronunciation to see if you got it right.

   a   *Mädchen* (girl), *Äpfel* (apples), *Bär* (bear)
   b   *möchte* (want), *hören* (to listen to), *schön* (pretty)
   c   *für* (for), *üben* (to practise), *Bücher* (books)

Speaking fluently doesn't mean speaking quickly, but **keeping the language flowing**. To help you get into that flow, give yourself the chance to think about what you want to say, while using natural filler words. Think of them as a boost of several 'extra' seconds to gather your thoughts! You'll find it easier to maintain a steady flow if you aim to speak at a slower rate.

CONVERSATION STRATEGY: filler words

You will see some occasional 'filler words' used in these conversations. While they don't add meaning to the conversation, just like how we say 'well …', 'so …', 'y'know …' in English, in German you'll hear similar filler words in natural conversations. When you need to hesitate, use filler words to make your conversation feel more natural!

na ja   nun (na)   ähm   also

1   ◀)) 02.13 Listen to the audio with a speaker talking without using any filler words. Then you'll hear the phrases repeated, but with the added filler words above. Notice how the filler words change the flow of the language.

2   Repeat the audio to mimic the speaker, and fill in the gaps with the filler words you hear.

   a   *Ich wohne in Berlin, _____ Ich möchte viel Deutsch sprechen.*
   b   *_____ … Ich lerne Spanisch _____ Ich möchte in Santander studieren.*
   c   *Ich lese gern Tolkien _____ Ich bin ein Tolkien-Fan.*
   d   *Ich möchte noch viel reisen, _____ Ich möchte Land und Leute _____ kennenlernen.*

GRAMMAR EXPLANATION: creating the *ich* (I) and *du* (you) verb forms

In Conversation 3, you met a lot of new verbs used in different ways. Now let's see how to change them into different forms.

From the dictionary form of a verb, you can usually easily figure out the *ich* and *du* forms:

···⟩ Step 1: Remove the ending (**-en**) from the dictionary form.
···⟩ Step 2: For the **ich** form, **add** -e; For the **du** form, **add** -st.

Examples:

lieben
(to love)
→ **ich** liebe
↘ **du** liebst

wohnen
(to live)
→ **ich** wohne
↘ **du** wohnst

lernen
(to learn)
→ **ich** lerne
↘ **du** lernst

> Changing a verb from its dictionary form (*lieben*) to other forms (*ich liebe* or *du liebst*) is what language teachers typically refer to as conjugating the verb.
>
> Nearly all German dictionary forms of verbs end in -en.

Now, go back to the table in Exercise 3 and fill in the missing verb forms.

PRACTICE

1 Fill in the table with the *ich* and *du* forms for each verb.

Dictionary form	*ich* form	*du* form
schreiben (to write)	ich schreibe	du schreibst
verstehen (to understand)		
denken (to think/believe)		
gehen (to go)		
versuchen (to try)		
studieren (to study)		
beginnen (to begin)		

> **GRAMMAR: *du* vowel changes**
> Some German verbs change their vowel for the *du* form. The most common change is from *e to i*, which is done to make the words easier to pronounce!
> For example:
> *ich spreche* –
>   *du sprichst* and
> *ich helfe* –
>   *du hilfst*.
> More on this later!

2 Now fill in the blanks with the correct forms.

a _____ _____ *hier in Berlin, oder?*
   (**You live** here in Berlin, right?)

b _____ _____ *Russisch.* (**I'm studying** Russian.)

c _____ _____ *viel Deutsch sprechen.*
   (**I want** to speak a lot of German.)

d _____ _____ *Siddhartha?* (**Are you reading** Siddharta?)

3 Fill in the blanks with the missing word(s) in German.

a *Was* _____ *du?* (What do you **think**?)

b _____ _____ *gern Artikel für meinen Blog.*
    (I like to **write** articles for my blog.)

c _____ _____ _____ *in Berlin* _____ *in London?*
    (**Do you prefer to live** in Berlin or London?)

d _____ _____ *jeden Tag zum Sprachkurs?*
    (**Do you go** to the language course every day?)

e _____ _____ *jeden Tag ein bisschen Deutsch zu sprechen?*
    (**Do you try** to speak a little German every day?)

4 Practise what you know by translating these full sentences into German.

a I like to speak Italian, but I prefer to speak German.

    _____

b I think you should learn vocabulary every day.

    _____

c It's true! Russian is not easy.

    _____

d I find German easy!

    _____

PUT IT TOGETHER

Use what you've just learned, along with any new 'me-specific' vocab
you've looked up, to write four sentences about yourself.

⋯⊱ Use *ich möchte* to say something you want to do one day.
⋯⊱ Use *ich spreche* to mention a language you speak.
⋯⊱ Use *ich sollte* to say something you should do.
⋯⊱ Use *ich denke* to express an opinion.

_____

_____

_____

COMPLETING UNIT 2

Check your understanding

🔊 02.14 Go back and reread the conversations. When you're feeling confident:

···⊱ listen to the audio rehearsal, which will ask questions in German
···⊱ pause or replay the audio as often as you need to understand the
   questions
···⊱ repeat after the speaker until the pronunciation feels and sounds natural
   to you
···⊱ answer the questions in German (in complete sentences).

Remember you can always use filler words to give yourself time to think!

Show what you know ...

Here's what you've just learned. Write or say an example for each item in
the list. Then tick off the ones you know.

☑ Ask a 'yes' or 'no' question.   *Wohnst du in Berlin?*
☐ Create *ich* and *du* verb forms (e.g. *lernen*).
☐ Ask the question, 'How long have you been learning German?'
☐ Say how long you've been learning German.
☐ Give the numbers 1–10.
☐ Say what other languages you speak or want to learn.
☐ Use the opinion phrases 'I think' and 'I prefer'.
☐ Negate a sentence using *nicht* (e.g. *Das stimmt nicht.*).
☐ Give three filler words.
☐ Pronounce the 'soft *ch*' in *ich* and the 'hard *ch*' in *auch*.
☐ Pronounce the German ä, ö, ü (e.g. *ähm, möchte, üben*).
☐ Pronounce the German *s, st, sp* and *ß* (e.g. *seit, stimmt, sprechen, heißt*).
☐ Use mnemonics to remember tricky vocab.

COMPLETE YOUR MISSION

It's time to complete your mission: trick someone into thinking you speak
German for at least 30 seconds. To do this, you'll need to prepare to initiate
a conversation by asking questions and replying with your own answers.

STEP 1: build your script

Keep building your script by writing out some 'me-specific' sentences along with some common questions you might ask someone else. Be sure to:

- ⋯⟩ ask a question using *Seit wann?* or *Wie viele?*
- ⋯⟩ ask a question using the verb at the start – *Sprichst du …? Wohnst du …?*
- ⋯⟩ say how long you've been learning German using *seit*
- ⋯⟩ say whether or not you speak other languages and how well you speak them
- ⋯⟩ say what other languages you want/hope to learn.

Write down your script, then repeat it until you feel confident.

Momentum is a powerful tool. Once you get started, it's so much easier to keep going.

STEP 2: all the cool kids are doing it … *online*

You've put the time into preparing your script, now it's time to complete your mission and share your recording with the community. Go online to find the mission for Unit 2, and use the German you've learned right now!

STEP 3: learn from other learners

How well can you understand someone else's script? **Your task is to listen to at least two clips uploaded by other learners.** How long have they been learning German? Do they speak any other languages? Leave a comment in German saying which words you were able to understand and answering a question they ask at the end of their video. And ask them one of the questions you've prepared.

STEP 4: reflect on what you've learned

What did you find easy or difficult in this unit?

_____

_____

_____

_____

After only two missions, you've learned so many words and phrases you can use in real conversations. Don't forget that you can mix and match words and sentences to create endless combinations. Get creative!

HEY, LANGUAGE HACKER, DO YOU REALIZE HOW MUCH YOU CAN ALREADY SAY?

In the next few units, you'll learn more about how to have conversations in German – even if you have a limited vocab or haven't been learning for very long.

Es ist einfach, weißt du?

3 SOLVING COMMUNICATION PROBLEMS

Your mission

Imagine this – you're having a great time at the *Biergarten* when someone decides it's time to play a party game – describe something without saying the word itself!

Your mission is to use your limited language and win the game. Be prepared to **use 'Tarzan German'** and other conversation strategies to **describe a person, place and thing** of your choosing.

This mission will help you overcome the fear of imperfection and show you how with just a few words and a powerful technique, you can make yourself understood.

Mission prep

- ⋯➤ Use phrases for meeting new people. *Nett, dich kennenzulernen.*
- ⋯➤ Use survival phrases to ask for help with your German: *Ein bisschen langsamer, bitte.*
- ⋯➤ Describe your interactions with other people: *du … mir, ich … dir.*
- ⋯➤ Talk about what you have / need with *ich habe / ich brauche.*
- ⋯➤ Develop a new conversation strategy: use 'Tarzan German' to fill the gaps in your vocab with *Mann, Frau, Ort, Dings.*
- ⋯➤ Use question words to learn about who you meet: *Wo? Wann? Wie viele?*

BUILDING LANGUAGE FOR MEETING SOMEONE NEW

Practising your German with a tutor or teacher online, especially when you don't live in a German-speaking country, is one of the most effective (and affordable) ways to learn more German in a shorter amount of time. You can do this right away, even if you don't know many phrases yet. In this unit you'll learn strategic survival phrases you can use whenever there's something you don't understand, and you'll use 'Tarzan German' to communicate with limited language or grammar. Strategies like these help you become comfortable making mistakes when speaking, and help you have meaningful conversations despite being a beginner.

#LANGUAGEHACK
power-learn word genders with the word-endings trick

CONVERSATION 1

Having an online chat

Ellen has decided to take Jakob's advice and she's about to have her first online conversation with Martin, her new German teacher.

🔊 **03.01** Since this is Ellen's first time meeting Martin, she needs to introduce herself. How does Ellen greet Martin? How does she reply to *Wie geht's*?

Martin:	Hallo! Wie geht's?
Ellen:	Hallo! Mir geht es gut. Vielen Dank, dass du mir hilfst, Deutsch zu lernen.
Martin:	Kein Problem, ich helfe dir gern.
Ellen:	Wie heißt du?
Martin:	Ich heiße Martin. Und du?
Ellen:	Ich heiße Ellen.
Martin:	Dein Name ist sehr schön! Nett, dich kennenzulernen, Ellen!
Ellen:	Schön, dich kennenzulernen.
Martin:	Also, wo bist du gerade?
Ellen:	Äh … langsamer, bitte.
Martin:	Wo bist du jetzt?
Ellen:	Ach, ja. Ich bin jetzt in Berlin.

It's easy to have conversations with other German speakers right through your computer. I've done this for all the languages I've learned. See our Resources to learn how.

There are endless ways you can answer the question *Wie geht's?* – Alles in Ordnung! (Everything is good!), Gut! (Good!) and Nicht schlecht! (Not bad!) are just a few. Don't be surprised if Germans give you an honest answer – you asked for it!

VOCAB: *bitte* **'please', 'you're welcome' and more!** *Bitte* is a versatile little word. You've already seen it used as 'you're welcome', but it's also commonly used as 'please', as in *Ich möchte eine Pizza bitte*. It can also mean 'here you are'. So for example, you order your pizza – *Eine Pizza bitte* – and the guy hands you your change – *bitte* – then hands you your pizza – *bitte* again – to which you reply *danke*, and him: *bitte!*

- Wie geht's?
- Vielen Dank.. dass du mir hilft. Deutsch zu lernen.
- Schön. dich kennenzulernen.
- langsamer bitte

FIGURE IT OUT

1 Use context to figure out which statement is false.
   a Ellen asks Martin to repeat himself more slowly.
   b Martin wants to know why Ellen is learning German.
   c Martin asks where Ellen is today.

2 How do you say 'many thanks,' 'no problem,' and 'please' in German?
   _____ _____ _____

3 Highlight the phrases 'What's your name?' and 'My name is ...' in German?

4 Can you guess what *Nett, dich kennenzulernen* means in English?
   _____

NOTICE

🔊 **03.02** Listen to the audio and pay special attention to the pronunciation of *Wie heißt du? Vielen Dank*, and *Nett, dich kennenzulernen*.

Essential phrases for Conversation 1

German	Meaning
Hallo! Wie geht's?	Hi! How are you? (How goes-it?)
Mir geht es gut.	I'm fine. (To-me goes it good.)
Vielen Dank, …	Thank you very much … (Many thanks)
… dass du mir hilfst, Deutsch zu lernen	… for helping me learn German (that you to-me help, German to-learn)
Ich helfe dir gern.	I'm happy to help you. (I help to-you gladly.)
Wie heißt du?	What's your name? (How are-called you?)
Ich heiße Ellen.	My name is Ellen. (I am-called Ellen.)
Dein Name ist sehr schön!	Your name is very pretty!
Nett, dich kennenzulernen.	Nice to meet you. (Nice, you to-meet.)
Schön, dich kennenzulernen.	Lovely to meet you.
Wo bist du gerade?	Where are you at the moment?
langsamer, bitte	slower, please
Wo bist du jetzt?	Where are you now?
Ich bin jetzt in Berlin.	I'm in Berlin now.

In Unit 1 you learned to introduce yourself with *Ich bin …* (I am …). Another common way to give your name is to say *Ich heiße …* (I am called …) – the same way we'd switch between 'I'm Luke' or 'My name is Luke' in English.

PRONUNCIATION: *ei sounds like 'eye'* You've heard the *ei* sound in words like *seit* and *weil*. It's simply pronounced like the English word 'eye'. It's important to distinguish this from *ie*, in words like *viel* and *wie* which has the 'ee' sound (as in 'eel'). One way to remember the difference is that each one sounds like the English name of the second vowel. So *ei* sounds like the letter 'i' and *ie* sounds like 'ee'.

CONVERSATION STRATEGY: learn set phrases

It's important to learn and use new phrases *before* you learn to understand the meaning of each individual word or the grammatical rationale behind them. For instance, you need to learn to say 'nice to meet you' way before you need to learn why German uses the structure it does for that expression.

Learn these expressions now as **set phrases** – you'll use them all the time. We'll cover the hows and whys of them later on, when understanding the grammar behind them will help you expand your conversational abilities.

⋯⟩ *Nett / Schön, dich kennenzulernen.* – a chunk that means 'nice to meet you'. Germans don't say 'get to know' a person but 'learn to know' them!

⋯⟩ *Vielen Dank, dass du mir hilfst, Deutsch zu lernen.* – how you say 'thank you for helping me learn German!'

1 What phrase can you use when someone is speaking too fast? _____

2 How do you ask 'Where?' and 'How?' in German? _____ _____

3 Fill in the gaps to say in German:

   a Nice to meet you. _____ *, dich kennenzulernen.*

   b I'm fine. _____ _____ *es gut.*

   c I'm in London right now.   *Ich bin* _____ *in London.*

4 Write the English meaning of the German verb forms:

   a *Ich bin* _____   c *Ich helfe* _____

   b *Du bist* _____   d *Du hilfst* _____

PRACTICE

1 Fill in the gaps with the correct question word: *Wie* or *Wo.* (In some cases both question words are possible).

   a _____ *wohnst du?*   d _____ *lernst du Russisch?*

   b _____ *findest du die Lehrerin?* e _____ *lernst du Vokabeln?*

   c _____ *spielst du Basketball?*   f _____ *hörst du klassische Musik?*

2 Match the English question with its translation in German.

a	What's your name?	1	*Wohnst du in Deutschland?*
b	Where are you?	2	*Wie geht es dir?*
c	Do you live in Germany?	3	*Wie heißt du?*
d	How are you?	4	*Kannst du langsamer sprechen?*
e	How do you travel?	5	*Wo bist du?*
f	Can you speak more slowly?	6	*Wie reist du?*

3 Fill in the blanks with the missing word(s) in German.

a _____ *Name ist* _____ *schön.* (**Your** name is **very** pretty.)

b *Kannst du* _____ *sprechen?* (Can you speak **more slowly**?)

c _____ *arbeitest du* _____? (**Where** are you working **now**?)

d *Danke, dass du* _____ _____. (Thanks for **helping me**).

GRAMMAR EXPLANATION: *mir* (to-me) and *dir* (to-you)

In Conversation 1, you were introduced to the German 'object words' *mir* (me) and *dir* (you). To get used to using these words, it helps to think about them as 'to-me' and 'to-you'. For example:

⋯⋗ *ich helfe* (I'm helping)   *ich helfe dir* (I'm helping **you** / I (give) help **to-you**')
⋯⋗ *du hilfst* (you're helping)   *du hilfst mir* (you're helping **me** / you (give) help **to-me**')

Here's some new vocab that will help you better understand how to use these object words.

1 ◀)) 03.03 Listen to the audio and study the table.

Verbs with *mir / dir*

Dictionary form	Example	Meaning	Word-for-word translation
helfen	Du hilfst **mir**.	You help me.	You help **to-me**.
danken	Ich danke **dir**.	I thank you.	I thank **to-you**.
geben	Du gibst **mir** (eine DVD).	You give me (a DVD).	You give **to-me** (a DVD).
sagen	Du sagst **mir**.	You say to me.	You say **to-me**.
schreiben	Du schreibst **mir**.	You write to me.	You write **to-me**.
erzählen	Du erzählst **mir**.	You tell me.	You tell **to-me**.

Take a minute to repeat these words to yourself a few times, and you should have them down. To check yourself, cover the German and try to remember their translations. Move on when you've got it.

2 Complete the sentences with the correct object word in German.

  a *Ich gebe* _____ *das Buch.*   (I give **you** the book.)
  b *Kannst du* _____ *helfen?*   (Can you help **me**?)

3 Complete these sentences with the correct verb form and object in German.

  Example: <u>Schreibst du mir?</u>   (Will you **write to me**?)

  a *Ich* _____ _____ *viel.*   (I **tell you** a lot.)
  b _____ *du* _____ *das Geld?* (Do you **give me** the money?)
  c *Ich möchte* _____ _____ *,...* (I would like to **say to you** ...)

4 Put the words in the correct order to make complete sentences.

  a *mir / du / möchtest / schreiben / ?*   (Do you want to write to me?) _____
  b *du / mir / sagen / kannst / ?*   (Can you tell me?) _____
  c *danken / dir / möchte / ich*   (I want to thank you.) _____

PUT IT TOGETHER

1 Now write a few sentences about yourself in German. Use your dictionary to look up new words you need, and try to answer the questions:

      ⋯⫶ *Wie heißt du?*   ⋯⫶ *Wo bist du gerade?*
      ⋯⫶ *Wie geht's dir heute?* ⋯⫶ *Was machst du jetzt?*

  _____

  _____

  _____

2 Imagine you are talking directly to a friend, how would you two typically interact? Use the verbs you've seen in this unit in combinations of *Du... mir* or *Ich... dir.*

  _____

  _____

  _____

CONVERSATION 2

I don't understand

As Ellen continues her online class, she has trouble understanding Martin.

🔊 03.04 How does Martin rephrase his sentences when Ellen asks for help?

Martin: Was meinst du mit „Ich bin jetzt in Berlin"? Wohnst du in einer anderen Stadt?

Ellen: Es tut mir leid. Ich verstehe nicht.

Martin: Warum bist du in Berlin?

Ellen: Ah, ich verstehe jetzt. Ich bin hier, um Deutsch zu lernen!

Martin: Wirklich? Sehr interessant!

Ellen: Und du? Wo bist du?

Martin: Ich bin auch in Deutschland, in Köln. Ich wohne und ich arbeite hier.

Ellen: Kannst du das wiederholen, bitte?

Martin: Ich wohne in Köln. Ich bin also in Deutschland.

Ellen: Einen Moment, bitte …Warte mal … Ich kann kaum etwas hören.

> **VOCAB: *also* and *auch* – 'false friends'**
> While we've seen lots of German words that are the same or very similar to English, there are also those known as 'false friends' which mean something different. One such example is *also*, which means 'so' (*auch* is 'also').
>
> You may also come across:
> ⋯⟩ *Bad* ('bath' – *schlecht* actually means 'bad'),
> ⋯⟩ *fast* ('almost' – *schnell* actually means 'fast') and
> ⋯⟩ *Gymnasium* ('secondary school' – *Sporthalle* is one way to say 'gym').

FIGURE IT OUT

1 *Richtig oder falsch?* Select the correct answer.

   a Martin asks Ellen why she is in Berlin.   *richtig / falsch*

   b Ellen says she is in Berlin for work.   *richtig / falsch*

   c Martin lives in Berlin.   *richtig / falsch*

2 Highlight the phrases in which:

   a Ellen says why she's in Berlin.   b Martin says 'so I am in Germany'.

3 What word does Martin use to express surprise? What word have you seen that means the same? _____ _____

4 Find a new cognate and guess its meaning. _____

5 What is the meaning of these phrases?

    a *Wohnst du in einer anderen Stadt?* _____

    b *Kannst du das wiederholen bitte?* _____

    c *Einen Moment bitte ... Ich kann kaum etwas hören.*

    _____

6 Find one word in the conversation that you don't understand and use context to infer its meaning. Look the word up in a dictionary and check!

NOTICE

🔊 **03.05** Listen to the audio and study the table. Repeat the phrases to try to mimic the speakers. Pay special attention to the way the speakers pronounce the words:

verstehe   jetzt   wirklich?   wiederholen   hören

GRAMMAR TIP: *um ... zu* – 'in order to' German uses the expression *um ... zu* to express the meaning of 'in order to', with the *zu* coming before the verb at the end of the sentence.
*Ich habe jeden Tag Unterricht, **um** schnell Deutsch **zu** lernen.*
(I have a class every day, **in order to** learn German quickly!)

Ich kann is a bit irregular, but luckily for us as English speakers, it's still an easy word to remember! And the *du* form of the verb is exactly as you'd expect it: *du kannst.*

Essential phrases for Conversation 2

German	Meaning
Was meinst du mit ...?	What do you mean by ...? (What mean you with?)
Wohnst du in einer anderen Stadt?	Do you live in another city?
Es tut mir leid.	I'm sorry.
Ich verstehe nicht.	I don't understand.
Warum bist du in Berlin?	Why are you in Berlin?
Ich verstehe jetzt.	Now I understand.
Ich bin hier, um Deutsch zu lernen!	I'm here to learn German! (I am here, in-order German to to-learn.)
Wirklich?	Really?
Ich arbeite hier.	I work here.
Kannst du das wiederholen, bitte?	Can you repeat that, please?
Einen Moment ...	One moment ...
Warte mal ...	(Just) Wait ...
Ich kann kaum etwas hören.	I can barely hear anything.

1 Remember the German word for 'why?' Notice how Ellen answers using 'in order to …'. Write out the missing words.

a _____ bist du in Berlin?

Ich bin hier, _____ .

b Based on this, ask 'Why are you learning German?' then give two different reasons. _____

c (in order to) study in Berlin. _____

d (in order to) work in Germany. _____

2 Use examples from the phrase lists and the language you know to write out each of the pairs.

a The *ich* and *du* forms of *wohnen* (to live). _____ _____

b The *ich* and *du* forms of *sein* (to be). _____ _____

c The *du* forms of *können* (to be able to / can) and *sagen* (to say).
_____ _____

d The *ich* forms of *arbeiten* (to work) and *verstehen* (to understand).
_____ _____

e The dictionary form (infinitive) of the verb 'to hear'. _____

3 Ellen uses several 'survival phrases' to tell Martin she's having trouble with her German. Write them out in German in the cheat sheet.

Your survival phrases cheat sheet

German	Meaning
	Slower, please.
	I'm sorry.
	I don't understand.
	Can you repeat that?
	One moment.
	I can barely hear anything.

GRAMMAR TIP: *zu* (without *um*)

Here you're practising using *um … zu* as 'in order to'. But there are some cases where you'll see *zu* used on its own, when a phrase does *not* convey the meaning of 'in order to'.

Look at these examples to help you see the difference:

Warum lernst du Deutsch?
(Why are you learning German?)

⋯▸ *Ich lerne Deutsch um mit meiner Oma zu sprechen.*
(I'm learning German (in order) to speak with my Grandmother.)

Was machst du?
(What are you doing?)

⋯▸ *Ich helfe dir, Deutsch zu lernen!*
(I'm helping you to learn German!)

Survival phrases are your secret weapon for 'surviving' any conversation in German, even when you're having trouble understanding. Learn these phrases, and you'll never have an excuse to switch back to English.

PRACTICE

1 You've now seen most of the main questions words used in German!
   Fill in the cheat sheet.

Question words cheat sheet

Meaning	German	Meaning	German
Why?		Who?	Wer?
What?		How long ?	
How?		Since when?	
Where?		How much?	
Which?	Welche?	How many?	Wie viel(e)?
When?	Wann?		
Can you?		Do you want?	

Have you noticed that most of the 'wh-' question words in English have 'w' equivalents in German?

2 What question words would you ask in German to get the following
   answers?

   a *Samstag.* _____   d *Zu Hause.* (At home.) _____

   b *14.* _____   e *Seit Dienstag.* _____

   c *Martin.* _____

3 Read the answers and select the correct question word.

   a **Wie viele / Was** *Sprachen kannst du sprechen? – Drei.*
   b **Warum / Was** *möchtest du? – Das Buch, bitte.*
   c **Seit wann / Wann** *lernst du Deutsch? – Seit Oktober.*
   d **Wann / Seit wann** *gehst du zum Deutschkurs? – Jeden Montag.*
   e **Warum / Wo** *bist du in Berlin? – Weil … na ja, ich möchte einen Job finden.*
   f **Wer / Welche** *bist du? – Ich bin Ellen.*
   g **Welche / Was** *Sprache sprichst du lieber, Englisch oder Spanisch? –*
      Spanisch.

4 Combine words you know to create new sentences in German.

a Where do you live? _____

b What are you saying? _____

c Why do you want to work in Berlin? _____

d What do you mean by 'I'm a designer'? _____

e How long have you been working in Stuttgart? _____

GRAMMAR EXPLANATION: 'Tell me!' – the command form

When you want to tell someone to 'watch', 'repeat' or 'go', you'll need to use the 'command' (or imperative) form. You saw this used in Unit 2, when Ellen asked Jakob, *Sag mal, sprichst du auch Englisch?* You'll hear a handful of words used this way again and again, such as:

Schau mal / Siehe! (Look!)	*Hör mal!* (Listen!)	*Komm!* (Come!)
Sag mir! (Tell me!)	*Hör mir zu!* (Listen to me!)	*Hilf mir!* (Help me!)
Warte mal! (Wait!)	*Sei vorsichtig!* (Be careful!)	*Sei still / ruhig!* (Be quiet!)

To use the command form, just **remove the final -st from the *du* form** of a verb. With some verbs you can also attach *mir / dir* to the end as an object.

An important exception is the verb *sein* (to be), which becomes *sei* in the command form.

Example: *sagen* (to say / tell) → *sagst* → *Sag!* (Tell!) → *Sag mir!* (Tell (to) me!)

It's good to know a few of the most common verbs in the command form, but there's a #languagehack you can use to easily get by without using this form: just add 'can you' before any dictionary verb you know.

Example: *Sprich!* → *Kannst du sprechen?* (Can you + to speak)
    Hilf mir! → *Kannst du mir helfen?*
    Komm mit! → *Kannst du kommen?*

GRAMMAR TIP: *vowel changes*
Verbs that have a vowel change in the middle (i.e. *ich helfe* → *du hilfst*) usually keep this in the command form. So we get *Hilf mir!* (Help me!)

Germans often add little 'filler words' to the command form to soften the command. *Mal* and *doch* are two of the most common. On their own, their meanings work differently, but in commands, they make you sound less bossy! So *Warte mal* (Wait a sec, would you?) sounds much softer to the German ear than *Warte!* (Wait!)

◀)) 03.06 Can you guess how to say the following command phrases in German? Write them out below, then listen to the audio to check your answers.

a Learn the language! _____

b Speak German, please! _____

c Repeat, please? _____

d Think! _____

PUT IT TOGETHER

Use what you've learned in Conversations 1 and 2, as well as new 'me-specific' vocab you look up in your dictionary, to create new sentences about yourself in German. Be sure to include:

⋯⋗ where you're from, but where you live now (use *aber* and *jetzt*)
⋯⋗ how long you've lived there (use *seit*)
⋯⋗ where you work (use *arbeite* + *in* and the name of the town
⋯⋗ how long you've worked there (use *seit*).

_____

_____

_____

_____

_____

_____

CONVERSATION 3

A bad connection

Ellen and Martin start having Internet connection problems.

🔊 03.07 How does Ellen say that her connection is bad?

Tut mir leid (I'm sorry) is the same as Es tut mir leid. The es often gets dropped from such phrases in casual usage.

> **Ellen:** Ich denke, meine Verbindung ist schlecht. Tut mir leid!
>
> **Martin:** Ist nicht schlimm! Möchtest du deine Webcam deaktivieren?
>
> **Ellen:** Meine Webcam ist nicht das Problem. Ich muss mein … du weißt schon … uff … Wie sagt man auf Deutsch? … Ich weiß das Wort nicht mehr! Also, mein Internet-Dings!
>
> **Martin:** Dein Computer? Oder dein WLAN?
>
> **Ellen:** Mein WLAN! Ja! Ich muss mein WLAN neu starten.
>
> **Martin:** Denkst du, das ist eine gute Idee?
>
> **Ellen:** Vielleicht … Hörst du jetzt besser?
>
> **Martin:** Nicht gut.
>
> **Ellen:** Tut mir leid. Mein Computer ist alt. Ich brauche mehr RAM. Können wir nächste Woche wieder sprechen?
>
> **Martin:** Kein Problem! Wann möchtest du wieder anrufen? Am Samstag?
>
> **Ellen:** Das passt! Bis dann!
>
> **Martin:** Okay, bis zum nächsten Mal!

VOCAB: *man*
'one'* or *'people in general'
Man is a common German word (not to be confused with *Mann* ('man' or 'husband') that you'll see and hear all the time. Literally it means 'one' as in 'someone / a person'. It's a handy word that avoids the confusion we have with 'you' in English. If someone asks, *Kann man hier schwimmen?* (Can one swim here?), it's very clear they are asking if people in general can swim there, and not if you specifically are able to swim (which would be: *Kannst du schwimmen?*).

FIGURE IT OUT

1 There are several German words in the conversation that are the same or similar to English. Highlight at least four cognates you recognize.

2 Did you highlight the following phrases? Can you guess their meanings?

deaktivieren   *neu starten*   *WLAN*   *Dings*   *alt*

If you ever need to access someone's WLAN (wifi, pronounced [veh-LAN]), just ask for their Passwort: Was ist das WLAN-Passwort? (What is the wifi password?)

3 Which one of the following statements about the conversation is *falsch*?

    a The problem is with Ellen's webcam.

    b Martin can't hear Ellen well.

    c Ellen and Martin agree to talk another time.

4 Answer the following questions in German.

    a How does Ellen describe the quality of her Internet connection? _____

    b How do you apologize in German? *Tut* _____

    c What are two ways of saying 'goodbye' in German? _____ _____

    d How do you say 'I don't know' and 'I know' in German? _____ _____

5 What do you think the words *mein(e)* and *dein(e)* mean? _____ _____

Mistakes are a necessary part of the process. In fact, they aren't just inevitable, they're important for making progress. In games like chess, players are advised to lose 50 games as soon as possible. Why not take this philosophy to the extreme and aim to make 200 mistakes a day in German? Get them out of your system sooner, and you can improve so much faster.

CONVERSATION STRATEGY: 'Tarzan German'

As a beginner, you won't always know how to say exactly what you want to say. Instead of feeling frustrated, focus on *getting your point across*, rather than speaking eloquently. This means getting comfortable making mistakes.

That's why I recommend you embrace 'Tarzan German'. Find ways to convey your ideas that are understandable, even if your grammar or word choice isn't beautiful. You can still get your meaning across if you know just the *key words*.

For example, if you want to say 'Could you tell me where the bank is?' *(Kannst du mir sagen, wo die Bank ist?)* you could convey the same meaning with only two words, 'Bank ... where?' (*Bank ... wo?*) Just like Tarzan.

1 Try out your 'Tarzan German'. Look at these sentences and isolate the key words. Then use 'Tarzan German' to convey the same meaning.

Example: *Ich verstehe nicht. Kannst du das bitte wiederholen?* →
<u>*Wiederholen, bitte.*</u>

a *Es tut mir leid, kannst du bitte langsamer sprechen?* (I'm sorry, would you mind speaking more slowly?) _____

b *Kannst du mir sagen, wie viel das kostet?* (Can you tell me how much this costs?) _____

c *Entschuldigung, weißt du, wo der Supermarkt ist?* (Excuse me, do you know where the supermarket is?) _____

> I call the fear of making mistakes 'perfectionist paralysis'. Perfectionism is your enemy because it will hold you back from actually communicating. If you wait to say everything perfectly, you'll never say anything at all!

CONVERSATION STRATEGY: memorize the power nouns *Mann / Frau, Ort, Dings*

These words are 'power nouns'. So, by definition, they encapsulate pretty much all other nouns, and you can use them in a huge number of situations when you want to describe something but don't know the German word.

For example: If you can't remember the words for:

⋯⋗ 'taxi driver' (*Taxifahrer*), you could say: 'taxi … man' – 'Taxi-Mann'
⋯⋗ 'singer' (†) (*Sängerin*), you could say: 'sing … woman' – 'sing-Frau'
⋯⋗ 'train station' (*der Bahnhof*), you could say: 'train … place' – 'Zug-Ort'
⋯⋗ 'bed' (*das Bett*), you could say: 'sleep … thingy' – 'schlaf-Dings'.

1 Look back at Conversation 3. Where does Ellen use this trick when she forgets the word for 'WLAN'? _____

2 Try it out. How could you convey your meaning using power nouns?

Example: Pen? → 'write thing' <u>Schreib-Dings</u>

a Library? → 'book place' _____

b Waitress? → 'restaurant woman' _____

c Actor? → 'film (*Film*) man' _____

NOTICE

🔊 03.08 Listen to the audio and study the table.

Essential phrases for Conversation 3

German	Meaning
Meine Verbindung ist schlecht.	My connection is bad.
Ist nicht schlimm.	No worries. (Is not severe.)
Meine Webcam ist nicht das Problem.	My webcam is not the problem.
… du weißt schon	… you know (you know already)
Wie sagt man ... auf Deutsch?	How do you say ... in German?
Ich weiß das Wort nicht mehr!	I can't remember the word anymore! (I know the word not more)
mein Internet-Dings	my internet thingy
Dein WLAN?	Your wifi?
Ich muss mein WLAN neu starten.	I have to restart my wifi. (I must my wifi new to-start)
Denkst du, das ist eine gute Idee?	Do you think that's a good idea? (Think you that is a good idea?)
Hörst du jetzt besser?	Can you hear better now? (Hear you now better?)
Nicht gut.	Not well.
Ich brauche mehr RAM.	I need more RAM.
Können wir nächste Woche wieder sprechen?	Can we speak again next week? (Can we next week again to-speak?)
Kein Problem.	No problem.
Wann möchtest du wieder anrufen?	When do you want to call again?
Das passt! Bis dann!	That works! See you! (Until then!)
Bis zum nächsten Mal!	Until next time!

Use the verb *müssen* for 'to have to' in German. Think of *ich muss* as 'I must!' in English.

There are many ways to sign off or say goodbye to someone. You could say *tschüss* (bye), *ciao*, *bis zum nächsten Mal* (until the next time), *bis dann* (until then), or just *bis* + day/time (like *bis morgen!* for 'see you tomorrow!').

1 Use the conversation to fill in the gaps with the missing verb forms.

a *hören* (to hear) → _ich höre_ (I hear) → _____ (you hear)

b *brauchen* (to need) → _____ (I need) → _____ (you need)

c *denken* (to think) → _____ (I think) → _____ (you think)

d *müssen* (must) → _____ (I must) → _du musst_ (you must)

2 Study the structure of the sentences *denke*, *brauche* and *muss* appear in.
Then put the following words in the correct order to make complete sentences.

a *ein Smartphone / ich / brauche* _____

b *kannst / kaum etwas / ich denke, / du / hören* _____

c *Peter / ich / anrufen / wieder / muss* _____

d *sprechen / können / auf Deutsch / wir* _____

3 Notice the connector words in the phrase list.

a If someone says, *Es tut mir leid*, and you want to tell them 'it's OK,'
you could use two phrases from the phrase list. One is given. Find
the other and write it out.

kein Problem _____

b 'That works' is an extremely versatile connector word in German.
Find it in the phrase list and write it out here in German.

_____

4 In this conversation, Ellen also uses two new survival phrases. Find them
in the phrase list, then add them to the your survival phrase cheat sheet.

English once used
word genders, too!
We lost them over
time, but sailors
still refer to the
ocean and boats as
'she' – a modern
remnant of old
English word genders.

⚙ #LANGUAGEHACK: power-learn word genders
with the word-endings trick

As you may have noticed, German words are divided into masculine, feminine or neuter.

Masculine:	*der Mann*	(the man)	*der Sport*	(the sport)
Feminine:	*die Frau*	(the woman)	*die Sprache*	(the language)
Neuter:	*das Tier*	(the animal)	*das Museum*	(the museum)

But why is 'language' feminine? When you first start learning German, it can seem like
genders are assigned at random. For instance, *Männlichkeit* (masculinity) is feminine, and
Feminismus is masculine!

Don't try to learn the genders of words one at a time as you come across them. This will start to feel overwhelming fast. Instead, learn the simple patterns behind the genders. Word gender has nothing to do with whether the concept of the word is masculine or feminine. It's actually the spelling of the word, in particular the word's ending, that determines its gender. Here's the general rule for how to guess a word's gender based on its spelling:

⋯⟩ If a word ends in *-er, -ich, -ig, -ling, -us, -ismus*, it's probably masculine.

Examples: *der Bäcker* (the baker), *der Teppich* (the carpet), *der König* (the king), *der Feigling* (the coward), *der Campus* (the campus), *der Tourismus* (the tourism)

⋯⟩ If a word ends in *-e, -ie, -ei, -heit, -keit, -tät, -ung, -ur* or *-schaft* in its singular form, it's probably feminine.

Examples: *die Seite* (the page), *die Familie* (the family), *die Partei* (the (political) party), *die Freiheit* (the freedom), *die Möglichkeit* (the possibility), *die Universität* (the university), *die Übung* (the exercise), *die Kultur* (the culture), *die Gesellschaft* (the company)

⋯⟩ If a word ends in *-chen, -lein, -ment, -um* or *-en* (a verb used as a noun) it's probably neutral.

Examples: *das Mädchen* (the girl), *das Brüderlein* (baby brother), *das Element* (the element), *das Museum, das Essen* (food – from the verb **essen = to eat**)

This trick works most of the time, but there are always exceptions. If you're unsure, just guess! If you go for die/meine then you will be right more often than not. Even if you guess wrong, you will always be understood.

YOUR TURN: use the hack

1 Now you should be able to answer the question: Why is *Männlichkeit* feminine and *Feminismus* masculine?

_____

2 Guess the genders of the following words. Fill in the gap with either *der, die* or *das*.

a _____ *Journalismus*

b _____ *Computer*

c _____ *Wohnung* (apartment / flat)

d _____ *Schwierigkeit* (difficulty)

e _____ *Freundschaft* (friendship)

f _____ *Energie*

g _____ *Meinung* (opinion)

h _____ *Winter*

GRAMMAR EXPLANATION: noun genders

The gender of a word affects whether the word is prefaced with:

⋯➔ *der* (m), *die* (f) or *das* (n) → for 'the'

⋯➔ *ein* (m / n) or *eine* (f) → for 'a'

⋯➔ *mein / dein / kein* (m / n)

or *meine / deine / keine* (f) → for 'my / your / no'

VOCAB: *mein und dein*
'my' and 'your'
To remember how to say 'my' in German, just attach *m* in front of *ein / eine* – so:

⋯➔ *ein* becomes *mein*

⋯➔ *eine* becomes *meine*.
This also works for *dein* (your) and a few other words you'll see later!

Using 'the', 'a', 'my' and 'your' in German sentences

German				English			
die eine meine deine	Webcam (f) Verbindung (f)			webcam connection			good
		gut schlecht					good bad
der ein mein dein	Computer (m) Bildschirm (m)	ist (nicht)	schnell langsam neu	the a my your	computer screen	is (not)	fast slow new
das ein mein dein	Smartphone (n) Mikrofon (n) WLAN (n)		alt kaputt		smartphone microphone wifi		old broken

1 Use the table and the following prompts to create sentences as in the model:

Example: I think your screen is broken. → I think + **your** + **screen** + **is** + **broken** → <u>Ich denke, dein Bildschirm ist kaputt.</u>

  a I think the webcam is new. _____

  b I think my connection isn't good.

_____

There are also other forms you have seen, such as einen / einem. We will always give you the correct form, but don't stress about using it yourself. If you always use eine, Germans will understand you perfectly. In fact, some Germans don't use these forms correctly either!

c   Do you think the wifi is fast? *Denkst du,* _____?

d   Do you think your computer is slow? _____,

_____

Expressing what technology you have, need or want

German			English		
ich habe	eine (1) keine (0)	Webcam Verbindung			webcam connection
ich brauche	einen (1) keinen (0)	Computer Bildschirm	I have I need	a (1) no (0)	computer screen
ich möchte	ein (1) kein (0)	Smartphone Mikrofon WLAN WLAN-Passwort	I want you have you need		smartphone microphone wifi wifi password
du hast					
du brauchst	zwei (2) drei (3) ...	Computer Bildschirme Webcams	you want	two three ...	computers screens webcams
du möchtest	zwanzig (20) ...	Verbindungen Smartphones Mikrofone		twenty ...	connections smartphones microphones

PRACTICE

1 Use the table to create sentences as in the model:

Example: I don't have a connection. → I have + no + connection
→ Ich habe keine Verbindung.

a   I don't have a wifi password, you know?

_____

b   I don't need any wifi; I don't have a smartphone.

_____

c   I don't have a webcam, but I have a microphone.

_____

d I have a smartphone and I don't need a computer.

_____.

e Do you have a computer or a smartphone?

_____?

2 Fill in the missing words in German.

a _____ du deinen _____ neu starten? (Can you restart your **computer**?)

b Du _____ _____ helfen. (You **must** help me.)

c Ich _____ am _____ wieder _____. (I **would like to call** again on **Saturday**.)

d _____ _____ meine Hilfe? (Do **you need** my help?)

PUT IT TOGETHER

Use the new phrases you've learned to create two sentences about yourself in German. Be sure to look up new 'me-specific' words in your dictionary so that you're practising phrases that you'd use in a real conversation. Describe in German:

⋯⇥ your opinion of the newest smartphone on the market (use _ich denke_)
⋯⇥ what devices you have now (use _ich habe_)
⋯⇥ some things you need or would like to buy (use _ich brauche_).

_____

_____

_____

_____

_____

This exercise gives
you a chance to
practise your
listening skills, which
is very important.
But remember –
this isn't a school
exam! Judge your
results based on
how well you're able
to **understand the
audio**, rather than
whether you spell
everything perfectly.

COMPLETING UNIT 3

Check your understanding

🔊 **03.09** Review the conversations from this unit, and when you're feeling confident:

⋯⋗ listen to the audio and write down what you hear
⋯⋗ feel free to pause or replay the audio as often as you need.

Show what you know ...

Here's what you've just learned. Write or say an example for each item in the list. Then tick off the ones you know.

- [ ] Say 'hello' and 'nice to meet you'.
- [ ] Give two phrases for saying goodbye.
- [ ] Say 'I understand' and 'I don't understand'.
- [ ] Say something that you have and something that you need.
- [ ] Use the survival phrases, 'Can you repeat that?', 'How do you say in German?' and 'Slower, please?'
- [ ] Use the question words When?, Where?, Why?, Who?, Which?, and How much?
- [ ] Use German object words (e.g. 'Can you help me?').
- [ ] Use the German words for 'person', 'place' and 'thing' to convey your meaning 'Tarzan-style'.

COMPLETE YOUR MISSION

It's time to complete your mission: using 'Tarzan German' to play (and win!) the word game. To do this, you'll need to prepare phrases for describing a German-speaking person, place or thing that other people could guess – without knowing the word itself.

STEP 1: build your script

Let's embrace 'imperfectionism' with today's script. Highlight the key words you need to convey your point, then look them up in your dictionary – but don't try to have perfect grammar! If you come across a complex expression, try to think of simpler words to convey the same idea.

Keep building your script using 'Tarzan German' and the unit conversation strategies. Be sure to:

···⟩ say whether you're describing a person, place or thing
···⟩ for a person, describe him / her with any words you know (What is / her job? Where is he / she *gerade*?)
···⟩ for a thing, describe whether it's something you have (*ich habe*), need (*ich brauche*), like or dislike
···⟩ for a place, describe what types of people live there or things associated with it.

For example, you could say:

> Weißt du ... ein Hollywood-Mann ... Film ... ein Pirat ...
> Azteken-Gold ... gerne viel sprechen ... Wo ist Rum?

Write down your script, then repeat it until you feel confident.

STEP 2: practice makes perfect ... *online*

Getting over the embarrassment of 'sounding silly' is part of language learning. Use your 'Tarzan German' to help you overcome these fears! Upload your clip to the community area, and you'll be surprised at how much encouragement you'll get.

It's time to complete your mission and share a recording with the community. Go online to find your mission for Unit 3 and see how far you can get with your 'Tarzan German'.

STEP 3: learn from other learners

Can you guess the words? After you've uploaded your own clip, get inspiration from how others use 'Tarzan German'. **Your task is to play the game and try to guess the words other people describe.** Take note of the clever ways they use the conversation strategies from the unit, and stash them away as a mental note to try later on your own.

If you get stuck, you're probably struggling with perfectionist paralysis. Take a step back, and remind yourself that your script is supposed to be imperfect today!

Really! The more time you spend on a task, the better you will get! (Studies show that you will be 30% better than your peers who don't practise their speaking regularly.)

HACK IT: *change your search preferences to Deutsch*
Did you know that many major websites automatically detect your language from your browser settings, and adjust accordingly? You can change these settings to *Deutsch*, and you'll instantly notice your search engine, social networking sites and video searches will automatically change to German!
You can also simply go to google.de (and click *Deutsch*) to search German-language websites around the world ... then be sure to type your keywords in German!

STEP 4: reflect on what you've learned

Did you learn about new places and people from the community? Write down anything interesting that you might want to look into later – a famous actor you might want to look up, or a film you may want to see. What gaps did you identify in your own language when doing your mission? What words do you reach for over and over? Are there any words you hear frequently, but don't understand? Keep note of them!

_____

_____

_____

_____

HEY, LANGUAGE HACKER, YOU'RE ON A ROLL!

By learning to work around a limited vocab, you really can start speaking German with other people in no time. It's not about learning all the words and grammar. It's about communicating – sometimes creatively. By finishing this mission, you've learned valuable skills that you'll use again and again in the real world.

Next, you'll learn to talk about your plans for the future.

Mach weiter so!

4 DESCRIBING YOUR FUTURE PLANS

Your mission

Imagine this – you want to spend a few weeks exploring Europe, but you can only afford the trip if your German-speaking friend comes with you and splits the cost.

Your mission is to make an offer they can't refuse! **Describe the trip of your dreams** and convince a friend to take the trip with you. Use *Lass uns ...* to draw the person in and say all the wonderful things you'll do together. Be prepared to **explain how you'll get there** and **how you'll spend your time**.

This mission will help you expand your conversation skills by talking about your future plans and using new sequencing phrases for better German flow.

Mission prep

····⟫ Develop a conversation strategy for breaking the ice: *Sprechen Sie Deutsch? Stört es, wenn ...?*
····⟫ Talk about your future travel plans with *Ich werde ...*
····⟫ Describe your plans in a sequence: *zuerst, dann, danach ...*
····⟫ Learn essential travel vocab: *besuchen, reisen, mit dem Zug/Bus fahren.*
····⟫ Use the 'slingshot' words *dass*, *wenn* and *weil*.
····⟫ Memorize a script that you're likely to say often.

BUILDING LANGUAGE FOR STRIKING UP A CONVERSATION

It takes a bit of courage to get started practising your German. But preparing 'ice breakers' in advance helps a lot! In this unit, you'll build a ready-made script you can use to start any conversation. You'll learn how to make conversations with German speakers more casual, and hopefully even make a new friend or two!

#LANGUAGEHACK
say exponentially more with these five booster verbs

Excuse me, do you speak German?

Ellen is back at her local language group. Today she wants to build up her confidence to approach someone new and strike up a conversation.

🔊 04.01 What phrases does Ellen use to approach someone new?

> **Ellen:** Entschuldigung, sprechen Sie Deutsch?
>
> **Judith:** Ja, ich komme aus Österreich.
>
> **Ellen:** Klasse! Stört es, wenn ich mit Ihnen ein bisschen Deutsch übe?
>
> **Judith:** Kein Problem – gerne!
>
> **Ellen:** Können wir uns duzen?
>
> **Judith:** Wie du möchtest – warum nicht? Ich heiße Judith.
>
> **Ellen:** Super! Ich heiße Ellen. Ich bin noch Anfängerin.
>
> **Judith:** Aber du kannst schon so viel auf Deutsch sagen!
>
> **Ellen:** Danke, aber ich muss noch viel üben.
>
> **Judith:** Das macht nichts. Ich habe viel Geduld. Lass uns also anfangen!

FIGURE IT OUT

1 Use context and familiar words to answer the questions:

   a Where does Judith come from? _____

   b Why does Ellen approach Judith? _____

2 Find and highlight the phrases in the conversation where:

   a Judith tells Ellen where she's from.

   b Ellen asks to practise German with Judith.

   c Ellen says she needs to practise more.

   d Judith says 'let's begin'.

3 Can you deduce the meaning of the word *Entschuldigung*?

   _____

4 Now find these three words in the conversation and highlight them.

   a practise   b patience   c beginner

5 When someone makes a request of you, rather than simply saying *ja*, how else could you reply? Write out the following phrases:

a With pleasure! _____ c No problem! _____

b Why not? _____ d Great! _____

VOCAB: *Ihnen* **formal 'you'** You've seen *dir*, used for 'you' as an object. In this conversation *Ihnen* is used instead, as the formal equivalent of *dir*.

NOTICE

🔊 **04.02** Listen to the audio and study the table. Pay special attention to the way Ellen pronounces the phrases *Stört es, wenn ...* and *Können wir ...?*

Essential phrases for Conversation 1

German	Meaning
Entschuldigung.	Excuse me.
Sprechen Sie Deutsch?	Do you speak German?
Klasse!	Great!
Stört es, wenn ...?	Do you mind if ...? (Bothers it, if ...?)
... ich mit Ihnen ein bisschen Deutsch übe?	... I practise a bit of German with you? (... I with you a bit German practise?)
Können wir uns duzen?	Can we use first names?
Ich bin noch Anfängerin.	I'm still a beginner.
Du kannst schon so viel auf Deutsch sagen!	You can already say so much in German.
Ich muss noch viel üben.	I still need to practise a lot. (I must still a-lot to-practise.)
Das macht nichts.	That doesn't matter.
Ich habe viel Geduld.	I have a lot of patience.
Lass uns also anfangen!	So let's start! (Let us so to-start.)

CONVERSATION STRATEGY: introducing yourself

This well defined transition between formal and informal language in German has actually helped me see those I count as friends in an even more obvious way, compared to people I simply know as aquaintances or conduct business with. Believe it or not, I miss the switch in English!

If you meet a stranger and see an opportunity to practise, it's safer to introduce yourself using the formal (polite) form, *Sie*, at first.

But here's a handy tip: Open the discussion with a set phrase like *Sprechen Sie Deutsch?* Then quickly ask *Können wir uns duzen?* If the other person is about the same age as you and the situation isn't formal, they'll nearly always say *ja*. In fact, it's such a common transition that German has this special word for using the *du* form: *duzen*.

1 Write out two phrases from the phrase list you can use when approaching someone to practise German.

a _____

Now rewrite them in casual form using *mit dir* and *sprichst du*.

b _____

2 Match the phrases with the correct forms (formal or casual).
   a *Wie Sie möchten.*   1 Can you ...? (formal)
   b *Können Sie ...?*   2 Can you ...? (casual)
   c *Kannst du ...?*   3 As you like. (formal)
   d *Wie du möchtest.*   4 As you like. (casual)

3 What is the question you should ask in German to change a conversation from formal to casual?

   _____

4 Complete the set in German:

   ___ich kann___ (I can) ⋯⟩ *du kannst* (you can)
   _____ (we can) ⋯⟩ *Sie können* (you can (formal))

GRAMMAR EXPLANATION: *wir* (we) and *Sie* (you formal)

You've now also met the German word *wir* meaning 'we', as in *Können wir ...?* (Can we ...?). Here's some good news: using *wir* and *Sie* forms is incredibly easy, as their verb forms are the same as the dictionary form!

*The only exception to this is **sein** 'to be' which uses the wir/Sie form: sind.*

Wir and *Sie* verb forms

Dictionary form	Meaning	We/You (formal)	Meaning
singen	to sing	wir/Sie singen	we/you sing
essen	to eat	wir/Sie essen	we/you eat
wissen	to know	wir/Sie wissen	we/you know
sein	to be	wir/Sie sind	we/you are

Example: *Wir sind Studenten und Sie sind der Professor.* (We're students and you're the professor.)

1 Highlight the correct *du* or *Sie* verb form in the sentences.

    a **Möchtest/Möchten** du nächste Woche wieder sprechen?

    b Was **denkst/denken** Sie?

    c **Verstehen/Verstehst** du Englisch?

    d Wo **wohnst/wohnen** Sie?

    e Wie viele Sprachen **sprechen/sprichst** du?

2 If you're speaking to someone you don't know, or are in a formal setting, how would you say the following?

    a Can you repeat that, please? _____

    b What do you like to eat? _____

    c What are you doing in Berlin? _____

    d Can you hear better now? _____

    e Can you please help me? _____

    f Do you want to start practising? _____ _____ *anfangen zu üben?*

PRACTICE

1 Mix and match phrases you've learned with new vocab. Use the phrases given in the box to create six new sentences in German.

> *wir sind* (we are), *wir arbeiten* (we work/we are working), *wir gehen* (we go/we're going), *wir essen* (we eat/we're eating), *im Supermarkt* (at the supermarket), *zum Strand* (to the beach), *die ganze Zeit* (all the time), *zusammen* (together), *auf eine Reise* (on a trip)

a _____   b _____

c _____   d _____

e _____   f _____

GRAMMAR TIP:
du arbeitest
Based on what you learned about *du* forms in Unit 2, you'd expect the *du* form of *arbeiten* to be 'arbeitst'. The problem is, that would be very tricky to pronounce! German solves this problem in cases like this, by **adding an -e** whenever the dictionary form of the verb ends in **-ten** or **-den**. This means that the *du* form of *arbeiten* becomes **du arbeitest**, which is much easier to say! *Findest du das logisch?*

2 The phrase *Ich bin noch Anfänger(in)* is a useful phrase, but you can also modify it to say countless other phrases. Practise using *noch* to create new sentences using the words given.

Example: I am still young. (*jung*) Ich bin noch jung.

a I'm still living in Europe. (*wohne/in Europa*)
   _____

b Are you still working at the bank? (*arbeitest/in der Bank*)
   _____

c I am still going to class! (*gehe/zum Unterricht*)
   _____

d Can we still practise? (*können/üben*)
   _____

e I am still quite tired. (*müde*)
   _____

3 Fill in the blanks with the missing words in German.

a *Wir_____ _____ unsere Tickets für das Konzert in _____ Monaten.*
   (We're **already buying** our tickets for the concert in **seven** months!)

b *_____ _____ mein Handy benutzen, _____ _____ _____.*
   (**You** (formal) **can** use my phone, **if you want**.)

c *_____ _____, _____ 'airport' _____ _____ist?*
   (Do **you know what** 'airport' is **in German**?)

d *Es ist_____, _____ zu sein!* (It's **cool** to be **here**!)

e *_____ _____ vor der Reise _____ so viel _____.*
   (**I still have to practise** so much before the trip.)

f *_____ _____, _____ ich eine Frage stelle?* (Do **you mind if** I ask a question?)

CONVERSATION STRATEGY: memorize regularly-used scripts

A lot of people get nervous speaking to someone new for the first time – especially in another language. But when you plan out what you'll say in advance, you have less to worry about. Luckily, many conversations follow a similar pattern, and you can use this to your advantage.

Learn set phrases

Sometimes you may want to say a complicated phrase that you haven't learned the structure of yet. But just because you don't know the grammar behind a phrase doesn't mean you can't use it. In these cases, you can simply memorize the full phrase as a *chunk* so you can use it whenever you need to – even if you don't fully understand all the individual words.

Try this with the very useful power phrase, *Stört es, wenn ...?*, which can be used in a variety of situations and conversation topics.

Memorize a script

When you learn set phrases that are specific to you and combine them together, you create a personal 'script' you can use over and over again.

For instance, over the course of my travels I'm frequently asked, 'Why are you learning this language?' and I'm often asked about my work as a writer, which isn't easy to explain as a beginner. Because I know these questions are coming, I don't need to answer spontaneously every time. Instead, I craft a solid response in advance so I can speak confidently when the question inevitably comes up.

For you, it may be your upcoming travels to Germany, or the personal reasons you're learning the language. Ultimately, if you know you'll need to give an explanation or mini-story frequently, memorize it to have ready when it's time to produce.

- ⋯▸ **First decide what you want to say.** Make it personal to you. Then simplify it as much as possible to remove complicated expressions. If possible, *try to do this in German from the start*. Think of key words and phrases and jot them down. Then you can fill in the script later. If you find this tricky, think of it in English and then try to translate that.
- ⋯▸ **Finally, when you have your final script,** recite it as often as you can until you commit it to memory.

You can ride a bike without understanding aerodynamics, you can use a computer even if you don't know the physics of how circuits work ... and you can use German phrases at the right time, **even if you don't understand each word** and why they go together the way they do!

GRAMMAR TIP: wenn
If you use *wenn* (if) in a sentence like this, the key verb will typically go to the end of the sentence.

You can even **have a native speaker review your scripts** and refine them to good German. It's fine to speak spontaneously with mistakes, but you may as well get it right if you're memorizing it in advance. It's easy and free when you know where to look. See our Resources to find out how to get free online help.

PUT IT TOGETHER

Don't forget to put the key verb at the end of the sentence, such as ... wenn ich mein Buch hier *lese* (if I *read* my book here).

1 Imagine that you're planning to visit Germany. In what situations might you need to ask the question, *Stört es Sie, wenn …?* Use this phrase along with your dictionary to create sentences you could use:

⋯⋗ at a social event (e.g. '… if I speak with you?')
⋯⋗ at a café (e.g. '… if I sit here?')
⋯⋗ in the park (e.g. '... if I smoke?')
⋯⋗ at someone's house (e.g. '… if I use the bathroom?').

2 Pick one of the following situations, then prepare a short script you can use without having to think on the spot.

This is a great memorized script to have in your back pocket. You'll use it loads. You may know a few phrases that you can use to discuss this, but it's good to **have a go-to answer for this question memorized.**

⋯⋗ Situation 1: Memorize a few words you can say any time someone unexpected hits you with German. Suggestions: 'Ah, you speak German!' 'I'm still a beginner.' 'I've been learning German for …'

⋯⋗ Situation 2: Someone asks you to give a mini life story, or asks why you are learning German. Suggestion: 'I think the language is beautiful!'

⋯⋗ Situation 3: You need to interrupt someone on the street to ask a question in German. Suggestions: 'Excuse me.' 'Do you mind if I ask a question?'

CONVERSATION 2

Where are you going?

Since Ellen and Judith are both visitors to Berlin, travel is a natural conversation topic. In fact, as you learn any new language, you'll likely be asked (or want to ask someone) about travelling to different places.

🔊 04.03 What phrase does Judith use to ask, 'Do you travel a lot?'

> **Judith:** Also, seit wann bist du in Berlin? Reist du viel?
>
> **Ellen:** Nein, eigentlich nicht … Ich bin jetzt ein paar Monate in Berlin. Danach möchte ich 'zu' Italien fahren.
>
> **Judith:** Du meinst, du möchtest nach Italien fahren?
>
> **Ellen:** Genau, ja. Danke!
>
> **Judith:** Du solltest Österreich besuchen. Die Natur in Österreich ist fantastisch.
>
> **Ellen:** Vielleicht im Sommer. Ich möchte hier in Deutschland noch so viel sehen.
>
> **Judith:** Ich sollte mehr reisen. Ich möchte andere Städte in Deutschland besuchen, wie Hamburg und München. Jetzt oder nie!
>
> **Ellen:** Das stimmt, aber hier in Berlin kann man so viel unternehmen!

FIGURE IT OUT

1 What phrase does Judith use to correct Ellen when she makes a mistake?

_____

2 Use context along with words you know to figure out:
   a where Ellen is going after Berlin _____
   b where Judith suggests that Ellen visit _____

3 Can you guess the meaning of the phrase: *Ich möchte andere Städte in Deutschland besuchen*? _____

4 Find and highlight the following phrases:
   a How long have you been in Berlin?   b Not really   c for a few months

---

GRAMMAR TIP:
nach versus *zu*
Both *nach* and *zu* can mean 'to', but *nach* is mostly used with geographical place names (*nach Deutschland/Berlin*) and directions like *nach Osten* (to the east) and *nach links* (to the left). It's OK to get them mixed up, since you will get help if you forget … like Ellen does here!

VOCAB: *das stimmt*
Das stimmt is a great chunk meaning 'that's right'. You'll often hear this without *das* as just *Stimmt!* 'Right!'

VOCAB: *unternehmen*
'under' + 'take'
You'll start to see a cool trick for understanding new German vocab by recognizing when different words come together as one. Here for instance, you may recognize *unter* (under) and *nehmen* (to take). Together they mean 'to undertake', which, let's face it, is simply a fancy way of saying 'to do'!

5 What phrase could you use to recommend a place someone should visit?

_____

NOTICE

🔊 04.04 Listen to the audio and study the table.

Essential phrases for Conversation 2

German	Meaning
Reist du viel?	Do you travel a lot?
eigentlich nicht	not really
Ich bin jetzt ein paar Monate in Berlin.	I have been in Berlin for a few months now.
Ich möchte nach Italien fahren.	I want to go to Italy.
Du meinst ...	You mean ...
Genau.	Exactly.
Du solltest Österreich besuchen.	You should visit Austria.
Vielleicht im Sommer.	Maybe in summer.
noch so viel sehen	still so much to see
Ich sollte mehr reisen.	I should travel more.
Ich möchte andere Städte besuchen.	I want to visit other cities. (I would-like other cities to-visit.)
wie Hamburg und München	like Hamburg and Munich
Jetzt oder nie!	(It's) now or never!
Man kann so viel unternehmen!	There's so much to do! (One can so much to-undertake.)

VOCAB: *meinen* '*to mean*'
In German, the way to say 'you mean ...' is *du meinst ...* You may hear this as you're learning and getting corrections from others. You can also say *ich meine* to clarify something you've said.

VOCAB: *wie*
You've seen that *wie* means 'how' in questions, but it also doubles up to mean 'like' or 'as'. Handy!

1 How would you correct yourself in German by saying 'I mean ...'?

_____

2 How would you ask in German, 'Do you mean ...?'

_____

3 Notice how the word *wie* can be used in different ways. How would you say the following?

    a I like (eating) fruit (*Obst*) like bananas (*Bananen*) and apples (*Äpfel*).

    _____

    b How do you do that? _____

    c. How many dogs (*Hunde*) do you have? _____

    d You are like my brother (*Bruder*). _____

4 Match up the German phrases with the correct English translations.

a	*du reist viel*	**1**	you should visit …
b	*du meinst*	**2**	you can do …
c	*du solltest … besuchen*	**3**	you travel a lot
d	*noch so viel*	**4**	you mean
e	*jetzt oder nie*	**5**	still so much
f	*man kann … unternehmen*	**6**	now or never

5 Highlight the correct translation for each word or phrase:

a	*seit wann*	maybe/ since when	**d**	*vielleicht*	never/maybe
b	*nie*	afterwards/never	**e**	*so viel*	more/so much
			f	*mehr*	other/more
c	*danach*	other/afterwards	**g**	*andere*	never/other

Here's some additional vocab you can use to talk about your own travel plans.

Travel vocab

German		Meaning	
ich nehme du nimmst	den Zug, den Bus, die S-Bahn, ein Taxi	I take/I'm taking you take/you're taking	the train, the bus, the metro, a taxi
ich fahre du fährst	mit dem Zug/ Auto	I go/I'm going you go/you're going	by train/by car

GRAMMAR EXPLANATION: vowel changes

You may have noticed that some verbs in the *du* form change around their vowels. In fact, these changes follow a distinct pattern:

···▸ e in the *ich* form changes to *i* or *ie*:
 ich esse → du isst, ich gebe → du gibst, ich lese → du liest
···▸ a in the *ich* form **adds an umlaut**:
 ich wasche → du wäschst (I wash / you wash).

1 These common verbs each require a vowel change. Practise changing them into the *du* form.

 a *schlafen* (to sleep) → *ich schlafe → du* _____ (a → ä)

 b *sehen* (to see) → *ich sehe → du* _____ (e → ie)

 c *helfen* (to help) → *ich helfe → du* _____ (e → i)

 d *sprechen* (to speak) → *ich spreche → du* _____ (e → i)

PRACTICE

> There isn't a huge number of verbs that work like this, but the ones that do tend to be used a lot. You will soon get a feel for what sounds right!

1 Use the phrase list to determine how to say the following in German. (Hint: both *nehmen* and *fahren* change vowels in the *du* form.)

 a I want to take _____   d I want to go _____

 b I take _____   e I go _____

 c you take _____   f you go _____

2 Now practise creating new sentences with the vocab you've just learned.

 a I'm taking the train. _____

 b You're taking the bus. _____

 c I'm going by car. _____

 d You're going by train. _____

3 Fill in the blanks with the missing words in German.

    a *Du* _____ *die U-Bahn zum Alexanderplatz* _____.
        (You **should take** the metro to Alexanderplatz.)

    b *Mit dem Zug* _____ *du so* _____!
        (By train you **see** so **much!**)

    c *Ich möchte* _____ *Städte* _____, _____
        München und Frankfurt.
        (I want **to visit other** cities, **like** Munich and Frankfurt.)

    d _____ _____, *mit dem* _____ *ist es nicht*
        schnell genug?
        (**You mean**, by (the) **car** is not fast enough?)

    e *Ich bleibe* _____ *lange in Italien im* _____!
        (I **never** stay long in Italy in **summer!**)

PUT IT TOGETHER

Read the questions as well as the prompts in German, then reply in sentences
relevant to your life. Use your dictionary to look up the 'me-specific' vocab you need.

a Do you travel a lot? (... *ein bisschen* ... *nie*)

    Ich reise _____

b Where are you going for your next trip?

    Ich fahre nach _____

c How long are you going for? (... *für ein paar Tage* ... *für ein paar Wochen*)

    Ich fahre _____

d When are you going? (... *diesen/nächsten Monat* ... *dieses/nächstes Jahr*)

    Ich fahre _____

e How are you going to travel? (... *mit dem Auto* ... *ich fliege*)

    Ich _____

CONVERSATION 3

What are you doing this weekend?

As the conversation between Ellen and Judith progresses, they start talking about their plans for the weekend.

🔊 04.05 Notice how the phrases *zuerst werde ich* and *wir werden* are used to talk about future plans. How does Judith ask, 'What are you going to do?'

VOCAB: *ja* for 'indeed'
Sometimes you'll see *ja* in the middle of phrases like this. Rather than a rogue 'yes', this is actually used to show how confident the speaker is in what he or she is saying, and used in the sense of 'indeed' in English, but with a more casual connotation.

Handy in German doesn't mean 'convenient/useful', but is the German word for 'mobile phone'. While most people may own *ein Smartphone*, you'd still use *Handy* in ways like this to get someone's number.

This *Denglisch* (funny mixture of German and English) can be seen in other words like *Wellness* (spa), *Mobbing* (bullying), *Beamer* (projector), *Smoking* (tuxedo) and *Oldtimer* (vintage car).

> **Judith:** Also, was machst du am Wochenende?
>
> **Ellen:** Na ja, zuerst werde ich das Brandenburger Tor sehen. Dann werde ich ein Stück Torte im Café Lebensart essen, das ist in der bekannten Straße Unter den Linden. Danach möchte ich auf den Fernsehturm am Alexanderplatz. Von dort hat man einen Blick über ganz Berlin. Und ich werde natürlich die ganze Zeit Deutsch üben!
>
> **Judith:** Das ist ja toll! Du hast ja so viel vor! Kann ich mitkommen?
>
> **Ellen:** Gerne! Ich freue mich, dass ich eine neue Freundin habe! Wir werden die Stadt zusammen entdecken!
>
> **Judith:** Ich denke, ich habe morgen Zeit, aber ich weiß es noch nicht. Kann ich dir eine SMS schicken?
>
> **Ellen:** Ja, natürlich. Meine Handynummer ist 0151/2718281.
>
> **Judith:** Cool, danke. Tschüss!

FIGURE IT OUT

1 Read the statements to determine which are *richtig* and which are *falsch*. For any *falsch* statements, write in the correct German word(s).

Example: Judith is sure she is free tomorrow.

falsch: ich weiß es noch nicht

a   Judith is going to call Ellen. _____

b   Ellen won't be practising her German at the weekend.
    _____

c   Judith doesn't want to go with Ellen and visit these places.
    _____

d   Ellen is happy to have a new friend. _____

CULTURE TIP: *giving your phone number*
Many Germans will give their phone number in single digits, which is easy. However, you may hear a number given in two-digit forms. These have a 'backwards' feel to them as a German would say 'four and twenty'. It's absolutely fine for you to stick to using single digits though.

2   Use your understanding of the conversation to put the things Ellen wants to do in the correct order.

a   ____ see the Brandenburger Tor
b   ____ see Alexanderplatz
c   ____ go to a café

3   Now give the answers to the following questions in German, starting with the prompted phrase.

a   Why is Ellen going to the café?
    Weil … na ja … sie möchte _____
b   Why is Ellen going to the Fernsehturm?
    Von dort hat man _____

4   Find these phrases in the conversation and write them out in German.

a   What are you going to do this weekend? _____
b   Can I come along? _____
c   That's great! _____

5   How would you arrange the German words to correctly form the sentence: 'We will discover the city together'?

    wir werden (we will)   *entdecken* ((to) discover)
    zusammen (together)   *die Stadt* (the city)

    _____

CULTURE TIP: *zwo*
When on the phone, Germans will sometimes say *zwo* instead of *zwei* to avoid any confusion with *drei*.

6   🔊 04.06 Listen to the audio and note down the number. Note that *zwei* is often said as *zwo* on the phone.
    Meine Handynummer ist __ __ __ __ / __ __ __ __ __ __

Some word combinations in German can be shortened. Take *am Wochenende* and *im Sommer*, for example. In full, they would be *an dem Wochenende* and *in dem Sommer*. However, just as we shorten the words 'do not' to 'don't' in English, German does the same with *am* and *im*. Other notable contractions are

···⟩ *ins (in das)*

···⟩ *zum (zu dem)*

···⟩ *zur (zu der)*

···⟩ *vom (von dem)*

You'll see these in phrases such as *Ich gehe ins Kino* and *Ich gehe zum Bahnhof*.

Broken up into pieces, **mit-kommen** means 'with-come', or 'to come along'. In German, you'll find many verbs with the head **mit-** and they all express the notion of 'along', or of doing something together: mitgehen, mitsingen, mitspielen, mitreisen, mitessen and mittrinken.

◀)) 04.07 Listen to the audio and study the table.

Essential phrases for Conversation 3

German	Meaning
am Wochenende	at the weekend
Zuerst werde ich ...	First, I'll ... (First will I)
Dann werde ich ...	Then I will ...
Danach möchte ich ...	Afterwards I want to ...
ein Stück Torte im ... essen	eat a piece of cake at ...
Von dort hat man einen Blick über ganz ...	From there you have a view of … (From there has one a view over all)
Und ich werde natürlich ...	And of course I will ...
die ganze Zeit Deutsch üben	practise German the entire time (the entire time German to-practise)
Du hast ja so viel vor!	You have so much planned!
Kann ich mitkommen?	Can I come along? (Can I with-come?)
Ich freue mich ...	I am happy ... (I please myself)
... dass ich eine neue Freundin habe!	... that I have a new friend (f)! (that I a new friend (f) have)
Wir werden die Stadt zusammen entdecken.	We will discover the city together. (We will the city together to-discover.)
Ich denke, ich habe morgen Zeit	I think that I have time tomorrow
Kann ich dir eine SMS schicken?	Can I send you an SMS? / Can I text you?
Meine Handynummer ist ...	My mobile phone number is ...

1 Match the German phrases with the correct English translations.

   a *Kann ich dich anrufen?*   1 Can you email me?
   b *Kann ich dir eine E-Mail schicken?*   2 Can I text you?
   c *Kann ich dir eine SMS schicken?*   3 Can I call you?
   d *Kannst du mich anrufen?*   4 Can you text me?
   e *Kannst du mir eine E-Mail schicken?* 5 Can I email you?
   f *Kannst du mir eine SMS schicken?*   6 Can you call me?

2 What are the German words for 'first', 'then' and 'afterwards'?

   a first _____   b then _____   c afterwards _____

3 Notice the new vocab you can use to talk about the future, then turn
   these sentences into a future equivalent in German.

Example: *Ich lese dein Buch.* (I'm reading your book.)

   → Ich werde dein Buch lesen. (I will read your book.)

   a *Wir sprechen auf Deutsch.* _____

   b *Ich schreibe dir.* _____

   c *Du wohnst in München.* _____

Hint: **werden** is an
e → i vowel changing
verb in the du form.

GRAMMAR EXPLANATION: word order in German

When I was learning German in school, I kept asking myself 'Why do they have to say it like that?' But with the benefit of hindsight, I've grown to love how German word order works! It's actually **more flexible than English** in many ways, but it does take a bit of practice to get used to the different ways it works. So while we're getting used to it, let's have some fun with it!

'Named must your fear be, before banish it you can!'

Here's the big question: Why do you see *ich kann* in some instances in German, but *Vielleicht kann ich ...* (Maybe can I) in others?

In both German and English, sentences like 'I can' and 'I will' put the *verb in the second position: Ich kann, Ich werde.* German *really* likes it there though, so it keeps it in that position no matter what. This means that whenever you add any word – or even a short phrase – to the start of a sentence, the verb will stay in the second position.

Examples:

Eines Tages möchte ich ...	(lit. 'One day want I')
Heute spiele ich ...	(lit. 'Today play I')
Im Sommer esse ich ...	(lit. 'In-the summer eat I')

Notice that the words in the *'first position'* can be more than one word – think of it as the first 'piece' of the phrase, not the first word. This works with:

    normalerweise (usually)   *im Park* (in the park)   *natürlich* (of course)

    dieses Wochenende (this weekend)   *nächste Woche* (next week)

1 Highlight the first 'piece' of the sentence for the three examples above.

2 Now look back at the phrase list and notice the German phrases that use this word order:

    a _____ (First I will ...)

    b _____ (Then I will ...)

    c _____ (Afterwards I want to ...)

3 Try it yourself! How do you think you would say in German:

    a Usually I take the bus. _____

    b At the weekend, I will see *Schloss Neuschwanstein.*

        _____

    c Next week I want to read a book. _____

'SLINGSHOT WORDS': *dass, weil, wenn*

Until now we've been cleverly using filler words (*weil ... na ja*) to keep German word order familiar. This is because in German, certain words act as 'slightshots' that send the second verb in a sentence straight to the end – requiring you to switch the word order from what you're used to. The most common slingshot words in German are:

dass (that)   *weil* (because)   *wenn* (if)

Take a look at how *dass* affects the word order in the sentence:

*Ich weiß, **Yoda** kommt aus Deutschland.*
(I know, **Yoda** comes from Germany.)

*Ich weiß, dass **Yoda** aus Deutschland kommt.*
(I know, *that **Yoda*** from Germany *comes*.)

1 Refer to the phrase list from Conversation 3 to find the phrase that uses *dass*. How would the phrase *Ich denke, ich habe morgen Zeit* change if you added *dass*?

Ich denke, dass _____

2 We've previously used the filler word *na ja ...* after *weil* to 'reset' the sentence. This time, use *weil* with natural (slingshot) word order to translate the sentence:

a _____
(I'm learning German because I have family in Germany.)

Now try again using *wenn* for 'if'.

Example: <u>Wenn du jetzt arbeitest, kannst du später spielen.</u>
        (If you work now, you can play later.)

b _____
(I will practise English with you if you practise German with me!)

Practise using this word order from now on, but when in doubt, you can avoid the word order change with connector words and filler words!

Dass (that) is one of those German words that Yoda would have loved! You may remember this from the phrase Vielen Dank, dass du mir hilfst.

Notice how adding dass slingshots the word kommt (comes) to the end of the sentence

⚙ #LANGUAGEHACK: say exponentially more with these five booster verbs

You've seen by now that saying things right in German means learning how to form verbs differently for *ich, du, wir* and so on. And that's even before you start changing from present to past forms and dealing with separable verbs … which is when things can really get messy! Sometimes – especially when you're just starting out – it can feel overwhelming.

But don't panic! You will eventually learn to handle even the messiest of verb forms, but for now here's a handy trick you can use to press the snooze button on learning endless German conjugations. Learn these five 'booster' verbs and their forms, and they can do the heavy lifting. Then simply put the second verb you want to use at the end of the sentence in its dictionary form.

Booster verb + **dictionary form**

1 *Ich möchte* for what you want
You've seen *ich möchte* and *du möchtest* used again and again in our conversations – precisely because they are such useful phrases. Imagine that you wanted to say 'You're running a marathon!'- but you don't know the *du* form of *laufen* (to run).

You can just use *Du möchtest* as a booster verb. In this case, if you know that 'to run' in its dictionary form is *laufen*, you can combine it with *Du möchtest* to express the same idea:

Du möchtest	*(einen Marathon)*	+	***laufen***
You'd like	(a marathon)	+	to run
(Booster verb)		+	**(dictionary form)**

*Eines Tages **möchte** ich München **besuchen**.* (One day I want to visit Munich.)
*Ich **möchte** zwei Wochen **bleiben**.* (I'd like to stay for two weeks.)

2 *Ich sollte* for intentions
You can talk about what you are supposed to do using *ich sollte* (I should).
*Mama sagt, ich **sollte** weniger Kaffee **trinken**.* (Mum says I ought to drink less coffee.)
*Ich **sollte** mehr Gemüse **essen**.* (I should eat more vegetables.)

3 *Ich muss* for necessities
This very handy verb can be used to say you 'have to' or 'must' do something. For example, instead of saying, 'I will work tomorrow', why not say:
*Ich **muss** morgen **arbeiten**.* (I have to work tomorrow.)

4 *Ich kann* for abilities and possibilities

To express yourself better, use this verb to clarify that you 'can' or 'are able to' do something. For instance, saying 'I play chess' isn't as expansive as:

> *Ich kann gut Schach* **spielen**. (I can play chess well.)
> *Vielleicht kann ich Zeit* **finden**. (Maybe I can find the time.)

5 *Ich werde* for future tense

Germans often use the present form to talk about the future. But another option you've seen is *Ich werde* (I will), which works exactly like all the other booster verbs. For example:

> *Ich werde im Sommer nach Frankreich* **fahren**. (I will go to France in the summer.)
> *Wirst du Tennis mit mir* **spielen**? (Will you play tennis with me?)

YOUR TURN: use the hack

1 Use booster verbs to convey the idea of each sentence in a different way, then fill in the gaps with the correct verb forms.

Example: I'm working late on Monday. → I have to work late on Monday.
(to work = arbeiten) → <u>Ich muss am Montag spät arbeiten.</u>

a Are you swimming? → Can you swim? (to swim = *schwimmen*)
_____

b Why don't you leave work early? → Can you leave work early? (to leave = *verlassen*)
_____ _____ *die Arbeit früh* _____?

c I'm attending a meeting. → I have to attend a meeting. (to attend = *teilnehmen*)
_____ _____ *an dem Treffen* _____.

d Have you tried yoga? → You should try yoga! (to try = *probieren*) _____ _____ Yoga _____!

e One day I'm moving to Germany! → One day I'd like to move to Germany! (to move = *umziehen*)
Eines Tages _____ _____ *nach Deutschland* _____!

2 Use *ich werde* + verb to create sentences in the future form.

a I will be busy! (*beschäftigt*) _____

b I'll take a taxi. _____

c Will you travel to Spain in the summer? _____

d Will you go to the restaurant? _____

e I won't travel to Frankfurt. _____

PRACTICE

1 Fill in the blanks with the missing words in German.

  a *Moment, _____ _____ dir meine _____ geben.*
     (Hold on, **I'm going to** give you my (mobile) **phone number**.)

  b *_____ habe ich keine _____, aber am Wochenende _____ _____ mit dir _____!*
     (**Tomorrow** I don't have **time**, but **I can come** with you at the weekend!)

  c *Natürlich _____ _____ _____ Deutsch sprechen.*
     (Of course **I will** speak German **there**.)

  d *_____! Ich _____ mich, _____ _____ so gute Freunde _____.*
     (With pleasure! I **am happy that I have** such good friends.)

2 Use the vocab in the box to create sentences about upcoming plans.

> *dieses Wochenende* (this weekend)   *diese Woche* (this week)   *morgen* (tomorrow)   *nächste Woche* (next week)

  a This weekend I'm dancing with you. _____

  b First I want to send an SMS. _____

  c This week I will eat a piece of cake. _____

  d Next I will discover the city. _____

  e Next week I have to visit Munich. _____

  f Then I can come along. _____

  g Tomorrow I should find time. _____

  h After that I'm travelling to Italy. _____

PUT IT TOGETHER

1 In Conversation 2, you described the next trip you're planning. Now, go more in depth to describe what you'll do when you get there. Try to include:

  ⋯▹ what you think you'll do first, then next   *So wird meine Reise! Zuerst …*

  ⋯▹ where you plan to visit, eat, or drink

  ⋯▹ something you want to see.

2 Imagine you've met someone you'd like to hang out with later. How would you:

  ⋯▹ give them your email address and phone number

  ⋯▹ ask them to call, text or email tomorrow (*Kannst du …?*).

COMPLETING UNIT 4

Check your understanding

To check that you understand the audio, don't forget that you can always look at the transcript online!

🔊 04.08 You know the drill! Listen to the audio rehearsal, which will ask you questions in German. Use what you've learned to answer the questions in German with details about yourself.

Show what you know ...

Here's what you've just learned. Write or say an example for each item in the list. Then tick off the ones you know.

- ☐ Give three phrases for politely starting a conversation (using *Sie*).
- ☐ Ask a polite question using 'Do you mind if ...'?
- ☐ Use *ich werde* + dictionary form to say something you will do tomorrow, this weekend or next year.
- ☐ Form verbs using *wir* and *Sie*.
- ☐ Give two sentences, one using 'still' and one using 'already'.
- ☐ Give three forms of travel in German.
- ☐ Give the three German words to say 'first', 'then' and 'afterwards'.
- ☐ Give one sentence each for the German words for 'that', 'because' and 'if'.
- ☐ Give one sentence each for the booster verbs:
  - ☐ 'I should'
  - ☐ 'I want to'
  - ☐ 'I can'
  - ☐ 'I will'
  - ☐ 'I have to'

COMPLETE YOUR MISSION

It's time to complete your mission: convince your friend to go with you on your adventure. To do this, you'll need to describe the trip of your dreams, using *wir* forms to say how you and your friend would spend your trip.

CULTURE TIP: *know before you go!* This is a good time to expand on your script with some of your own research! There are many beautiful cities in Germany, Austria and Switzerland. Look into what sights there are and what you can do when you get there. If you can, talk to someone who lives there to get the inside scoop. Your language partners can be a great resource for tips and stories on travel and culture! Plus, travel aspirations are a great conversation starter.

Travel is a popular topic among language learners, so this is a script you'll want to make sure you have down solid.

STEP 1: build your script

Create a script you can use to tell other language hackers about your travel plans. Incorporate as many new words or phrases from this unit as possible – *schon*, *am Wochenende*, *vielleicht*, etc. Be sure to say:

⋯⇥ where you're going and what you plan to do when you get there

⋯⇥ what you want to see first (what are you most excited to explore?)

⋯⇥ when you'd like to go and how long you'd like to be there

⋯⇥ how you'll get there and how you'll get around once you're there.

Give recommendations to other language hackers for things to do at this destination! Write down your script, then repeat it until you feel confident.

STEP 2: feedback promotes learning ... *online*

Give and get feedback from other learners – it will massively improve your German! When the opportunity presents itself in real life, you won't always have notes at the ready, so let's emulate this by having you speak your script from memory.

This time, when you make your recording, you're not allowed to read your script! Instead, speak your phrases to the camera, relying on brief notes, or even better, say your script from memory. Make sure to revise it well!

STEP 3: learn from other learners

How do other language hackers describe their travel plans and dreams? **Your task is to listen and choose a holiday you'd like to join in on.** Say why you think the place and plans sound good.

STEP 4: reflect on what you've learned

What would you like to add to your script next?

CULTURE TIP:
Your language partners can be a great resource for tips and stories on travel and culture! Plus, travel aspirations are a great conversation starter.

HEY, LANGUAGE HACKER, LOOK AT EVERYTHING YOU'VE JUST SAID!

Isn't it easier when you already know what you want to say? If you take advantage of how predictable some conversations can be and prepare answers you'll give often, you can be confident in what you say. Next, let's build on your script to talk about your friends and family.

Toll!

5 TALKING ABOUT FAMILY AND FRIENDS

Your mission

Imagine this – your good friend develops a serious crush on a German pal of yours and asks you to play matchmaker.

Your mission is to casually talk up your friend and spark the interest of this *Freund* to get those two out on a date! Be prepared to **describe your relationship with your friend – how you know him/her, where he/she lives and works, and the kinds of things he/she likes to do.**

This mission will get you comfortable talking about other people and using new verb forms as well as descriptive language.

Mission prep

⋯⋗ Talk about 'he' and 'she' using *er/sie* forms.

⋯⋗ Talk about 'they' using *sie* forms.

⋯⋗ Use phrases to describe things you do with other people: *verbringen wir die Woche zusammen …*

⋯⋗ Learn essential family vocab: *Mutter, Schwester …*

⋯⋗ Use the two forms of 'to know': *wissen* and *kennen*.

⋯⋗ Use *mir/mich, dir/dich* (me, you).

BUILDING LANGUAGE FOR DESCRIBING YOUR RELATIONSHIPS

Until now, our conversations have focused on describing *ich, du* and *wir*. We'll build on that now with vocab you can use to talk about anyone else.

#LANGUAGEHACK
use clues and context to understand much more than you think

CONVERSATION 1

What do you (two) have planned?

Ellen has been taking online German classes for a few weeks. Today she's practising with Mia, a German tutor from Switzerland, and she's excited to talk about the new friend she made at her language group.

🔊 05.01 Notice how Mia greets Ellen. Which phrase means 'How's it going'?

CONVERSATION STRATEGY: the 'Captain Jack Sparrow' technique
Hesitation is unavoidable when you start learning a new language. Filler words can make things smoother, but another good option is to summon your inner Captain Jack Sparrow! When you start a sentence and need to gather your thoughts, don't just hesitate – *pause* – as if you're deep in thought. Hesitating with confidence makes it seem you're about to say something extremely interesting – even if you're just describing your day!

> **Mia:** Hallo Ellen, meine Lieblingsschülerin! Wie läuft's?
>
> **Ellen:** Super! Stell dir vor, diese Woche unternehme ich etwas mit einer neuen Freundin.
>
> **Mia:** Das ist wunderbar! Wer ist sie? Wie heißt sie?
>
> **Ellen:** Sie heißt Judith. Sie kommt aus Österreich und sie ist Ingenieurin. Ich kenne sie von meinem Sprachkurs.
>
> **Mia:** Okay. Seit wann ist sie in Berlin?
>
> **Ellen:** Sie ist erst eine Woche in Berlin.
>
> **Mia:** Und was möchtet ihr unternehmen?
>
> **Ellen:** Morgen planen wir, auf den Fernsehturm zu fahren. Danach verbringen wir die Woche zusammen, um die Stadt zu entdecken. Sie möchte unbedingt Döner essen. Und ich glaube, ich besuche sie … nächstes Wochenende in Österreich.
>
> **Mia:** Wie interessant! Mein Mann ist Österreicher. Er fährt jeden Sommer nach Salzburg. Sein Bruder wohnt dort.

FIGURE IT OUT

1 Find and highlight the German phrases:

a Who is she?
b What's her name?
c her name is
d she comes from
e she is
f she wants

2 The following statements about the conversation are *falsch*. Highlight the incorrect parts, then write the correct phrase in German.

   a Judith works as a lawyer. _____

   b Judith has been in Berlin for only a month. _____

   c Tomorrow, Ellen and Judith are going to a restaurant. _____

   d This weekend, Ellen is going to see Judith in Austria. _____

3 You've learned a lot of words that tell you *when* something is happening. Find the following words and write their German translations.

   a this week _____
       d after that _____

   b next weekend _____
       e every summer _____

   c tomorrow _____

4 Can you guess the meaning of these phrases?

   a *Lieblingsschülerin* _____
       c *Morgen planen wir* _____

   b *Mein Mann ist* _____

PRONUNCIATION EXPLANATION: *au, eu, äu*

When certain vowels are combined in German, they create a new sound all of their own. And because German is a phonetic language, you can expect these sounds to be consistent whenever you see these combinations. Here are three that end in *u*:

⋯⟩ *au* is pronounced 'ow' as in 'ouch!', so *Auge* (eye) is 'ow-guh'
⋯⟩ *eu* is pronounced 'oy', so *neu* (new) sounds like 'noy'
⋯⟩ *äu* is also pronounced 'oy', so *Häuser* (houses) sounds like 'hoy-zer'.

🔊 05.02 Practise pronouncing these vowel combinations. First say each out loud, then listen to the audio to check your pronunciation, and repeat.

⋯⟩ *Euro*   *Deutsch*   *heute*
⋯⟩ *braun*   *Haus*   *auch*
⋯⟩ *Fräulein*   *Mäuse*   *träumen*

NOTICE

🔊 **05.03 Listen to the audio and study the table. Repeat the phrases to mimic the speakers.**

Essential phrases for Conversation 1

German	Meaning
Wie läuft's?	How's it going?
diese Woche	this week
unternehme ich etwas mit	I'm doing something with
einer neuen Freundin	a new friend (f)
Wer ist sie?	Who is she?
Wie heißt sie?	What's her name?
Sie heißt ...	Her name is ...
Sie kommt aus ...	She's from ...
Ich kenne sie von ...	I know her from …
Sie ist erst eine Woche in Berlin.	She has been in Berlin for one week.
Was möchtet ihr unternehmen?	What do you want to do?
Morgen planen wir ... zu fahren.	Tomorrow we are planning to go ...
Danach verbringen wir die Woche zusammen.	Then we'll spend the week together.
Sie möchte unbedingt ...	She absolutely wants to ...
Und ich glaube, …	And I believe …
... ich besuche sie ...	... I'll visit her ...
nächstes Wochenende	next weekend
Mein Mann ist ...	My husband is ...
Er fährt …	He goes …
... jeden Sommer nach Salzburg.	... to Salzburg every summer.
Sein Bruder wohnt dort.	His brother lives there.

GRAMMAR: *zu as 'to'*
Have you seen that some German sentences include the word *zu* before the second verb? This happens with most verbs in German, except booster verbs (*möchte, werde,* etc.). In these sentences, *zu* simply indicates 'to', as in ***wir planen ins Kino zu gehen*** (we are planning to go to the cinema).

As with most things in German, if you forget to add in the *zu* in the conversation, the world will not end (... and you will still be understood!).

1 Write out the new phrases you can use to talk about your plans with someone else:

    a I'm doing something with ... _____

    b We'll spend the week ... _____

    c What do you (pl) have planned? _____

    d We plan to ... _____

2. Most German sentences with two verbs include a *zu* before the second verb – unless there's a booster verb. Fill in the gaps, and decide whether or not you need to use *zu*.

   a *Ich versuche, ein* _____ (I'm trying to find a hotel this weekend.)

   b *Ich plane, mit Jan* _____ (I'm planning to speak German with Jan.)

   c *Ich möchte* _____ (I want to visit Ireland.)

3. This conversation introduces forms for talking about 'he' and 'she' in German. You'll also see a new word for 'you plural'. Write out each of the following words in German:

   a he _____

   b she _____

   c we _____

   d you _____

   e you formal _____

   f you plural _____

4. Use the examples to translate the English sentences.

   a *Du bist Designerin.* (You are a designer.) _____ (She is an engineer.)

   b *Wir kommen aus England.* (We come from England.)

   _____ (She comes from Germany.)

   c *Ich möchte die Stadt sehen.* (I want to see the town.)

   _____ (She wants to visit the city.)

   d *Sie heißen …* (Your (formal) name is …) _____ (Her name is …)

   e *Du wohnst in der Schweiz.* (You live in Switzerland.)

   _____ (He lives with a friend (m).)

   f *Wir fahren oft nach Italien.* (We often go to Italy.)

   _____ (He goes to Italy every summer.)

   g *Was möchtet ihr unternehmen?* (What do you (pl) want to do?)

   _____ (What does he want to do?)

5. Put the words in the correct order to make complete sentences. Be sure to put the verb in the second position (with *ich* or *wir* after the verb).

   a *nehme/diese Woche/nach Hamburg/den Zug/ich*

   _____

   b *besuchen/in Irland/nächstes Wochenende/wir/Fiona*

   _____

   c *ich/zu/morgen/machen/eine/plane/Party*

   _____

Similar to what happens with *du* **arbeitest**, an extra -e is added into these er/sie and ihr forms when the dictionary form ends in -ten and -den.

GRAMMAR TIP: *sie, sie, sie and Sie*
There are actually several kinds of sie in German, such as 'she', 'her', 'you (formal)', 'they' and 'them'. You can tell the difference by looking at the verb ending: the 'she' form ends in **-t** and the 'they' form ends in **-en**. For the formal 'you' the verb ending is always the same as the 'they' form, but the **Si**e is capitalized.
⤳ **sie** *heißt* (she is called)
⤳ **sie** *heißen* (they are called)
⤳ **Sie** *heißen* (you (formal) are called)

sie is also used as an object word:
⤳ *Ich kenne* **sie**.
(I know **her**.)
⤳ *Das ist für* **sie**. (That is for **them**.)
⤳ *Stört es* **Sie**, *wenn* …? (Do **you** mind (lit. Bothers it you) if …)

GRAMMAR EXPLANATION: 'he', 'she', 'you plural'

In many cases, you can create the *er* (he) and *sie* (she) form of the verb by starting with the dictionary form. For instance, from *spielen* (to play):

Step 1: Remove the -en: → spiel~~en~~ → spiel.

Step 2: Then **replace the -en with** -t → er/sie spiel**t** (he/she plays).

You've seen these forms in the conversation: *sie heißt* and *sie kommt*, for example. As a bonus, the exact same form works for *ihr* (you plural) – handy!

> Examples: ***ihr spielt, ihr kommt, ihr heißt, ihr arbeitet***

Vowel changes

You've seen that a few verbs change their vowel for the *du* form. The same happens for the *er/sie* form, but not for *ihr* forms, so they will be spelled/pronounced differently:

werden (for future: will)	er/sie wird	ihr werdet
sprechen (to speak)	er/sie spricht	ihr sprecht
lesen (to read)	er/sie liest	ihr lest
fahren (to travel)	er/sie fährt	ihr fahrt

1   Use the table to practise creating *er/sie* and *du/ihr* forms yourself. Some forms have been filled in for you.

Dictionary form	ich form	du form	er/sie form	ihr form
lernen	ich lerne	du lernst	er lernt	ihr lernt
können	ich kann			
helfen		du hilfst		
schlafen			er schläft	
planen		du planst		

2   Fill in the gaps with the correct form of the verb given.

Example: **Sie** _____ **Berlin.** (lieben) → *Sie liebt Berlin.* (She loves Berlin!)

a   *Stefan* _____ *Spanien jeden Sommer.* (besuchen)

b   *Ihr* _____ *Deutsch, um in Berlin zu studieren.* (lernen)

c   *Sie (she)* _____ *zu Hause.* (lesen)

d   *Jonas und Paul, ihr* _____ *viel!* (tanzen)

PRACTICE

Here's some new vocab you can use to talk about your family.

1 🔊 **05.04** Listen to the audio and follow along with the table. Repeat the words as you hear them.

> Grammatical genders (*der* or *die*) for people tend to be the same as the person's gender. 'The brother' is *der Bruder*; 'the sister' is *die Schwester*.

Family / die Familie

German	Meaning	German	Meaning
Eltern	parents	Sohn / Tochter	son / daughter
Mutter / Vater	mother / father	Kinder	children
Mama / Papa	mom / dad	Großvater / Großmutter	grandfather / grandmother
Bruder / Schwester	brother / sister	Opa / Oma	grandpa / grandma
Geschwister	siblings	Großeltern	grandparents
Freund / Freundin	friend (m), boyfriend / friend (f), girlfriend	Onkel / Tante	uncle / aunt
bester Freund / beste Freundin	best friend (m/f)	Cousin / Cousine	cousin (m) / cousin (f)
Mann / Frau	husband / wife	Mitbewohner(in)	flatmate (m/f)
Partner(in)	partner (m/f)	Hund	dog
Ich bin single	I'm single	Katze	cat
Das ist kompliziert	It's complicated	das Krokodil	crocodile

2 Use your dictionary to fill in the last two rows of the Family members table with words for family members (or pets!) close to you, or other phrases to describe your personal situation.

You saw in Unit 3 that words like 'the / a / my / your' change depending on the words around them. For instance, the word 'my' has six versions: *mein, meine, meinen, meiner, meinem, meines.*
Learning when to use the correct one isn't a high priority for now. If you're unsure, the safest bet is to guess *meine*. But, it's a good idea to know the different ways 'my' appears in German, so you can start getting a feel for the patterns.

3 Fill in the blanks with the missing words in German.

a *Hast du* _____? (Do you have (any) **siblings**?)

b _____ *ist mein* _____! (**He** is my **favourite nephew**!)

c *Mein* _____ *Jim und ich* _____ _____ *eine Reise machen.*
(My **friend** Jim and I **will** take a trip **together**.)

d *Meine* _____ _____ *als Ärztin.* (My **mum works** as a doctor.)

e *Ich möchte* _____ *Zeit mit meinen* _____ *verbringen.*
(I'd like to spend **more** time with my **parents**.)

f *Ich spreche oft mit meinem* _____. (I talk to my **brother** often.)

g *Wo* _____ *dein* _____? (Where does your **dad work**?)

h _____ _____ *joggt* _____ _____. _____ *liebt es.*
(**My girlfriend** jogs **every day**. **She** loves it.)

VOCAB: *Freund(in)*
The word *Freund(in)* in German makes it ambiguous whether someone is talking about a platonic friend or a boyfriend/girlfriend. The distinction is usually made by adding a possessive (*mein Freund* = 'my boyfriend', or *ein Freund von mir* = 'a friend of mine').

4 Use the phrase list from Conversation 1 to answer the questions and practise creating sentences about someone close to you.

Example: *Woher kennst du deinen besten Freund / deine beste Freundin?*
(From-where know you your best friend?)
⋯⟶ Ich kenne meinen besten Freund, Mark, aus der Schule.

a *Woher kennst du deinen besten Freund / deine beste Freundin?*
_____

b *Wie heißt er / sie?* _____

c *Wo arbeitet er / sie?* _____

5 Describe plans you have for a weekend together with a family member or friend. Refer back to the phrase list from Conversation 1 and practise using these phrases:

ich verbringe Zeit mit ...   wir planen ... zu ...

Example:

> **Dieses Wochenende** verbringe ich Zeit mit meiner Freundin Ellen. Wir planen ins Kino zu gehen. Sie sagt, dass der Film sehr gut ist.

a *Mit wem verbringst du dieses Wochenende Zeit?*

Dieses Wochenende _____ ich _____

_____

b *Was plant ihr (zu machen)?* Wir _____

_____

GRAMMAR TIP:
von deiner / mit meinem
If you want to challenge yourself to more complicated grammar, try to remember that the translations of 'a', 'the', 'my' and 'your' end in *-m*, or if feminine, in *-r*:
···› *Ich fahre mit mein**em** Bruder.* (I'm travelling with my brother.)
···› *Die Fotos von dein**er** Stadt sind schön!* (The photos of your town are pretty!)
···› *Ich fahre mit d**em** Auto.* (I'm travelling by car / lit. 'I travel with the car'.)

PUT IT TOGETHER

1 Look up the 'me-specific' verbs you need to talk about the people close to you, then write at least three sentences to talk about:

···› where you or members of your family live.
   Example: Ich wohne ..., meine Familie ...
···› what some friends (Jan, Karl ...) or family members like to do or do for work.
   Example: Ich schreibe ..., Thomas ...

2 Who is your favourite person? Who do you spend your time with? Use your dictionary and new vocab to write out details like:

···› What is his / her name? Where does he / she live?
···› Who does he / she live with? (e.g. *mit Peter*)
···› What does he / she like to do, or do for work?

_____

_____

_____

You might be tempted to talk about where you 'met' someone, but we haven't learned how to talk about things that happened (past tense) yet. It's coming up in Unit 7. In the meantime, practise rephrasing sentences so you can convey the same idea with what you know now. This is an invaluable skill in language learning.

CONVERSATION 2

Who do you know?

Let's build on the language you can use to talk about people in your life. The conversation continues as Ellen and Mia talk about their families.

🔊 05.05 How does Ellen ask 'how long' Mia has been married?

> **Ellen:** Also, du bist verheiratet, oder?
>
> **Mia:** Ja, mein Mann heißt Jan.
>
> **Ellen:** Seit wann seid ihr zusammen?
>
> **Mia:** Wir sind schon lange zusammen. Ich kenne ihn und seine Familie seit zwanzig Jahren. Bist du verheiratet?
>
> **Ellen:** Nein, ich bin single.
>
> **Mia:** Wohnst du allein?
>
> **Ellen:** Du meinst in England? In England wohne ich mit Anna. Anna ist meine Schwester.
>
> **Mia:** Jan und ich wohnen mit Rambo! Rambo ist Jans Hund und er ist ganz süß und klein.
>
> **Ellen:** Hunde haben mich nicht gern und ich habe Hunde nicht gern! Außerdem machen sie alles kaputt.
>
> **Mia:** Rambo macht nichts kaputt, er ist ganz klein. Besuche mich doch und schau selbst!
>
> **Ellen:** Super, danke schön! Also, wann kann ich Rambo besuchen?

FIGURE IT OUT

1 Answer the questions about the conversation.

a *Ist Mia verheiratet?* _____

b *Wie heißt der Mann von Mia?/Mias Mann?* _____

c *Seit wann kennt Mia Jan und seine Familie?* _____

d *Wohnt Ellen allein in England?* _____

e *Wie heißt Ellens Schwester?* _____

f *Warum hat Ellen Hunde nicht gern?* _____

2 Which article do you use with the word *Familie*? *Der, die* or *das*?

NOTICE

🔊 **05.06** Listen to the audio and study the table.

Essential phrases for Conversation 2

German	Meaning
Du bist verheiratet, oder?	You are married, right?
Seit wann seid ihr zusammen?	How long have you (pl) been together?
Wir sind schon lange zusammen.	We've been together for a long time. (We are already long together.)
Ich kenne ihn und seine Familie seit zwanzig Jahren.	I have known him and his family for 20 years.
Ich bin single.	I'm single.
Wohnst du allein?	Do you live alone?
Anna ist meine Schwester.	Anna is my sister.
Jans Hund	Jan's dog
Er ist ganz süß und klein.	He is very sweet and small.
Hunde haben mich nicht gern	Dogs don't like me (Dogs have me not gladly)
ich habe Hunde nicht gern	I don't like dogs
Außerdem ...	Besides ...
... (er) macht nichts kaputt	... (he) doesn't break anything. (makes nothing broken)
Besuche mich doch ...	Come visit me ...
... schau selbst	... see for yourself

1 Find these words in the conversation and write them here.

a married _____

b single _____

c twenty _____

d him _____

e for a long time _____

f besides _____

2 How do you say these phrases in German?

a Come visit me ... _____

b Do you mean ... _____

c See for yourself. _____

d Jan's dog. _____

GRAMMAR TIP: *ihr habt / seid* (you (pl) have / are) You've learned how to create *er, sie* and *ihr* forms for most verbs, but two important exceptions are **haben** (to have) and **sein** (to be). For these verbs, you'll use: ⋯⋯> *er / sie hat* (he / she has), which is totally irregular, whereas *ihr habt* (you (pl) have) follows the normal rule. ⋯⋯> *er / sie ist* (he / she is) and *ihr seid* (you (pl) are) are irregular.

GRAMMAR TIP: *s* and *von* – *possessives* In German, to talk about something that belongs to a person, you can add an *-s* to their name just like in English (but there's no need for the apostrophe), for example, *Toms Auto* = (Tom's car). You can also use *von* to indicate 'of', or to add emphasis, as in *das Auto von Tom* (the car of Tom).

3 Write the correct words to complete the sentences.

a *Ich kenne _____ aus Italien.* (I know **him** from Italy.)

b _____ _____ _____ *auch in Frankreich.* (**Ellen's sister** also **lives** in France.)

c *Dein Bruder _____ immer _____ _____.* (Your brother **always breaks everything**.)

d *Jan _____ sie _____ _____.* (Jan **visits** her **every summer**.)

e *Ich spreche so viel mit meinem Lehrer. _____ ist Deutsch sehr leicht.*
   (I speak a lot with my teacher. **Besides**, German is very easy.)

GRAMMAR EXPLANATION: me, you, him, her

> *Ich gebe dir das Buch* (I give you the book – lit. 'I give to-you the book.')
> *Ich helfe dir*   (I help you – in the sense of 'I (give) help to-you.')

Many examples you've seen so far reflect the translations of these words *mir* and *dir* as (essentially) 'to-me' and 'to-you'. But now consider the sentences:

> *Markus kennt dich.* (Markus knows **you**.)   *Verstehst du mich?* (Do you understand **me**?)

Here, the words for 'me' and 'you' don't convey the meaning of 'to' that we've seen. German uses the words *mich* and *dich* instead to clarify that difference.

Object	Example	Object	Example
mir (to me)	*Wie interessant!* **Erzähl mir mehr!** (How interesting! Tell (to) me more!)	**mich** (me)	**Besuche mich** *mal in Sankt Petersburg!* (Why don't you visit me in Saint Petersburg?) (lit. 'Visit me (then) in Saint Petersburg!')
dir (to you)	*Ich **helfe dir** immer gerne.* (I'm always glad to help you.) (lit. 'I help to-you always gladly.')	**dich** (you)	*Rambo, ich **habe dich** gern!* (Rambo, I like you.) (lit. 'Rambo, I have you gladly.')
ihm (to him)	*Sie **schreibt ihm** eine E-Mail/SMS.* (lit. 'She writes (to) him an e-mail/SMS.')	**ihn** (him)	*Das **stört ihn** nicht.* (This doesn't disturb him.) (lit. 'This disturbs him not.')
ihr (to her)	*Er **gibt ihr** vor dem Eiffelturm einen Ring.* (He's giving her a ring in front of the Eiffel Tower.) (lit. 'He gives to-her in-front of-the Eiffel-Tower a ring.')	**sie** (her)	**Kennst** *du **sie?*** (Do you know her?) (lit. 'Know you her?')

You'll recognize *ihr* as meaning 'you plural'; here it's also the word for 'to her'. It will be easy to see which is implied from context.

> **GRAMMAR TIP:** *für dich* – 'for you' / *ohne mich* – 'without me'
> You'll also notice that *mich* and *dich* are used after the words *für* (for) and *ohne* (without). In most other cases, you'll use *mir* and *dir*: **mit dir** (with you), **von ihm** (from him). Fortunately, **uns** (us) doesn't change.
> **Examples:**
>
> ⋯⟫ *Meine Freundin reist am Montag mit mir, aber sie reist am Dienstag ohne mich.*
>   (My girlfriend travels on Monday with me but she travels on Tuesday without me.)
>
> ⋯⟫ *Gehen sie mit uns oder ohne uns?* (Are they going with us or without us?)

This is something that comes with time and practice – but for now it's good for you to know the meaning of these words when you hear them used in conversation!

1 Fill in the gaps with the appropriate object word *mich, dich, ihn* or *sie.*

   a *Ich sehe _____.* (you)

   b *Ist das Geschenk für _____?* (me)

   c *Seit wie lange kennst du _____?* (her)

   d *Gehst du ohne _____?* (him)

2 Now fill in the gaps in the sentences with the correct word, drawing from all eight of the object words you've learned.

   a *Ich kenne _____ seit ...* (I have known **him** since ...)

   b *Meine Schwester sagt _____ immer ...* (My sister is always telling **me** ...)

   c *Er besucht _____ im Sommer.* (He visits **her** in the summer.)

   d *Kannst du _____ sagen ...* (Can you tell **her** ...)

   e *Ich möchte _____ fragen ...* (I want to ask **you** ...)

   f *Fährst du mit _____ nach Frankfurt?* (Are you going with **him** to Frankfurt?)

For now, try to recognize these words as you see and hear them used, but when you're speaking as a beginner you don't need to worry about getting these words exactly right, as you will still be understood. (It would be similar to saying 'this book is for she' in English – not right, but perfectly understandable).

3 Read through this sample telephone conversation and highlight the correct word.

> **A:** Hörst du (a) mich/mir?
>
> **B:** Ja, ich verstehe (b) dich/dir gut.
>
> **A:** Ich möchte (c) dir/dich etwas erzählen. Kennst du Anna?
>
> **B:** Anna? Peters Schwester? Ja, ich kenne (d) sie/ihr.
>
> **A:** Wir sehen (e) sie/ihr immer beim Yoga. Glaubst du, sie gibt (f) mir/mich eine Chance?
>
> **B:** Sie ist mit Kai zusammen. Kennst du (g) ihn/ihm nicht?

4 Use what you know to translate these full sentences. (Tip: reuse the vocab from the other exercises.)

a   How long have you known her? _____

b   Are you going without me? _____

c   I see him every Monday. _____

VOCAB EXPLANATION: *wissen* and *kennen* (to know)

German has two ways of saying 'to know'. Most of the time you'll use *wissen*, which implies that you know a piece of information, or how to do something. The other form, *kennen*, implies that you are familiar with something, or that you know a person.

Generally, you'll use *kennen* instead of *wissen* if you can replace the word 'know' with 'know of' or 'be familiar with'. For example, you can't really say, 'I know of what time it is,' but you can say 'I am familiar with Berlin' (*Ich kenne Berlin*) or 'I know of the film.' (*ich kenne den Film*).

> Example: *Ich weiß, du kommst aus Deutschland.* (I know you come from Germany.)
> *Ich kenne dieses Lied!* (I know this song!)

PRACTICE

1 Choose between *wissen* and *kennen* for each sentence below.

a   *Ich **kenne** / weiß dieses Buch.*

b   ***Kennst** / Weißt du wann das Konzert beginnt?*

c   *Wir **kennen** / wissen Alexander seit Jahren.*

d   *Kennen / **Wissen** Sie, wann der Bus kommt?*

2 Practise answering questions about your relationships with other people.

a *Hast du Geschwister?* or *Wie viele Geschwister (Brüder und Schwestern) hast du?*
Ja / Nein, ich habe (keine Geschwister).

b *Bist du verheiratet, single, oder hast du einen Freund / eine Freundin?* Ich bin / habe

c *Hast du Kinder? Wie viele?* Ja / Nein, ich habe (keine Kinder)

d *Wohnst du allein?* Ja / Nein, ich wohne allein / mit

PUT IT TOGETHER

Use the new vocab you've learned to build on the script you wrote in Conversation 1. Write four sentences about someone close to you, in which you describe things like:

····⟩ how long you've known him / her (*kennen + seit*)
····⟩ how long you've been friends, together or married (*seit + zusammen*)
····⟩ what you plan to do together (*wir fahren, wir planen ... zu ...*)
····⟩ how your typical interactions go (*er sagt mir…, ich sehe ihn / sie …*).

CONVERSATION 3

How do you say ... in German?

The conversation gets more detailed now, as Mia talks about her family.

🔊 05.07 How does Mia say, 'their names are'?

VOCAB: *irgendwann*
Irgend- is a useful word head to know, and is like 'some' in English. This gives *irgendwann* ('sometime', or literally 'somewhen'), *irgendwie* (somehow), *irgendwo* (somewhere / anywhere).

Ellen: Habt ihr Kinder?

Mia: Ja, wir haben zwei wunderbare Kinder. Sie heißen Hans-Jürgen und Günter.

Ellen: Oh, das ist toll! Ihre Namen sind sehr schön!

Mia: Möchtest du irgendwann Kinder haben?

Ellen: Ich bin nicht so sicher. Vielleicht eines Tages.

Mia: Und wenn du einen charmanten Deutschen in Berlin triffst? Werdet ihr dann für immer hier bleiben?

Ellen: Sehr lustig! Ich treffe viele Deutsche, aber sie sind oft ... 'nicht für mich'? Wie sagt man auf Deutsch? Nicht mein 'type'?

Mia: Sie sind nicht dein Typ. Ja, ich verstehe. Aber man weiß nie! Alles ist möglich!

FIGURE IT OUT

1 Highlight the relevant phrases, then answer the questions.

   a How many children does Mia have? _____

   b Does Ellen want to have children some day? _____

2 Look at the conversation. What do the following words/phrases mean?

   a *einen charmanten Deutschen* _____   c *oft* _____

   b *Ich bin nicht so sicher.* _____   d *Man weiß nie.* _____

3 What two phrases does Ellen use to get around not knowing the right word?

   _____   _____

4 Find and highlight these phrases in the conversation.

   a Their names are (they are called)   b Their names are pretty   c Oh, that's great!

NOTICE

🔊 05.08 Listen to the audio and study the table.

Essential phrases for Conversation 3

German	Meaning
Habt ihr Kinder?	Do you (pl) have children?
wir haben zwei wunderbare Kinder	We have two wonderful children.
Sie heißen ...	Their names are ... (They are-called)
Ihre Namen sind sehr schön.	Their names are very pretty.
Möchtest du irgendwann Kinder haben?	Would you like to have children sometime?
Ich bin nicht so sicher.	I am not so sure.
Vielleicht eines Tages.	Perhaps one day.
Und wenn du einen charmanten Deutschen in Berlin triffst?	And if you meet a charming German man in Berlin?
Werdet ihr dann für immer hier bleiben?	Then will you stay here forever? (Will you (pl) then for always here to-stay?)
Sehr lustig!	Very funny!
Ich treffe viele ...	I meet a lot of ...
sie sind oft ... nicht mein 'Typ'	they are often ... not my 'type'
man weiß nie	you never know (one knows never)
Alles ist möglich!	Anything is possible!

1 Use the phrase list to complete the missing question-answer phrases.

a Q: _____

   A: *Nein, aber meine Schwester hat zwei wunderbare Kinder.*

b Q: *Wie heißen sie?*   A: _____ *Agne und Holly.*

2 How would you say these phrases in German?

a I'm sure! _____   b Anything's possible! _____

3 Translate these useful phrases using the word *man*.

a You never know. _____

b How do you say 'bye' in German? _____

c That can be done (one can do that). _____

d In Germany, people don't say that. _____

4 Match the German phrases with the correct English translations.

a *wir gehen*	e *sie sind*	1 we are	5 you are (pl) going
b *ihr geht*	f *werdet ihr*	2 you (pl) are	6 they are going
c *sie gehen*	g *wir wissen*	3 they are	7 we know
d *wir sind*	h *ihr seid*	4 we are going	8 will you (pl)

GRAMMAR EXPLANATION: possessives

Let's have a look at how to use words of possession. Here are the key words you'll need:

Possessives – 'my', 'your', 'his', 'her', etc.

German	English	Example	Meaning
mein	my	*meine Wohnung*	my apartment
dein	your (sing.)	*dein Land*	your country
sein	his / its	*sein Job / sein Bein*	his job / its leg
ihr	her	*ihre Familie*	her family
unser	our	*unser Haus*	our house
euer	your (pl)	*eure Eltern*	your (pl) parents
ihr	their	*ihre Stadt*	their city
Ihr	your (formal)	*Ihre Hilfe*	your (formal) help

Euer will change to *eure* before feminine and plural forms, to make it easier to pronounce.

They work just like *ein*, so if something is feminine or plural, you'll say *meine*, *deine* and so on.

1 Using this table, work out how to say the following:

a her brother _____   c our dog _____   e his nephew _____

b their children _____   d your (formal) wife _____

2 Select the correct option between the two possessives given in the story:

Alexanders / Alexander's Familie ist sehr interessant. Ich kenne **seine / ihre** Eltern schon lange. **Ihr / Euer** Haus ist sehr groß, aber Alexander sagt mir und meiner Schwester oft: „**Eure / Deine** Eltern sind nicht reich, aber sie haben viel Zeit."

PRACTICE

1 Fill in each question–answer pair using *er/sie/sie* (he/she/they) and the appropriate verb form.

   a *Ist dein Bruder mein Typ? Nein, _____ _____ bestimmt nicht dein Typ!*

   b *Wie heißt deine beste Freundin? _____ _____ Stefanie.*

   c *Versteht ihr die Deutschen? Nein, _____ _____ _____ absolut nicht!*

   d *Trefft ihr deine Eltern oft? Nein, _____ _____ _____ nicht oft.*

2 Now fill in the gaps using the possessive words and family vocab you've learned.

   a *_____ Vater besucht jeden Sommer _____ Bruder.*
     (**My** father visits **his** brother every summer)

   b *_____ _____ und ich, _____ _____ nicht _____.*
     (**My girlfriend** and I, we don't **often travel**.)

   c *Heute hat _____ _____ Geburtstag.*
     (Today is **my mother's** birthday. (Literally: Today my mother has birthday)

   d *Fahrt ihr _____ _____ _____?* (Are you (pl) going **with his friend**?)

   e *Ich _____ _____ besten _____ schon _____.*
     (I have **known my** best friend for a **long time**.)

3 How would you ask the following in German?

   a Do you (pl) want to go to the cinema (*ins Kino*) sometime?

     _____

   b Are they here? _____

   c He has two dogs. (*Hunde*) _____

   d Her parents don't know me. _____

4 Practise creating your own sentences in German! Use:

   a *Ich treffe* to talk about someone you're meeting with soon.

     _____

   b *Sie sind* to talk about a group of your friends or several family members.

     _____

   c *Ihre Namen sind* to talk about some people you work with.

     _____

#LANGUAGEHACK: use clues and context to understand much more than you think

Getting into German can feel overwhelming when you think there are so many words and sentence structures you don't know yet. But even as an absolute beginner, you have a huge head start. Here are four strategies you can use to help you understand when you are spoken to in German, even when a dictionary is nowhere in sight:

1 Get clues from the theme of the conversation

It's highly unlikely that you'll find yourself in a German conversation where you have no idea what the subject is. You can tune your ear to listen for particular themes – like hobby or interest words (*Sport, Musik, Kochen*, etc.) that give you clues to what other people might be saying, even if you're not able to understand most of the words.

Simply knowing what **word category** to expect can make a huge difference. For instance, if you aren't sure whether a person said *Suppe* (soup) or *super* (great), then the fact that you're talking in a restaurant should make it obvious!

A conversation is almost never about 'anything'. There are topics people are more likely to discuss in a given conversation.

2 Use visual markers to infer meaning

Suppose you're at a restaurant on your first day in Germany, the waiter arrives and you hear "&%$## @@[|ç/&?".

If you pay attention to the additional context you're getting from **visual markers**, then you can infer the meaning of new words and phrases

···⋗ Where is the person looking? Is the waiter looking at your glass?

···⋗ Where are their hands or body pointing?

···⋗ What facial expression do they have? What kind of reply is he looking for from you?

···⋗ Is he looking to see if you're satisfied? Or is he waiting for some specific information from you?

As well as visual markers, intonation will also tell you whether something is a question, a request, a command or a casual comment.

3 Look for signpost words at the beginnings and ends of sentences

The same way that you'll see signs alerting you when you're entering or leaving certain areas, conversations often work the same way. For instance, if you hear phrases along the lines of:

> *Wo ... Smartphone* (Where ... smartphone)
> *Neulich ... Buch* (Recently ... book)
> *Freitag ... Kino* (Friday ... cinema)

you can get a pretty good idea of the gist of the phrase as a whole. Each word brings you closer to the truth – even if you only recognize the beginning and ends!

Some common **signpost words** to look out for are:

⋯⋗ question words: *wer, wann, wo* (who, when, where)
⋯⋗ time indicators: *diese Woche, normalerweise* (this week, usually)
⋯⋗ booster verbs: *Möchtest du? Kann ich?* (Would you like? Can I?).

4 Rely on connector words for hints to what's next

Can you deduce how the following sentence will end?

> *Wenn das noch einmal passiert ...* (If that happens again ...)

> *Ich trinke meinen Kaffee mit Milch aber ohne ...* (I like my coffee with milk but without ...)

Connector words function to connect one part of a sentence with another, which makes them very reliable signposts for what type of information is to come!

In the examples, *aber* is a big hint that the speaker doesn't like coffee with sugar, and *wenn* most likely indicates a threat of some consequence. When you hear these words you can confidently infer that:

⋯⋗ *aber*: there's contradiction of what was previously said. If you understood either statement, you can guess the other is opposing in some way
⋯⋗ *wenn*: something unsure may happen, and you may hear a positive / negative consequence of it
⋯⋗ *weil*: the first statement happened as a result of the second.

YOUR TURN: use the hack

1 ◀)) **05.09** Listen to the audio and try to figure out the 'theme' the person might be talking about. In the text below, highlight any keywords that give you clues to the theme.

   a *Ich möchte einen neuen Computer kaufen. Mein Computer ist langsam, weil er nicht genug RAM hat. Ich kann nur zwei Programme gleichzeitig benutzen.* Theme: _____

   b *Heute reise ich mit meinem Freund und seiner Mutter. Sie spricht immer über ihre Cousine.* Theme: _____

   c *Im Sommer fahre ich nach Australien. Ich sollte meinen Pass nicht vergessen, weil das Ticket sehr teuer ist!* Theme: _____

   d *Ich lerne Spanisch seit einem Monat. Ich finde die Sprache leicht, aber ich spreche nur mit meinem Lehrer.* Theme: _____

2 ◀)) **05.10** Listen to the audio, and use signpost words or connector words to guess what sentence you think will follow.

   a *… ich lerne gern Deutsch. / … Deutsch zu lernen.*

   b *… das Wetter nicht gut ist. / … wir jeden Tag Basketball spielen.*

   c *… Tennis ist mein Lieblingssport. / … heute möchte ich zu Hause bleiben.*

PUT IT TOGETHER

Create a script of at least four sentences that's true for you about:

⋯⋗ your parents or family – their names, ages, or where they live (using *sie* + verb)

⋯⋗ your children, nephews or cousins – their names, ages, what they're doing or what they like (using *er / sie / sie* (plural) + verb)

⋯⋗ your friends – how long you've known them for, what they do or what they like (using *er / sie / sie* (plural) + verb)

⋯⋗ your co-workers – what they usually say (using *er/sie/man/sie* (plural) + verb)

⋯⋗ your pets, people you admire, or anyone else you want to talk about!

You should now have most of the 'me-specific' vocab you need to talk about your family or group of friends!

COMPLETING UNIT 5

Check your understanding

🔊 05.11 Listen to this audio rehearsal, which asks questions in German, followed by a short answer.

⋯⋗ Combine the answer with the verb in the question to give the full answer.
⋯⋗ Feel free to pause or replay the audio as often as you need.

Example: *Wohnt ihr schon lange zusammen? Nein, erst seit einem Monat.*
→ Wir wohnen seit einem Monat zusammen.

Show what you know ...

Here's what you've just learned. Write or say an example for each item in the list. Then tick off the ones you know.

- [ ] Give the German phrases for:
  - [ ] 'my mum' and 'my dad'
  - [ ] 'your sister' and 'your brother'
  - [ ] another family member of your choice.
- [ ] Give two phrases you can use to express how you 'spend time' or what you 'plan' to do.
- [ ] Give one sentence each using:
  - [ ] the *er* verb form to describe what someone (m) you know works as
  - [ ] the *sie* verb form to say what some friends of yours are doing now.
- [ ] Say something you plan to do with another person using *wir* and *zusammen*.
- [ ] Use *kennen* to say something or someone you 'know' (are familiar with).
- [ ] Give a sentence each using *mir, dir, mich, dich*.

COMPLETE YOUR MISSION

It's time to complete your mission: talk up your friend to spark a love connection between him / her and your German pal. To do this, you'll need to prepare a description of your friend, explain the story of how you met and all the good things about him or her.

STEP 1: build your script

Wer ist die wichstigste Person in deinem Leben? (Who is the most important person in your life?)

Use the phrases you've learned and 'me-specific' vocab to build scripts about your favourite person. Be sure to:

····⋗ say who it is (*mein Freund, meine Schwester, mein Cousin*)
····⋗ explain why the person is so important to you (*er, sie*)
····⋗ describe things you do together (*wir* and *zusammen*)
····⋗ say how long you've known each other (*kennen + seit*)
····⋗ describe their characteristics, jobs, family, etc. (*sein, ihr*).

Write down your script, then repeat it until you feel confident.

Use your language to communicate with real people! You need to speak and use a language for it to start to take hold in your long-term memory. And it's the best way to see and feel your progress.

STEP 2: keep it real ... *online*

This is a script you'll use over and over to talk about your nearest and dearest in German. Start using it right away to fill the gaps. Go online, find the mission for Unit 5, and share your recording with the community.

STEP 3: learn from other learners

Remember, your missions help you, but also help others expand their vocab. **Your task is to ask a follow-up question in German to at least three different people,** to inspire them to build on their scripts just a little bit more.

STEP 4: reflect on what you've learned

What new words or phrases did you realize you need to start filling gaps?

_____

_____

_____

HEY, LANGUAGE HACKER, YOU'RE HALFWAY THERE!

You've successfully overcome one of the biggest challenges in language learning: getting started and then *keeping it up*. Momentum will take you a long way in learning German quickly, so you should feel good about how far you've come. Always focus on what you can do today that you couldn't do yesterday. Next up: you'll apply what you know to prepare for conversations at the German dinner table.

Nicht nachlassen!

6 HAVE SOME FOOD, DRINK AND CONVERSATION

Your mission

Imagine this – you've discovered an incredible restaurant near your *Haus*, so you invite a new German friend to join you there. You can't wait to show off your *Insiderwissen*. But it turns out, to your horror, that your friend has heard bad things about it! *Bäh*, he says, *es ist langweilig ...*

Your mission is to **convince your friend to come with you** to the restaurant. Be prepared to **give your opinion** and **say why you disagree**. Back it up with details of why the place is so *beliebt* – **describe food you like** and why you like it.

This mission will help you get comfortable agreeing or disagreeing and explaining your point of view, as well as talking about food and restaurants – a very important topic.

Mission prep

···} Learn phrases and etiquette for dining out: *ich nehme, ich möchte*.
···} Use food and drink vocab: *Wasser, ein Glas Wein*.
···} Use expressions for giving opinions and recommendations: *meiner Meinung nach, das stimmt nicht*.
···} Learn about the building blocks to making and understanding longer German words: *Speisekarte, Mittagessen, Geburtstagsgeschenk*.
···} Make comparisons using *kleiner als, interessanter als, besser als*.

BUILDING LANGUAGE FOR GERMAN DINNER CONVERSATION

Having a long meal filled with fun discussion is a key part of German culture. To blend in, it's important for you to be able to proudly share your opinions. A lot of your conversations will take place in cafés or restaurants, so let's make sure you also understand the different ways you'll interact with waiters, as well as with your dinner companions!

#LANGUAGEHACK
sound more fluent with conversation connectors

Around 6 p.m. in Germany, the formal greeting changes from *Guten Tag* to *Guten Abend* (good evening). If you're talking to your colleagues, you might say, more informally, *Tach* during the day and *N'Abend* in the evening – these are shortened versions of the full greetings.

CULTURE TIP:
Mineralwasser
When you order *Mineralwasser* or even *Wasser*, you'll probably get sparkling mineral water which is the default choice in most parts of Germany. And be careful, because *Stille Quelle* and *Classic* are also different kinds of sparkling water, though it's easy to think otherwise. To play it safe, specify *Wasser* either *mit* or *ohne Kohlensäure* (carbonation).

CULTURE TIP: *Schnitzel*
A *Schnitzel* is a typical German food – a cutlet coated with beaten egg and breadcrumbs, then fried. The meat used in a *Wiener Schnitzel* (meaning 'of Vienna') is veal (*Kalb*) but other types of *Schnitzel* are also common, especially pork (*Schwein*) and chicken (*Hähnchen*).

CONVERSATION 1

For me, I'll have …

Ordering in German restaurants may be different from what you're used to. When interacting with waiters, or any professional in public that you don't know, you'll need to use formal German – the *Sie* form.

◀)) 06.01 Ellen and her friend Judith are sitting down to eat at a café in Berlin. What phrase does the *Kellner* (waiter) use to ask, 'Are you ready?'

Ellen:	Ich habe Hunger! Ah, hier ist der Kellner.
Kellner:	Guten Abend, meine Damen. Ein Tisch für zwei?
Judith:	Guten Abend. Ja, wir sind zwei Personen.
Kellner:	Hier ist Ihr Tisch und hier ist die Speisekarte.
Judith:	Sehr gut. Wir nehmen zuerst Mineralwasser. Vielen Dank.
Kellner:	Möchten Sie bestellen?
Judith:	Ja, danke! Wir wissen schon, was wir möchten.
Kellner:	Was möchten Sie essen?
Ellen:	Also, für mich ein Schnitzel bitte.
Judith:	Und ich nehme Salat mit Hähnchenbrust.
Kellner:	Und zu trinken?
Judith:	Möchtest du etwas trinken?
Ellen:	Ich möchte gern ein Pils. Und du, Judith? Trinkst du etwas?
Judith:	Für mich einen Weißwein bitte.
Kellner:	Kommt sofort!

FIGURE IT OUT

1 Highlight the phrases Ellen and Judith use to order:
   a *ein Schnitzel*   c *Mineralwasser*
   b *Salat mit Hähnchenbrust*   d *einen Weißwein*

2 What do you think *Weißwein* means? _____

3 Use what you find in the conversation to write out in German:

   a A table for two. _____   c A table for three. _____

   b And to drink? _____   d And to eat? _____

4 Each of these translations from the conversation is *falsch*. Determine what makes each one *falsch* and correct it.

    a *Guten Abend* → Good day _____

    b *Trinkst du etwas?* → Are you eating something? _____

    c *Weißwein* → red wine _____

    d *Hier ist Ihr Tisch.* → Here is your table (informal). _____

NOTICE

🔊 **06.02 Listen to the audio and study the table. Pay special attention to the pronunciation of *Ein Tisch für zwei?* and *die Speisekarte*.**

CULTURE TIP: *formal language*
While you can expect to hear this kind of formal language from waiters in restaurants or at fancy hotels, in casual social situations this would sound old-fashioned.

Essential phrases for Conversation 1

German	Meaning
Ich habe Hunger!	I'm hungry! (I have hunger.)
Guten Abend, meine Damen.	Good evening ladies.
Ein Tisch für zwei?	Table for two?
Hier ist Ihr Tisch	Here is your table
... die Speisekarte.	... the menu.
Möchten Sie bestellen?	Would you like to order?
Wir nehmen zuerst ...	First we'll have ... (We take first)
Wir wissen schon ...	We know already ...
was wir möchten.	what we would like.
Was möchten Sie essen?	What would you like to eat?
Ich nehme ...	I'll have ... (I take)
... Salat mit Hähnchenbrust.	... the salad with chicken breast.
Und zu trinken?	And to drink?
Trinkst du etwas?	Are you going to drink something?
Für mich einen Weißwein, bitte.	For me a white wine, please.
Kommt sofort!	Right away! (Coming immediately.)

*Notice that while in English we'd say 'I'll have,' Germans would say **ich nehme**, 'I'm taking'.*

1 Look at *I'm hungry* in the phrase list. How does German express this feeling differently?

_____

2 Write out three phrases in the conversation that are used to place an order.

_____ _____ _____

3 Find and write out at least two different formal forms in the conversation.

_____ _____ _____

4 What do the phrases and questions mean? Write the English.

a *Ich weiß schon ...* _____

b *Ich nehme ...* _____

c *Wir wissen schon ...* _____

d *Wir nehmen ...* _____

e *Weißt du ... ?* _____

f *Nimmst du ...?* _____

g *Möchten Sie bestellen?* _____

h *Trinkst du etwas?* _____

Remember to use the German verb **nehmen** for 'to take' to order food or drinks (whereas in English we would say 'have').

PRACTICE

1 Fill in the blanks with the missing words in German.

a _____ Sie _____ ?
(Would you (formal) **like to order?**)

b _____ _____ einen _____, bitte.
(**For me, a red wine, please.**)

c Ich _____ eine Cola und sie nimmt _____ ohne Kohlensäure.
(I'll **have** a cola and she'll have non-fizzy **water.**)

d _____ _____ nichts, was ich möchte, auf der _____.
(I can't **find** anything that I want on the **menu**).

e Ich _____, _____ _____ etwas Leichtes.
(**I think I'll have** something light.)

f Hast du _____ _____ ?
(Are you **already hungry?**)

g _____ _____, was _____ _____.
(**We know** what we're having.)

h _____ _____ mein _____ platz!
(**Here is my favourite place!**)

I'd suggest you also bring a pocket dictionary or use a dictionary app / site on your phone, (see some recommendations in our Resources). You may want to try something on the specials board!

Here's some more important vocab related to eating and drinking to give you a solid base. Before you head to a German restaurant, it's a good idea to learn the names of your favourite dishes in advance.

Eating and drinking vocab

German	Meaning	German	Meaning
Hunger haben / Ich habe Hunger	to be hungry / I'm hungry	das Essen / die Mahlzeit	food / meal
Durst haben / Ich habe Durst	to be thirsty / I'm thirsty	lecker	delicious
essen / ich esse	to eat / I'm eating	das Frühstück / Ich frühstücke	breakfast / I'm having breakfast
trinken / ich trinke	to drink / I drink	das Mittagessen / ich esse zu Mittag	lunch / I'm having lunch
das Getränk	(the) drink	das Abendessen / ich esse zu Abend	dinner / I'm having dinner
kochen	to cook	das Fleisch	meat
Vegetarier, vegetarisches Essen	vegetarian (person), vegetarian food	das Hähnchen(fleisch)	chicken
glutenfrei / alkoholfrei	gluten-free / alcohol-free	das Rindfleisch	beef
mit / ohne	with / without	das Schweinefleisch	pork
Was empfehlen Sie?	What do you recommend?	der Fisch	fish
ich bin allergisch gegen Erdnüsse	I'm allergic to peanuts.	die Meeresfrüchte	seafood
Können Sie das ohne ... machen?	Can you make that without ...?	das Gemüse	vegetables
		Früchte	fruit
		Orangensaft	orange juice

2 What are your favourite foods? What can you imagine yourself asking for in a German restaurant? Add more food or drink items you would order in German to the table. Then add more phrases you could use to interact with the waiting staff.

GRAMMAR EXPLANATION: compound nouns

GRAMMAR TIP: *the hierarchy of compound nouns*

When you put two nouns together, the last one decides the gender and nature of the newly-created noun. Even though *die Orange* is feminine, *der Saft* (m) decides what the result of putting them together would be. So *der Orangensaft* is masculine!

Here's a really fun part of German: combining words together to make new words!

You've already seen a few compound nouns like *Telefonnummer* (telephone number), *Lieblingsschülerin* (favourite student), *Mineralwasser* (mineral water), *Hähnchenbrust* (chicken breast) and *Weißwein* (white wine). You've also seen *Speisekarte*, and although it just translates as 'menu', it means 'dish menu', as opposed to a *Getränkekarte* (drinks menu).

Creating your own German words

To create compound nouns, most of the time you simply put the two words together that you'd like to combine. So if you want to say orange juice, just combine *Orangen* (oranges) with *der Saft* (juice) to make *der Orangensaft*.

This also works for words like:
- *Arbeitgeber* (employer / lit. 'work-giver')
- *Arbeitnehmer* (employee / lit. 'work-taker')
- *Straßenbahn* (tram / lit. 'street-rail')
- *Hauptstadt* (capital city / lit. 'main-city').

LEARNING STRATEGY: break down compound nouns
You can see this just from words using the word *Tier* (animal):

- *das Haustier* (pet/ 'house-animal')
- *das Faultier* (sloth/'lazy animal')
- *das Stinktier* (skunk/'stink animal').

In these examples, *Tier* is the last part of the word as each of these is a type of animal, where-as a *Tierarzt* is a type of doctor (can you guess what kind?). Figuring out German phrases from compound nouns can get very interesting. For instance, If you didn't know the word for 'gloves' in German and guessed 'hand ... shoes' (*Handschuhe*) you'd be right!

Compound nouns in German are often wonderfully descriptive, and you can even improvize (like Ellen did in Unit 3 with *Internet-Dings*) by picking words that describe what you mean. If you were learning English, you might struggle if you heard the word 'veterinarian' for the first time, as the word gives no real clue to its meaning. But in German, *Tierarzt* (animal doctor) is self-explanatory, as is *Krankenhaus* (sick-people house) for 'hospital'.

German speakers are so used to creating new words this way, no one will bat an eyelid if you make some up too!

1 **What do think the translation of the following words would be?**

   a *der Tomatensaft* _____   c *der Krankenwagen* _____

   b *der Sprachschule* _____

2 **Match the words in the columns to make compound nouns.**

a	*Speise*	1	*Nummer (die)*	_____
b	*Haus*	2	*Seite (die)*	_____
c	*Lieblings*	3	*Wein (der)*	_____
d	*Rot*	4	*Karte (die)*	_____
e	*Internet*	5	*Bus (der)*	_____
f	*Reise*	6	*Restaurant (das)*	_____

PUT IT TOGETHER

1 Role-play a conversation in which you order your favourite foods in German at a restaurant. Respond to the questions by ordering anything you like (as long as it's in German!). Take inspiration from what you've learned in this unit, and use your dictionary to look up new words.

You'll order a salad as a starter, a main course and two drinks.

Du hast Hunger und Durst heute! You've already seen die Speisekarte and it conveniently has all your favourite foods!

Kellner: Möchten Sie bestellen?

Du: a. _____

Kellner: Sehr gut. Noch etwas zu essen?

Du: b. _____

Kellner: Sie haben aber Hunger heute! Und zu trinken?

Du: c. _____

Kellner: Gern!

(30 Minuten später ...)

Du: (Call the waiter over.) d. _____

Kellner: Möchten Sie noch etwas bestellen?

Du: (You order another drink.) e. _____

Kellner: Kommt sofort! Sie haben aber Durst heute!

Du: f. _____

Kellner: ... Hier. Bitte schön!

Aber normally means 'but'. In this conversation, it's used to express surprise: 'But you are hungry today!' 'But you are thirsty today!' Used this way in the middle of a sentence, aber takes on the sense of 'wow', and is common in colloquial German.

2 Create three 'me-specific' phrases in which you describe your normal mealtime routine. Use the vocab you've learned in this unit, as well as any new words you need from your dictionary. Try to include:

···⟩ what you usually eat (*essen*) or drink (*trinken*)
···⟩ whether you normally cook (*kochen*), have dinner in a restaurant (*im Restaurant essen*), or microwave yesterday's pizza (*die Pizza von gestern in der Mikrowelle warm machen ...*).

_____
_____
_____

CONVERSATION 2

In my opinion …

Ellen and Judith discover they don't quite see eye to eye on where they should go in Berlin.

🔊 06.03 How does their disagreement get resolved?

VOCAB: *es gibt*
'there is' / 'there are'
The German phrase *es gibt* (lit. 'it gives') means both 'there is' and 'there are' – it doesn't change. So you could say *es gibt ein Buch* (there is a book) or *es gibt drei Bücher* (there are three books). Learn *es gibt* as a set phrase. You'll also see *dort sind* in the conversation, which is the literal 'there (in a physical location) are'.

Ellen: Also, wir müssen natürlich das Haus am Checkpoint Charlie besuchen.

Judith: Nein, dort sind die meisten Touristen! Es gibt doch so viele Museen in Berlin!

Ellen: Ich weiß, dass dort viele Touristen sind, aber es ist ein absolutes Highlight!

Judith: Ich bin nicht einverstanden. Meiner Meinung nach ist das Pergamon Museum besser und dann sind wir schon auf der Museumsinsel …

Ellen: Ja, dort sind weniger Menschen als im Haus am Checkpoint Charlie, aber es ist nicht so interessant!

Judith: Das stimmt nicht! Die Ausstellung ist einzigartig.

Ellen: Das stimmt schon … die Ausstellung ist schön, aber ich finde sie ein bisschen langweilig.

Judith: Du weißt, dass viele Berliner nie das Haus am Checkpoint Charlie besuchen.

Ellen: Na ja, … wir können einen Kompromiss schließen. Wir können morgen das Pergamon Museum besuchen, wenn du das interessanter findest. Wir können zum Haus am Checkpoint Charlie gehen, wenn weniger Touristen da sind, zum Beispiel am Montag.

Judith: Das klingt gut – einverstanden!

FIGURE IT OUT

1 Find the following details within the conversation, then write the answers in English.

a What are the names of the two museums being discussed?

_____   _____

b Where does Ellen think they should visit? _____

c What is Ellen's opinion of the Pergamon Museum? _____

d What phrase shows that Ellen and Judith will make a compromise?

_____

2 What do you think is the meaning of the phrase *es ist ein absolutes Highlight*?

_____

3 Find these phrases in the conversation and highlight them.

a on Monday

b of course we have to visit

c if you find that more interesting

d there are a lot of tourists

e That's not true!

4 Look at the phrases from the conversation and write out the meaning of the words in bold.

a *Nein, **dort sind** die meisten Touristen!* _____

b *... aber **es ist ein** absolutes Highlight!* _____

c *... aber **ich finde sie** ein bisschen langweilig.* _____

d *... wenn **weniger Touristen** da sind, ...* _____

e ***Ich weiß, dass** dort viele Touristen sind* _____

NOTICE

🔊 06.04 Listen to the audio and study the table. Pay special attention to the way *einverstanden* and *meiner Meinung nach* are pronounced.

In questions, you've seen that 'when' in German is **wann**. When used in statements about a potential future though, you would use **wenn** (which also means 'if').

Essential phrases for Conversation 2

German	Meaning
Wir müssen natürlich … besuchen.	Of course we have to visit … (We must naturally … to-visit.)
dort sind die meisten Touristen	there are the most tourists there (there are the most tourists)
Es gibt doch so viele Museen in …	But there are so many museums in … (It gives certainly so many museums in)
Ich weiß, dass dort viele Touristen sind.	I know that there are a lot of tourists there.
Ich bin nicht einverstanden.	I don't agree.
Meiner Meinung nach …	In my opinion …
… ist das Pergamon Museum besser …	… the Pergamon Museum is better … (is the Pergamon Museum better)
… und dann sind wir schon …	… and then we are already… (and then are we already)
… dort sind weniger Menschen als …	… there are fewer people there than …
… aber es ist nicht so interessant	… but it's not so interesting
Das stimmt nicht!	That's not true!
Die Ausstellung ist einzigartig.	The exhibition is unique.
Ich finde sie ein bisschen langweilig.	I find it a little boring. (I find her a bit boring.)
Wir können einen Kompromiss schließen.	We can make a compromise. (We can a compromise to-close.)
… wenn du das interessanter findest.	… if you find it more interesting.
Am Montag …	On Monday …
… wenn weniger Touristen da sind …	… when there are fewer tourists there …
Das klingt gut – einverstanden!	That sounds good – agreed!

1 Find the comparison words in the phrase list, then write them here.

a the most _____   c better _____

b less/fewer _____

2 How do you say 'more interesting than' in German?

_____

3 Based on this, how would you say these phrases?

a more active than (active = *aktiv*) _____

b more beautiful than (beautiful = *schön*) _____

c nicer than (nice = *nett*) _____

4 How would you write the following in German?

a I find _____

b I find the exhibition _____

c I find the museum is better _____

d you find _____

e if you find _____

f I know that _____

g I know that there are a lot of tourists there.

_____

5 This conversation expands on the vocab you can use to express your opinions. Use the phrase list as well as language you know to match each German phrase to its English counterpart.

a *Das stimmt nicht.*   1 Sounds good!

b *Meiner Meinung nach, ...*   2 Of course!

c *Ich bin nicht einverstanden.* 3 That's true.

d *Das klingt gut!*   4 In my opinion ...

e *Ich finde sie ...*   5 I don't agree.

f *Ich möchte (gern) ...*   6 That's not true.

g *Ich denke, dass ...*   7 I know that ...

h *Natürlich!*   8 I would like ...

i *Das stimmt.*   9 I think that ...

j *Ich weiß, dass ...*   10 I find it ...

VOCAB: *er / sie / es as 'it'*
Generally, the word you'll use in German for 'it' is *es* when you aren't actually referring to something specific you can name, as in *es regnet* (it's raining). In other cases, you can still use *es*, but you might also hear *er* (he) or *sie* (she) to refer to the gender German uses for that word. Here, *die Ausstellung* is feminine, so in **Ich finde sie ...**, *sie* is 'it'. On the other hand, *das Museum* is neuter, so you say *es ist ein absolutes Highlight*! As you can see, 'it' takes the same verb form as the *er / sie* forms.

PRACTICE

1 Use *es gibt* with the sentence endings given.

Example: There are not (enough hours in the day). ⟶ <u>Es gibt nicht genug Stunden am Tag!</u>

   a Are there (only three hotels (*Hotels*) here)?

   _____

   b There is (no wine at my house (*bei mir*)).

   _____

   c There are (a lot of schools (*viele Schulen*) in Germany).

   _____

2 Practise expressing your opinions! For each sentence, use a phrase from the box to express your own attitude toward the statement given.

> *Das stimmt!*   *Ich bin einverstanden*   *Das klingt gut!*
> *Das stimmt nicht!*   *Ich bin nicht einverstanden.*

   a *Möchtest du mit Bálint nach Hawaii reisen?* _____

   b *Die besten Dinge im Leben sind kostenlos (free).* _____

   c *Katzen sind intelligenter als Hunde!* _____

   d *Der Morgen ist die beste Tageszeit.* _____

   e *Frauen fahren besser als Männer.* _____

3 Now translate the sentences into German to create something that accurately expresses your opinion. (If you don't agree, add *nicht* to make the statement true for you).

   a _____ *zu viele Menschen in der Stadt gibt.*
     (I find that there are too many people in the city.)

   b _____ *wir weniger Kaffee und mehr Wasser trinken sollten.*
     (I think that we have to drink less coffee and more water.)

   c _____ *sind Hunde freundlicher als Katzen.*
     (In my opinion dogs are much friendlier than cats.)

   d _____ *die beste Eissorte natürlich Schokolade ist.*
     (I know that the best ice cream flavour is, of course, chocolate.)

GRAMMAR EXPLANATION: comparisons

Hopefully you're starting to see that German makes it very easy to compare things!

For 'bigger' or 'smaller', add -er

In German, as in English, you can describe something as bigg*er* or small*er* simply by adding *-er* to the word. But whereas in English we sometimes use 'more' instead (e.g. more boring, not 'boringer'), German is more straightforward, and pretty much always adds *-er*.

Examples: *lustig* (funny) + *er* = *lustiger* (funnier)   *billig* (cheap) + *er* = *billiger* (cheaper)

For 'biggest' or 'smallest', add -ste / -este

If you want to say something is 'the most / -est' (e.g. biggest, most intelligent, smallest), most of the time, you'll just add *-ste*, similar to English!

Examples: *schnell* (fast) + *ste* = *der/die/das schnellste* (the fastest)

teuer (expensive) + *ste* = *der/die/das teuerste* (the most expensive)

schwierig (difficult) + *ste* = *der/die/das schwierigste* (the most difficult)

For the rest of the time, if the adjective you're using ends in *t*, *d*, or *s*, you'll add *-este* instead.

Examples: *schlecht* (bad) + *este* = *der/die/das schlechteste* (the worst)

For 'more' and 'less', use *mehr* and *weniger*

When you want to compare amounts or numbers, that's when you'll use the words for 'more' and 'fewer' / 'less' in German: *mehr* and *weniger*.

Examples: *Ich sehe mehr Touristen heute.* (I see *more* tourists today.)

Ich habe weniger Geld Heute. (I have *less* money today.)

For 'better' and 'best', use *besser* and *beste*

Also similarly to English, German has unique words for comparing what's 'good', 'better', or 'best':

gut (good)   *besser* (better)   *der/die/das beste* (the best)

Example: *Dieses Café hat der/die/das beste Eis* (ice cream) *in ganz Berlin!*

For 'most' use *meisten*

To talk about 'the most', use *die meisten*:

Example: *Die meisten Leute können ein bisschen Englisch.* (*Most* people can speak a bit of English.)

For comparison, use *als* as 'than'

Finally, when you want to compare people or things, use *als*, which works like 'than' in English:

Example: *Ich finde Horrorfilme spannender als Actionfilme.*

(I find horror films more exciting *than* action films.)

1 Practise forming comparison words in German.

Example: nicer (*nett*) → _netter_   the nicest → _der/die/das netteste_

   a smaller (*klein*) → _____   the smallest → _____

   b more charming (*charmant*) → _____   the most charming → _____

   c lazier (*faul*)→ _____   the laziest → _____

   d more interesting (*interessant*)→ _____   the most interesting → _____

   e more difficult (*schwierig*)→ _____   the most difficult → _____

   f easier (*leicht*) → _____   the easiest → _____

2 Use all the comparison words you've learned to translate these phrases.

   a more books than _____   **d** the best restaurant _____

   b the most beautiful city _____   **e** the worst (*schlecht*) film _____

   c fewer people than _____   **f** It's better than … _____

3 Fill in missing words.

   a *Deine Stadt ist _____ _____ meine Stadt.* (Your city is **smaller than** my city.)

   b *Deine Stadt ist _____ _____ im Land.* (Your city is **the smallest** in the country).

   c *_____ _____ Französisch _____ _____ Italienisch.* (**I find** French **more beautiful than** Italian.)

   d *_____ Deutsch ist _____ _____ Sprache.* (**But** German is **the most beautiful** language.)

   e *Ich finde dieses Museum _____.* (I find this museum **bigger**.)

   f *Der Film ist _____ _____.* (The film is **the most interesting**).

   g *Dieses Restaurant ist _____ _____ das andere.* (This restaurant is **worse than** the other one.)

   h *Aber die neue Pizzeria ist _____ _____ Restaurant überhaupt.*
   (But the new pizzeria is **the worst** restaurant of all.)

PUT IT TOGETHER

1 *Welche Stadt möchtest du besuchen?* Recommend to a friend some things to do in a city you know or would like to visit. Use the vocab you learned in Conversation 2, as well as any new 'me-specific' vocab that you look up on your own. Try to include:

   ⋯⟩ the places would you like to visit (*besuchen*)   *Es gibt so viele Highlights in …*

_____

   ⋯⟩ the sites or experiences you think would be the best (*das beste*)

_____

   ⋯⟩ phrases for comparison (*mehr / weniger / besser …, als*)

_____

   ⋯⟩ phrases for expressing your opinion (*meiner Meinung nach*).

_____

CONVERSATION 3

What do you recommend?

Another important dinner topic in Germany is culture. You don't need to quote Shakespeare, but it's good to learn some phrases you can use to contribute to conversations and give your opinion about books, music, art or politics.

🔊 06.05 Now that their debate is settled, Ellen and Judith share their opinions on music and books and give one another suggestions. What phrase does Ellen use to say 'tell me'?

Ellen: Sag mal, Judith. Ich interessiere mich für deutsche Musik. Was kannst du mir empfehlen?

Judith: Das ist eine gute Frage! Meiner Meinung nach ist die beste deutsche Musik von Beethoven, Bach und Mozart ... Ich höre Klassik lieber als moderne Musik.

Ellen: Ich höre gern Tim Bendzko! Er singt „Keine Zeit", oder? Ich möchte seine Songtexte lernen.

Judith: Du solltest die deutsche Musik besser kennenlernen. Ich gebe dir ein paar Lieder. Kannst du mir dafür ein gutes Buch auf Englisch empfehlen?

Ellen: Sicher! Ich lese sehr viel. Ich lese gerade ein Buch und morgen gebe ich es dir. Ich bin ganz sicher, du wirst viel Spaß haben!

Judith: Danke!

Ellen: Ich danke dir auch!

Judith: Also, wo ist der Kellner? Lass uns zahlen, Ellen ... Entschuldigung? Die Rechnung bitte!

> **CULTURE TIP: going Dutch in Germany**
> 'Going Dutch', or the custom of everyone paying for their own meal expenses, is the default in most situations in Germany. In fact, paying separately is so common in Germany that some waiters ask if you'd like to pay *getrennt oder zusammen?* (separately or together) even before taking your order.

FIGURE IT OUT

1 Which topics do Ellen and Judith discuss in this conversation? Highlight all that apply.

   travel, politics, relationships, art, food, books, music

2 Answer the questions about the conversation with a short phrase in German.

   a What does Judith think is the best German music? _____

   b Which music does she not like as much? _____

   c What is Ellen going to give Judith? _____

3 There are five instances of *mir / dir* in the conversation. Highlight each verb associated with them.

4 How do you ask in German:

   a Where is the waiter? _____

   b The bill, please! _____

5 Find the following phrases in the conversation.

   a In my opinion … _____

   b I like listening to … more than… _____

   c What can you recommend? _____

NOTICE

◀)) 06.06 Listen to the audio and study the table.

Essential phrases for Conversation 3

German	Meaning
Ich interessiere mich für …	I'm interested in …
Was kannst du mir empfehlen?	What can you recommend to me?
Das ist eine gute Frage!	That's a good question!
Meiner Meinung nach ist die beste …	In my opinion, the best … is …
Ich höre Klassik lieber als moderne Musik.	I prefer listening to classical rather than modern music.
Du solltest … besser kennenlernen.	You should get to know … better.
Ich gebe dir ein paar Lieder.	I'll give you a few songs.
dafür	in exchange
Kannst du mir … empfehlen?	Can you recommend to me … ?
… das Buch, das ich gerade lese.	… the book that I've just read.
Ich bin ganz sicher, du wirst viel Spaß haben!	I am totally sure you will have a lot of fun!
Lass uns zahlen.	Let's pay.
Die Rechnung bitte!	The bill please!

1 How do you say the following in German?

   a to have fun _____   b in exchange _____

2 Match the German phrases with the correct English translations.

    a *Ich höre lieber*   **d** *Lass uns zahlen*   **1** I'll give you   **4** I'd like to learn

    b *Ich möchte lernen*   **e** *Ich bin sicher, dass*   **2** I'm sure that   **5** Let's pay

    c *Ich gebe dir*   **3** I prefer to listen to

3 Notice which phrases can be used to ask for recommendations and write them out in German.

    a Tell me … _____

    b What do you recommend? _____

    c Can you recommend to me … _____

PRACTICE

1 Practise adapting power phrases to use in a variety of different situations.

    a Power phrase: *Ich bestelle* (I'm going to ask for / asking for)

        … still mineral water. _____

        … a taxi. _____

        … the bill. _____

        … another drink. _____

    b Power phrase: *Ich möchte … (etwas) … besser kennenlernen.*
        What would you like to learn more about? Look up new words that you can use in combination with this power phrase, then write three different sentences.

2 Fill in the blanks with the missing words in German.

    a *Ich höre* _____ _____ _____ *moderne Musik.*
        (I listen to **classical music more than** modern music.)

    b *Welches Buch* _____ *deiner* _____ _____ *interessanter?*
        (**In your opinion**, which book is more interesting?)

    c *Ein Moment bitte,* _____ _____ _____ *unsere Adresse* _____!
        (One moment please, **I will give you** (informal) our address!)

#LANGUAGEHACK: sound more fluent with conversation connectors

Cushion your conversations to say much more

As a beginner, when you're asked a question in German, you may be tempted to give single word answers. Do you like this book? *Ja.* How is your food? *Gut.*

While you may not be able to give as detailed replies in German as you'd like to (yet), you can learn versatile phrases to use instead of brief answers.

Conversation connectors are a type of power phrase that you can tack on to nearly anything you say. You learn them once, and you can use them again and again in countless situations to help make conversations feel a lot less one-sided. For example, in Conversation 3, Judith uses the conversation connector *das ist eine gute Frage* during her discussion with Ellen.

How to use conversation connectors

Good conversation connectors should be versatile. They don't need to add any extra information to the sentence, but should expand on an otherwise short answer. For example, if someone asks you: *Wie findest du dieses Restaurant?* You could reply with: *Danke für dein Interesse. Ich finde dieses Restaurant sehr gut, und du?*

Here are some different conversation connectors you can use to get you started.

For giving your opinion
- *um ehrlich zu sein* (to tell the truth)
- *meiner Meinung nach* (in my opinion)
- *unter uns gesagt* (between us)
- *leider* (unfortunately)
- *so wie ich es sehe* (as I see it)
- *immer mehr* (more and more)
- *wie du vielleicht weißt* (as you perhaps know)
- *soweit ich weiß* (as far as I know)
- *das kommt darauf an* (it depends)

For elaborating on an idea
- *um genau zu sein* (to be precise)
- *zum Beispiel* (for example)
- *und deswegen …* (and that is why …)
- *und außerdem* (and moreover …)
- *ohne Zweifel* (without doubt)

For changing the subject
- *anderseits* (on the other hand)
- *übrigens* (by the way)

Here are a few more examples of how to use conversation connectors.
- If someone asks, *Wie alt bist du?* (How old are you?), you could say: *Ich bin 41,*

or:

Also … unter uns gesagt … leider … bin ich schon 41!

···⟩ If someone asks, *Warum lernst du Deutsch?* you could say: *Ich finde die deutsche Kultur interessant.*

or:

Meiner Meinung nach ist die deutsche Kultur sehr interessant! Und deswegen lerne ich Deutsch.

Conversation connectors help you expand on your answers, and give them a much chattier feel! For beginners, momentum helps conversations stay alive better than more words.

YOUR TURN: use the hack

Use the conversation connectors suggested to give lengthier replies to common questions.

Example: *Was meinst du, ist dieses Haus klein?*

Um ehrlich zu sein, finde ich dieses Haus sehr groß!

a   *Wie ist dein Essen?* _____

b   *Wo wohnst du?* _____

c   *Möchtest du etwas vom Supermarkt?* _____

d   *Trinkst du Kaffee?* _____

GRAMMAR TIP:
word order

For several of these conversation connectors, the verb will come immediately after the connector, a slightly different word order to English.

PUT IT TOGETHER

1   Prepare phrases you could use during real-life German dinner conversations, with culture as a central topic. Create 'me-specific' sentences in which you:

···⟩ say which music, art, or books you love and why (*... ist das schönste Buch, weil ...*)

···⟩ use phrases for offering your opinion (*meiner Meinung nach, ich finde, ...*)

···⟩ include power phrases (*Ich interessiere mich für ...*)

···⟩ use comparisons (*mehr / weniger ... als, beste*) and conversation connectors.

COMPLETING UNIT 6

Check your understanding

Listen to the audio, which will play sets of two statements in German. The first statement will give information about someone, and the second attempts to summarize that information.

🔊 **06.07** Based on what you understand, select *richtig* if the summary is correct or *falsch* if it's false. Listen to the example first.

Example: *Marie denkt, dass Düsseldorf schöner als Köln ist.* (*richtig*)/ *falsch*

Now listen and do the rest.

a Boris denkt, Yoga ist besser als Karate.	*richtig / falsch*
b Sarah findet die Museen in Berlin nicht interessant.	*richtig / falsch*
c Martin denkt, Japanisch ist nicht leicht.	*richtig / falsch*
d Mia findet, dass Online-Unterricht nicht praktisch ist.	*richtig / falsch*
e Alina möchte mit Tania zum Englischkurs gehen und Tania findet, das ist eine gute Idee.	*richtig / falsch*

Show what you know ...

Here's what you've just learned. Write or say an example for each item in the list. Then tick off the ones you know.

- ☐ Ask for a specific food item using 'I'll have'.
- ☐ Ask for a specific drink using 'I would like'.
- ☐ Use phrases in formal situations:
    - ☐ good evening, in formal and casual situations
    - ☐ please (formal)
    - ☐ thanks to you (formal).
- ☐ Say 'I agree', 'I disagree' and 'in my opinion'.
- ☐ Give one phrase each for giving and asking for recommendations.
- ☐ Give the comparison words 'more than', 'less than', 'most' and 'better than'.
- ☐ Give two examples of conversation connectors.

COMPLETE YOUR MISSION

It's time to complete your mission: convince your friend to try out your favourite restaurant. You'll need to prepare phrases for giving your opinions and explaining why you agree or disagree. Describe a restaurant you know and love, or research some restaurants in a German-speaking country you want to visit.

STEP 1: build your script

Keep building your script! Use opinion phrases and 'me-specific' vocab to:

···⋗ describe your favourite restaurant. Say what type of food and drinks they serve. Why do you like it so much? Which are your favourites and why?
···⋗ convince a friend to try it out by saying what makes it better than other restaurants in town (use comparisons)
···⋗ give or ask for recommendations
···⋗ include power phrases and conversation connectors.

Write down your script, then repeat it until you feel confident.

STEP 2: it's all about me! ... *online*

When you feel good about your script, go online to find your next mission, and share your recording with the community. This time, as you're speaking, use conversation connectors between phrases and while you're thinking to help your German flow better. By using these phrases right away, you'll also start burning them into your muscle memory, so they are at the tip of your tongue when you need them!

Yes, it is! Personalize your language to talk about yourself and what's important to you! Learning a language is easier when you can talk about things that are meaningful.

STEP 3: learn from other learners

Test out your debate skills with other language hackers! **Your task is to reply in German to at least three different people** to tell them whether you agree or disagree with the argument they made and why. Use the phrases *Einverstanden* or *Das stimmt* to let them know that you understand their point of view.

STEP 4: reflect on what you've learned

What did you find easy or difficult about this unit? Did you learn any new words or phrases in the community space? After every script you write or conversation you have, you'll gain a lot of insight for what words you need to fill in your script.

_____

_____

_____

_____

HEY, LANGUAGE HACKER, LOOK AT YOU GO!

Now you can share opinions, talk about food, make comparisons, and keep the conversation flowing – you've come a long way. Cherish this feeling and know that things can only improve from here!

Next, let's make a huge leap forward with the range of conversations you can have – by starting to talk about the past.

Du schaffst es!

7 TALKING ABOUT YESTERDAY ... LAST WEEK ... A LONG TIME AGO

Your mission

Imagine this – you've just joined a German meet-up group and you have to introduce yourself by sharing personal stories, but with a twist – it can be true or completely made up.

Your mission is to tell a true, but possibly unbelievable story or one completely made-up story in as convincing a way as possible. Be prepared to **describe a personal story** or a **life lesson you've learned from past experiences**, whether in learning a new language, moving to a new place, or taking a big risk.

This mission will help you expand the range of conversation topics you can confidently contribute to and allow you to use anecdotes to spice up your German repertoire!

Mission prep

···▹ Talk about the past in just two steps: *Ich habe ... gesprochen.*
···▹ Answer questions about the past: *Was hast du gestern gemacht? / Ich bin ... gegangen.*
···▹ Say how long ago something happened using *vor.*
···▹ Use the past tense to talk about your progress in German: *Habe ich das Wort richtig gesagt?*

BUILDING LANGUAGE FOR RICHER CONVERSATIONS

The range of what you can discuss in German has until now focused on what's happening now or in the future. By the end of this unit, you'll be able to give detailed descriptions of things you did in the past, which will help you have much richer conversations.

 #LANGUAGEHACK
time travel – talk about the past and future using the present

As you make friends with other German speakers, or practise with the same people regularly, a big question is often: **What am I going to talk about?** Being able to use and understand the German past tense is a great solution to this problem. You can use it to describe personal stories about your life, which makes for endless conversation topics.

VOCAB: *using über and vor*

When talking about physical locations, *vor* means 'in front of' and *über* means 'above'. They double to have other important meanings though:

⋯⟶ *vor* is used as 'ago', and it comes before the time rather than after it: *vor neun Wochen* (nine weeks ago)

⋯⟶ *über* is used as 'about' for conversation topics: *Er spricht über sein Auto.* (He's talking about his car.)

CONVERSATION 1

What did you do last weekend?

Ellen is talking again with Martin, one of her online teachers.

🔊 **07.01** How does Martin ask, 'What did you do last weekend?'

Martin:	Hallo Ellen! Was gibt's Neues? Was hast du am letzten Wochenende gemacht?
Ellen:	Judith und ich haben zusammen zu Abend gegessen … und wir haben über unsere Pläne für das Wochenende gesprochen. Gestern haben wir dann das Pergamon Museum gesehen … und wir haben auch viele andere Sehenswürdigkeiten fotografiert!
Martin:	Und, wie war es?
Ellen:	Es hat mir Spaß gemacht! Judith weiß viel über Geschichte und Politik; man kann richtig gut mit ihr plaudern! Und wir gehen morgen ins Haus am Checkpoint Charlie!
Martin:	Du hast doch Judith erst vor einer Woche getroffen, oder?
Ellen:	Das stimmt.
Martin:	Ich habe das Pergamon Museum in Berlin einmal vor vier Jahren besucht.
Ellen:	Hat es dir gefallen?
Martin:	Es war okay … vor allem das Café im Museum hat mir gefallen! Dort habe ich eine leckere Torte gegessen!

FIGURE IT OUT

1 Look for these phrases in the conversation and highlight them.

a last weekend
b had dinner together
c Yesterday, we saw …
d How was it?
e once four years ago
f It was OK.
g I ate a delicious cake there.
h we talked about our plans for the weekend

2 What is Martin's opinion of the Pergamon Museum?

a It's fun.   b It's not bad.   b It's one of his favourite museums.

3 *Richtig oder falsch?* Select the correct answer.

a Judith and Ellen only visited the museum yesterday.   *richtig / falsch*
b Judith knows a lot about history and politics.   *richtig / falsch*
c Yesterday, Ellen went to the Checkpoint Charlie Museum. *richtig / falsch*
d Ellen met Judith one week ago.   *richtig / falsch*

4 What do you think the phrase *richtig gut* means? _____

5 What are the German words for:

a yesterday _____ b today _____ c tomorrow _____

NOTICE

🔊 **07.02** Listen to the audio and study the table. Repeat to mimic the speakers.

VOCAB: *gefallen*
While you may expect
to see *gern* when
discussing what you liked
or didn't like, another
way to express 'I liked it'
is *das hat mir gefallen*.
(that has to-me pleased).

Essential phrases for Conversation 1

German	Meaning
Was gibt's Neues?	What's new?
Was hast du am letzten Wochenende gemacht?	What did you do last weekend? (What have you at-the last weekend done?)
Judith und ich haben zusammen zu Abend gegessen	Judith and I had dinner together
Wir haben über unsere Pläne für das Wochenende gesprochen.	We talked about our plans for the weekend. (We have about our plans for the weekend spoken.)
Gestern haben wir ... gesehen.	Yesterday, we saw ... (Yesterday, have we ... seen.)
wir haben ... fotografiert	we took photos (of) ... (we have ... photographed)
... auch viele andere Sehenswürdigkeiten	... a lot of other sights, too (also many other sights)
Es hat mir Spaß gemacht!	I had fun! (It has to-me fun made.)
Judith weiß viel über ...	Judith knows a lot about ...
wir gehen morgen ins ...	tomorrow we're going to ... (we go tomorrow to)
Man kann richtig gut mit ihr plaudern!	You can chat with her really well! (One can really good with her chat.)
Du hast doch Judith erst vor einer Woche getroffen.	You met Judith just a week ago. (You have certainly Judith first before a week met.)
Ich habe das Museum einmal vor vier Jahren besucht.	I visited the museum once four years ago. (I have the museum once before four years visited.)
Hat es dir gefallen?	Did you like it? (Has it to-you pleased?)
Es war okay	It was OK
Dort habe ich eine leckere Torte gegessen!	I ate a delicious cake there!

1 Find each example of the past in the phrase list, then write them out in German.

   a What did you do last weekend? _____

   b Judith and I ate dinner together. _____

   c We talked about our plans for the weekend. _____

2 Now highlight each of the following phrases in the German sentences you wrote in Exercise 1.

   a last weekend   b together   c about our plans for the weekend

3 Use the literal translations in the phrase list to fill in the missing past tense phrases in the table. The first one has been done for you.

Dictionary form	German – past tense phrase	Meaning
	Was hast du gemacht?	What did you do?
machen (to do / to make)		We made ... (plans).
		I had (fun)!
zu Abend essen (to eat dinner)		We ate dinner.
essen (to eat)		I ate.
sprechen (to talk)		We talked
sehen (to see)		We saw ...
treffen (to meet)		You met (her).
fotografieren (to photograph)		We photographed ...
besuchen (to visit)		I visited ...
gefallen (to like)		Did you like (it)?
		I liked (it)!

4 Look at the table in Exercise 3. What do the past tense forms tend to have in common? Write down any patterns you notice.

_____

5 Vor (ago) works like seit (since) in how it refers to numbers of days, months or years. Based on this, use vor to complete the following sentences.

   a Was hast du _____ _____ _____ gemacht? (What did you do three days ago?)

   b _____ _____ _____ habe ich meine Eltern besucht. (Four days ago, I visited my parents.)

c *Der Film hat* _____ _____ _____ *begonnen.* (The film began **ten minutes ago.**)

d *Ich habe ihn* _____ _____ _____ *in München getroffen.*

(I met him **six months ago** in Munich.)

e *Ich habe* _____ _____ _____ *schon in diesem Restaurant gegessen.*

(I already ate at this restaurant **two years ago!**)

GRAMMAR EXPLANATION: forming the past, with *haben*

For regular verbs – follow two easy steps

Forming the past tense in German is actually quite simple for many verbs. Here are the rules:

Step 1: start with the present form of the verb *haben* (to have), which by now you know well: *ich habe, du hast, er / sie / es hat, wir haben, ihr habt, sie / Sie haben.*

Step 2: add the verb you want to use, modified to the past form, which usually consists of *ge* + **the** *er / sie* **form**.

　　Example: *spielen* → *gespielt*

Step 3: put them together to create *ich habe gespielt* (I played).

With this you now know how to say *ich habe gefragt* (I asked), *du hast gesagt* (you said), *ich habe gewohnt* (I lived), and more!

Exceptions

There are exceptions to every rule, and not all German verbs follow this neat pattern. Take a look at some of the most important forms that don't follow this rule:

If you say *ich habe gesagt*, it can be translated as 'I said', 'I have said' or even 'I was saying'. German doesn't normally make this distinction, so learning the one version gives you all three ways of expressing yourself!

PRONUNCIATION: *geschrieben*

It's easy to miss the spelling change here, but remember that there's a definite difference in the pronunciation of *ei* and *ie*: in *schreiben*, the vowel sound rhymes with 'eye', whereas in *geschrieben* it rhymes with 'fee'.

Past tense exceptions cheat sheet

Pattern	Dictionary form	Past tense	Dictionary form	Past tense	Dictionary form	Past tense
	sehen (to see)	gesehen (saw)	geben (to give)	gegeben (gave)	essen (to eat)	gegessen (ate)
	trinken (to drink)	getrunken (drank)	finden (to find)	gefunden (found)	wissen (to know)	gewusst (knew)
	treffen (to meet)	getroffen (met)	helfen (to help)	geholfen (helped)	sprechen (to speak)	gesprochen (spoke)
(irregular)	nehmen (to take)	genommen (took)	schreiben (to write)	geschrieben (wrote)	denken (to think)	gedacht (thought)

For instance, if **denken** is 'to think', wouldn't you expect its past tense to be 'gedenkt'? Well, if you think about it, it isn't 'thinked' in English either! When a past form isn't as expected, it's very often when we do the same in English!

You also don't add ge- if in its dictionary form the last letters of the verb are -ieren. You also saw this when Ellen said **wir haben fotografiert** (we photographed).

Though these verbs are irregular, you can spot a few patterns that make them easier to remember. For example, *sprechen* (to speak) works similarly to English in that it changes to *gesprochen* (spoke). What other patterns do you see?

Past form with no *ge-*

Some past forms don't have *ge-* in them (as in *ich habe … besucht* which you saw in Conversation 1). Generally, don't add *ge-* for the past form when you see a verb that starts with:

⋯⋗ **be-** e.g. *bekommen* (to get) → *ich habe bekommen* (I got)
　　Also, *bestellen* (to order), *beginnen*, *besuchen* (to visit).
⋯⋗ **er-** e.g. *erklären* (to explain) → *sie hat es erklärt* (she explained it)
　　Also, *erfahren* (to experience).
⋯⋗ **ent-** e.g. *entscheiden* (to decide) → *ich habe entschieden* (I decided)
　　Also, *entdecken* (to discover).
⋯⋗ **ge-** e.g. *gefallen* (to please) → *es hat mir gefallen* (it pleased me / I liked it).
⋯⋗ **ver-** e.g. *verstehen* (to understand) → *Hast du verstanden?* (Did you understand?)
　　Also, *vergessen* (to forget), *vermissen* (to miss).

1　Fill in the gaps to make a past tense sentence with the verbs given.
　a　*Er _____ vor zwei Jahren Spanisch _____. (lernen)*
　b　*_____ ihr gestern Pläne _____? (machen)*
　c　*_____ du heute schon Deutsch _____? (üben)*
　d　*_____ Sie ein Buch von Tolkien _____ ? (lesen)*
　e　*Marius und Maria _____ einen Film im Kino _____. (sehen)*
　f　*Stefan _____ ihr einen Kuss _____. (geben)*
　g　*Wir _____ gestern ganz viel _____. (fotografieren)*
　h　*Ich _____ im Sommer meinen Bruder _____. (besuchen)*

2　Now practise using irregular verbs in the past to find out how the following story unfolds!
　a　*Stefan und ich _____ gestern in einem Restaurant zu Abend _____ (essen).*
　b　*Dabei _____ er zu viel Alkohol _____ (trinken).*
　c　*Ein Taxifahrer _____ mir _____ (helfen), Stefan ins Taxi zu tragen.*
　d　*Der Taxifahrer _____ bei Stefan einen Zettel mit einer Nummer _____ (finden).*
　e　*Was _____ Stefan _____ (schreiben)? Eine Telefonnummer?*
　f　*_____ er eine andere Frau _____ (treffen)?*
　g　*Ich _____ mein Handy _____ (nehmen), die Nummer getippt (typed) und mit einer Frau _____ (sprechen).*
　h　*Sie _____ nicht _____ (wissen), dass Stefan mein Freund ist.*
　i　*Ich _____ nie _____ (denken), dass Stefan sich für andere Frauen interessiert!*

PRACTICE

1 You can now create new types of full sentences! Write out in German:

   a The restaurant is great. I ate lunch there two days ago.

     _____

   b I spoke with Martin about Germany.

     _____

   c She visited her brother in Dublin.

     _____

2 Consider the phrase *Hat es dir gefallen?* (Did you like it?) from
Conversation 1. Based on the use of *dir*, how would you translate
these sentences?

   a Did he like it? _____
   b Did she like it? _____
   c I liked it! _____
   d We didn't like it. _____

PUT IT TOGETHER

Was gibt's Neues? Was hast du gestern / am letzten Wochenende gemacht?

Let's use the past forms you've just learned to create 'me-specific'
sentences that you could use in real conversations. Answer the questions
in German with real details about your life. You might include:

···┊ what you did, what you ate ...
···┊ who you saw, who you talked with ...
···┊ what you talked about.

CONVERSATION 2

When did you begin learning German?

Another great way to expand the scope of your German conversations is to learn to talk about your German progress, in German! People will definitely ask you these questions, so let's prepare you to answer them in German. Now that Ellen and Martin have caught up, they start discussing what Ellen has been doing to improve her German.

🔊 07.03 How does Martin ask, 'Did you study German this week?'

> **Martin:** Und, hast du diese Woche Deutsch gelernt?
>
> **Ellen:** Ja, ich habe ein bisschen gelernt. Ich habe ein paar neue Wörter gelernt und mit Judith ein paar Sätze geübt.
>
> **Martin:** Ausgezeichnet! Hast du deine Hausaufgaben gemacht?
>
> **Ellen:** Ja. Hier sind sie.
>
> **Martin:** Hast du dazu Fragen?
>
> **Ellen:** Ja! Was ist der Unterschied zwischen 'Apartment' und 'Wohnung'? Habe ich 'Wohnung' richtig gesagt?
>
> **Martin:** Es gibt keinen Unterschied! Und ja, du hast es richtig gesagt. Ich muss sagen, dass du eine ausgezeichnete Schülerin bist. Wann hast du begonnen, Deutsch zu lernen?
>
> **Ellen:** Ich habe erst vor ein paar Monaten begonnen. Letzten Sommer habe ich entschieden, ein Jahr lang zu reisen, also habe ich ein Ticket gekauft und bin nach Düsseldorf geflogen, und dann bin ich nach Berlin gereist.
>
> **Martin:** Stimmt, ich habe das vergessen – du hast mir das schon erzählt!

VOCAB: use *lang* 'for' a period of time
Ein Jahr lang can indeed work as the obvious 'a year long', but you'll see it much more frequently used to describe a period of time where you'd usually use 'for'. So here it means 'for a year'.

FIGURE IT OUT

1 Each of the following sentences are *falsch*. Highlight the words
   that make them incorrect and write out the correct replacements
   in German.

   a Ellen studied a lot of German over the weekend.   _____
   b Ellen began learning German only a few weeks ago. _____
   c Ellen flew to Berlin in January.   _____

2 Read the conversation and answer the questions.

   a What did Ellen do with Judith to help her German this week?

      _____

   b What is the meaning of the phrase *ich habe das vergessen – du hast
      mir das schon erzählt!*?

      _____

   c What phrase does Ellen use to check her pronunciation?

      _____

3 Use context to figure out the meaning of these words / phrases.

   a *Unterschied* _____

   b *ich habe entschieden* _____

   c *Hausaufgaben* _____ ←

   d *zwischen* _____

4 Highlight at least ten past tense forms in the conversation.

Did you notice the
compound noun,
Hausaufgaben? Try
to guess its meaning
from the context of
the conversation and
its component words
Haus (house) and
Aufgaben (tasks).

NOTICE

🔊 **07.04** Listen to the audio and study the table.

Essential phrases for Conversation 2

German	Meaning
Hast du diese Woche Deutsch gelernt?	Did you study German this week?
Ich habe ... geübt.	I practised ... (I have ... practised.)
ein paar neue Wörter	a few new words
ein paar Sätze	a few phrases
Ausgezeichnet!	Excellent!
Hast du deine Hausaufgaben gemacht?	Have you done your homework?
Hast du dazu Fragen?	Do you have (any) questions about it?
Was ist der Unterschied zwischen ...?	What is the difference between ...?
Habe ich 'Wohnung' richtig gesagt?	Did I say 'Wohnung' right? (Have I 'apartment' right said?)
Ich muss sagen, dass ...	I have to say that ...
Wann hast du begonnen, ...	When did you begin ...
Letzten Sommer habe ich entschieden, ...	Last summer I decided ...
ein Jahr lang zu reisen	to travel for a year
also habe ich ein Ticket gekauft	so I bought a ticket
und bin nach Düsseldorf geflogen	and flew to Düsseldorf
und dann bin ich nach Berlin gereist	and then I travelled to Berlin
Ich habe das vergessen.	I forgot that.
Du hast mir das schon erzählt.	You told me that already.

1 Find these power phrases in the phrase list, and write them out in German.

    a Did I say… right? _____

    b I have to say, that … _____

    c You told me that. _____

2 There's one use of 'you have' in the conversation that uses the present tense. Which is it? (Hint: look for a sentence without a second verb).

    Deutsch: _____   *Englisch:* _____

3 There are two past verb forms in the conversation, one starting with *ent-* and one with *ver-*, which therefore don't use *ge-*. What are they? _____ _____

4 Use the phrase list to help you recognize the past tense phrases in German. Choose the correct phrase from the list, then write it out next to its English counterpart.

> du hast gemacht   ich habe gelernt   ich habe entschieden
> du hast mir erzählt   ich habe geübt   ich habe gekauft
> du hast begonnen   ich bin geflogen   ich habe vergessen
> du hast gesagt   ich bin gereist

a   I learned / studied _____

b   I flew _____

c   I practised _____

d   I bought _____

e   I travelled _____

f   I forgot _____

g   I decided _____

h   you did _____

i   you told me _____

j   you said _____

k   you began _____

GRAMMAR EXPLANATION: using *sein* for movement

Most of the time, you'll use *haben* when talking about the past, but things change with verbs involving motion or 'transformation'. For example:

I **went** = *ich bin gegangen*   I **became** = *ich bin geworden*

we **flew** = *wir sind geflogen*   they **were born** = *sie sind geboren*

In these cases, you'll use *sein* (to be) in place of *haben*. But you'll otherwise be following the same two steps! For example, to translate 'Markus travelled to Italy yesterday':

sein (to be)   +   *ge* + *reist*   →   *gereist* (**travelled**)

Markus ist   +   *gereist*   →   *Markus ist gestern nach Italien **gereist**.*

Here are some of the most important verbs that work this way, along with their past forms:

Dictionary form	gehen (to go)	fahren (to go / drive)	kommen (to come)	fliegen (to fly)	laufen (to run)	werden (to become)
Past form	gegangen (went)	gefahren (drove)	gekommen (came)	geflogen (flew)	gelaufen (ran)	geworden (became)

1 Try it! Use *sein* + *ge-* to form the past tense phrase for 'I drove': _____

2 Using what you've learned about *haben* and *sein*, highlight the correct answer in German to form the past tense.

a   *Ich bin / habe mit dem Bus gefahren.*   (I went by bus.)
b   *Er ist / hat diesen Film gewählt.*   (He chose this film.)
c   *Bist / Hast du nach Italien geflogen?*   (Did you fly to Italy?)
d   *Wir sind / haben ins Kino gegangen.*   (We went to the cinema.)
e   *Habt / Seid ihr mit dem Auto gefahren?*   (Did you (pl) travel by car?)

3 Fill in the gaps with the past tense using *haben* or *sein*, and pay attention to the word order you use.

a   *Vor drei Monaten* _____ _____ *nach Kanada* _____.
    (Three months ago, **I travelled** to Canada.)
b   _____ _____ *das Museum sehr interessant* _____!
    (**I found** the museum very interesting!)
c   *Heute Morgen* _____ _____ *mit dem Zug* _____.
    (This morning **I went (drove)** by train.)

4 Use what you've learned about the past tense to fill in Sections 1 and 2 of the Past tense cheat sheet with key verbs in German. (Leave the rest of the cheat sheet blank for now).

Past tense cheat sheet

1. Regular verbs	Past form	2. Irregular verbs	Past form	3. Me-specific verbs	Past forms
I talked	ich	I went	ich		
I said	ich	I thought	ich		
I made	ich	I flew	ich		
I bought	ich	I forgot	ich		
I practised	ich	I decided	ich		
I learned / studied	ich	I knew	ich		
		I ate	ich		
		I began	ich		

PUT IT TOGETHER

1 Use the past tense to describe the details of a trip you took to another city. Draw from your own experiences to create sentences that answer the questions:

···⟩ *Wann bist du nach dieser Stadt gefahren? (Ich bin vor ... nach ...)*

···⟩ *Warum hast du entschieden, nach ... zu fahren? (Ich habe entschieden, nach ... zu fahren, weil ...)*

···⟩ *Hat es dir gefallen? Warum? (Es hat mir (nicht) gefallen, weil ich .... habe / bin ...)*

2 Imagine you're having a conversation with someone in German, when you casually mention an interesting anecdote and the other person says, *Toll! Was hast du genau gemacht? (Cool! What did you do exactly?)*

Answer the question with detailed sentences about a time in your life. You could write about somewhere you went, a film you saw, or anything else – but try to use new verbs you haven't used before. Try to include several past tense verbs in various forms to describe:

···⟩ specific details of what happened – who did what? (*Sie haben ... gelernt.*)

···⟩ specific details of conversations – who said what? (*Die Tochter hat gesagt, ...*)

···⟩ where you went, when you returned ... (*Ich bin ... gegangen.*)

CONVERSATION 3

Have I told you already …?

*You'll use **als** (when) to describe something in the past, and like wenn, dass, etc., it sends the verb to the end!*

The conversation continues between Ellen and Martin, as they use the past tense to discuss Ellen's progress in German.

🔊 **07.05** What phrase does Ellen use to ask, 'Have I told you already …'?

Anfangen means 'to start', which gives the German word for 'beginner' as Anfänger(in).

Ellen: Habe ich dir schon erzählt, dass ich Deutsch ein Jahr lang gelernt habe, **als** ich 13 Jahre alt war?

Martin: Wirklich? Ich habe gedacht, du bist Anfängerin.

Ellen: Ich habe alles vergessen, was ich in der Schule gelernt hatte. Deshalb glaube ich, dass ich noch Anfängerin bin.

Martin: Warum hast du nichts gelernt?

Ellen: Mein Lehrer hat nur Grammatik unterrichtet. Wir haben nie wirklich Deutsch gesprochen.

Martin: Ich glaube, man muss so viel wie möglich sprechen.

Ellen: Ich habe geglaubt, dass meine Aussprache schrecklich war! Ich wollte keine Fehler machen und ich war zu nervös, um zu sprechen.

Martin: Du hast keinen starken Akzent! Du sprichst gut und du kannst schon **so viel** auf Deutsch sagen.

Ellen: Danke, das ist nett von dir!

To avoid overusing sehr, work in other intensifiers like so (which means 'so', in English as well), and zu for 'too' (zu viel 'too much', zu nervös 'too nervous').

FIGURE IT OUT

1 *Richtig oder falsch?* Select the correct answer.

    a Ellen studied German in school for one year.   *richtig / falsch*
    b They spoke German often in her class.   *richtig / falsch*
    c Ellen's school teacher said her pronunciation was terrible. *richtig / falsch*

2 Highlight the following cognates and near cognates in the conversation.

    a nervous   b accent   c grammar

3 Now highlight each of these German phrases in the conversation.

    a Have I told you already that …?   e One should speak as much as
    b I forgot everything.   possible.
    c Why did you …?   f I was too nervous to speak!
    d I didn't want to make any   g when I was 13 years old
        mistakes.

4 What do you think the compound word *die Aussprache* means?

_____

In saying 'everything that', the word used for 'that' is normally **was** in German. If you keep this in mind, lots of other phrases are easy to recognize: *Ich weiß alles, was ich gelernt habe* (I know everything that I learned), *Wir haben alles, was wir brauchen* (We have everything that we need), *Ich verstehe alles, was du sagst* (I understand everything that you're saying).

GRAMMAR TIP:
nichts for 'anything' and 'nothing'

Both 'I don't have anything' and 'I have nothing' translate the same in German: *Ich habe nichts.*

GRAMMAR TIP:
unterrichtet for 'taught'

Like *be-* and *ver-* words that don't take *ge-* in their past form, words starting with **unter-** also often have a non *ge-* past – like **unterrichtet** (taught).

NOTICE

🔊 07.06 Listen to the audio and study the table.

Essential phrases for Conversation 3

German	Meaning
Habe ich dir schon erzählt …	Have I already told you …
dass ich Deutsch gelernt habe	that I learned German
als ich 13 Jahre alt war	when I was 13 years old
Ich habe gedacht …	I thought …
… du bist Anfängerin.	… you were a beginner (you are beginner).
… dass meine Aussprache schrecklich war!	… that my pronunciation was terrible! (that my out-speak terrible was!)
Ich habe alles vergessen.	I have forgotten everything.
was ich in der Schule gelernt hatte	that (what) I had learned at school
Warum hast du nichts gelernt?	Why didn't you learn anything? (Why have you nothing learned?)
Mein Lehrer hat nur Grammatik unterrichtet.	My teacher only taught grammar.
Wir haben nie wirklich Deutsch gesprochen.	We never really spoke German.
so viel wie möglich	as much as possible
Ich wollte keine Fehler machen.	I didn't want to make any mistakes.
Ich war zu nervös, um zu sprechen.	I was too nervous to speak.
Du hast keinen starken Akzent!	You don't have a strong accent! (You have no strong accent.)
Du kannst schon so viel auf Deutsch sagen.	You can already say so much in German.
Das ist nett von dir.	That's nice of you!

1 The following phrases can be adapted to use in a variety of different conversational situations. Find them in the phrase list and write them out.

   a Have I already told you _____

   b I thought that _____

   c I have forgotten _____

   d I had _____

   e when I was (13 years old) _____

2 Write out the German words for:

   a nothing _____   f really _____

   b everything _____   g so much _____

   c only _____   h too _____

   d never _____   i in _____

   e already _____   j of _____

3 Notice how the words 'that' and 'what' are used in the phrase list. Fill in the missing words to complete each sentence.

   a _____ _____ _____, ich habe dir die Antwort schon gesagt.
      (I **thought** (that) I already told you the answer.)

   b _____ _____ _____, _____ ich sagen wollte!
      (I **forgot what** I wanted to say!)

   c _____ _____ _____, _____ sie … war.
      (I **thought that** she was …)

   d _____ _____ _____ schon _____, _____ …
      (Did I ever **tell you what** …?)

4 Fill in the gaps with *alles* or *nichts*.

   a *Ich habe* _____ *vergessen.* (I forgot **everything**.)

   b *Ich werde* _____ *sagen, Ehrenwort!* (I'll say **nothing**, cross my heart!)

   c _____, *was ich will, ist ein Urlaub in Hawaii.*
      (**All** (that) I want is a holiday in Hawaii.)

GRAMMAR EXPLANATION: *war* (was) – *hatte* (had) – *wollte* (wanted) – *musste* (had to)

Since you need to use *haben* and *sein* to talk about the past, how do you say 'to have' and 'to be' in the past, as in 'I had' and 'I was'? Luckily, it's easy. German uses single word translations of these words in the past tense:

*Sein: ich war (**I was**), du warst, er / sie war, wir waren, ihr wart, sie waren*
*Haben: ich hatte (**I had**), du hattest, er / sie hatte, wir hatten, ihr hattet, sie hatten*

You can use these words as you might expect, and in fact you've already seen them in phrases like: *Es war okay* (**It was** OK) and *ich hatte gelernt* (**I had** learned).

Booster verbs in the past

Some of the booster verbs you saw in Unit 3 also get special past tense forms to themselves, and usually don't combine with *haben* and *sein* in the past. But luckily their use isn't complicated:

*Wollen: ich wollte (**I wanted**), du wolltest, er / sie wollte, wir wollten, ihr wolltet, sie wollten*
*Müssen: ich musste (**I had to**), du musstest, er / sie musste, wir mussten, ihr musstet, sie mussten*

PRACTICE

1 Go back and add: 'I was', 'I had', 'I wanted' and 'I had to' to your Past tense cheat sheet.

2 Complete the German phrases in the past tense.

a _____ *ein Taxi nehmen.* (He had to take a taxi.)

b _____ *nichts zu tun.* (I had nothing to do.)

3 How would you say these sentences in German?

a He was 31 years old when he met his wife. _____

b I wanted to talk with you about Germany. _____

c I wanted to learn German in Hamburg. _____

4 Use 'when I was' to create different phrases describing a past experience. Use ideas from the word box or others of your own.

> *in Brasilien* (in Brazil)
> *auf dem Weg zum Theater*
> (on the way to the theatre)
> *18 Jahre alt* (18 years old)
> *Manager bei der Firma Zamenhof*
> (manager at the Zamenhof company)

Example: **Als ich jünger war, habe ich gedacht, dass Deutsch zu schwer war.**
Jetzt denke ich das nicht!

(When I was younger, I thought that German was too hard. Now I don't think that!)

a _____

b _____

5 Now use the phrase *Habe ich dir schon erzählt …?* with *dass* (that) or *wie* (how) to create a sentence about your past.

Example: **Habe ich dir schon erzählt, dass ich immer Astronaut werden wollte?**

(Did I ever tell you that I always wanted to become an astronaut?)

_____

6 Use the vocab you've learned in this unit to fill in the gaps in German.

a *Kannst du mir sagen, was der* _____ _____ *den zwei* _____ *ist?*
(Can you tell me what the **difference** is **between** the two **words**?)

b _____ _____ *nur deutsche* _____ *in der* _____ _____.
(**We** only **learned** German **grammar** at **school**.)

c _____ *ist meine* _____? _____ _____ *einen* _____ _____ ?
(**How** is my **pronunciation**? **Do I have** a **strong accent**?)

7 Now test your knowledge of irregular past forms by completing the sentences.

a _____ *du mich* _____? *Ich* _____ _____,
_____ *ich Hunger habe!*
(Did you **understand** me? I **said that** I'm hungry!)

b *Ich habe* _____ _____ _____, _____ *wir*
_____ _____ *im Restaurant waren.*
(I **ate so much** when we were in the restaurant **last week**!)

c _____ _____ *die ganze Woche nur über Grammatik*
_____. _____ _____ *so … interessant!*
(**She** only **talked about grammar** all week! **It was** so … interesting!)

d _____ _____ *das Wort* _____. _____ _____
sollte ich eine Eselsbrücke benutzen!
(I **forgot** the word. **Next time**, I should use a mnemonic!)

e _____ _____ _____ *sehr* _____. *Danke!*
_____ _____ *meinen Hund nach dir* _____!
(**You helped** me a lot. Thank you! **I have** named my dog after you!) (named = *benannt*)

The German word for 'mnemonic', *Eselsbrücke* literally means 'donkey-bridge'. It comes from the idea that donkeys are so reluctant to cross the smallest streams that a bridge has to be built for them. The donkey-bridge – just like mnemonics – makes something that seems impossible much simpler!

#LANGUAGEHACK: time travel – talk about the past and future using the present

Language learning is a process, and as a beginner German learner, it's important to remember that you don't need to learn everything at once!

One of the truly fun aspects of languages is how flexible, fluid and creative they can be! Let's explore this now, by figuring out how many inventive ways you can express yourself in the past, even if you don't think you have the grammar or vocab for it yet.

1 Use *ich habe* ...
This is the most common way to form the past tense in German, which you've now seen used plenty of times! To form the past tense with 'I have', simply say *ich habe* using a past form, and you're done. Although some verbs require you to use *ich bin* instead (like *ich bin gegangen,* 'I went'), as a beginner it's OK if you use *ich habe* most of the time as your go-to past form while you learn.

This said, you're not limited to just using 'I have' to talk about the past. Let's get creative. Why not...

2 Use time indicators to travel through time
When you learned booster verbs, you saw that *ich werde* can be used for 'I will' to indicate something happening in the future. But a handy alternative that's also used frequently to refer to a future event is to use a time indicator! Notice the difference between:

Ich werde gut Deutsch sprechen. (I will speak German well.)

and

In einem Monat spreche ich gut Deutsch!
(In a month I'll speak (I speak) German well.)

3 Tell a story!

Once you've learned to use time indicators, you can build on them to form the past through 'storytelling'. For example, have you ever told a story that went something like this?

> 'So, the other day, there I am ... minding my own business, when someone comes up to me, and you'll never guess what happens!'

Though it's clearly an anecdote about something that happened in the past, the entire sentence actually uses present tense forms – 'there I am', 'someone comes up to me'. You can do the same thing in German! To make this narrative style work, you just need to:

⋯▸ give details that set the context of the situation to make it clear that it's a story. You can use time indicators, but other details work as well – say where you are, when it's happening, or what you're doing.

⋯▸ then simply say what happened, using the present form!

Examples:

Es ist letzten Montag und ich esse die beste Currywurst in Berlin ...
(It's last Monday, and I'm eating the best Currywurst in Berlin ...)

Also ich bin auf dem Markt und kaufe Tomaten ...
(So, I'm at the market, (and I'm) buying some tomatoes ...)

4 Just say it 'Tarzan' style!

If all else fails, the world won't end if all you can think of is a dictionary or other form of the verb. Though you will want to use this sparingly, people will get the gist of what you're saying even if all you can get out is something like:

> 'Gestern ... ich ... essen Pizza.' (Yesterday... I ... to-eat pizza.)

Always remember that saying something badly is miles better than saying nothing at all. And in fact, it's an opportunity to get corrections from a helpful German speaker!

I recommend you focus on improving one major aspect of your language skills at a time. Start with the most important ones first, then fine tune from there. Remember, people will see that you're a beginner, and they will forgive the error!

YOUR TURN: use the hack

While this #languagehack is very powerful, you only need to use it if you can't think of the past forms introduced in this unit. Use it as a crutch until you're confident!

1 Use time indicators to say in German:

   a I am watching the film now. _____

   b I am going to watch the film tomorrow. _____

   c I watched the film last week. _____

2 How would you attempt to tell the following implied story if you couldn't think of the past form of these verbs?
   Vor drei Tagen ... den Zug nehmen ... sehen .... einen Wolf !

   _____

3 Create 'me-specific' sentences in which you describe things you did at different time periods.

   a a week ago _____   c two years ago _____

   b last Saturday _____   d yesterday _____

Now say what you are going to do:

   e next Wednesday _____

   f in one year _____

PUT IT TOGETHER

1 Tell a story about a time you got nervous speaking German. Using what you've learned, describe those moments – what you were thinking ... doing ... saying … and what you learned. Be sure to include:

···▸ at least three of the following verbs: *denken, sprechen, lernen, machen, vergessen*, in the past

···▸ a specific time indicator (*Am letzten Wochenende ...*)

···▸ details of what you did to overcome your nerves (*Ich habe entschieden, langsam zu sprechen …*).

_____

_____

_____

_____

COMPLETING UNIT 7

Check your understanding

1 🔊 **07.07** Listen to this audio rehearsal first, in which a German speaker, Jan, describes meeting Mark, a tourist visiting Germany. ← *Feel free to take notes or listen to it multiple times.*

2 🔊 **07.08** Now listen to the second audio, which will ask you questions about Jan. Answer them out loud in German.

Show what you know ...

Here's what you've just learned. Write or say an example for each item in the list. Then tick off the ones you know.

- ☐ Say the past tense phrases:
    - ☐ 'I thought', 'I said', 'I went'
    - ☐ 'I learned' and 'I decided'
    - ☐ 'I was' and 'I had', 'I wanted' and 'I had to'
    - ☐ 'When I was...'
    - ☐ 'Have I ever told you that...'
- ☐ Give a sentence using *vor* to say how long ago you did something.
- ☐ Give time indicators for:
    - ☐ 'one time' and 'yesterday'
    - ☐ 'last week' and 'tomorrow'.

COMPLETE YOUR MISSION

It's time to complete your mission: put on your poker face and start your story. Try to fool the language hacking community as best you can.

STEP 1: build your script

Ich habe gedacht … Ich habe gelernt … Ich habe gesprochen.

Expand on your scripts by using 'me-specific' vocab to describe an important life lesson you gained from a past experience. Be sure to include:

⋯⋗ time indicators to describe when this happened (*vor …*)

⋯⋗ several past tense verbs in various forms to describe what you thought, what you wanted, what you learned, and more

⋯⋗ as many details as possible! (use the time travel #languagehack if you get stuck).

Write down your script, then repeat it until you feel confident.

Perhaps about an embarrassing situation when you used the wrong word in German, or a time when you overcame a personal struggle and felt really encouraged.

STEP 2: don't be a wallflower. Use language in real social contexts … *online*

If you're feeling good about your script, it's time to complete your mission! Go online to find your mission for Unit 7, and share your recording.

Research in learning emphasizes the importance of **social context** in facilitating language learning!

STEP 3: learn from other learners

Your task is watch at least two video clips uploaded by other hackers. Then ask three follow-up questions in German to see if they can keep the conversation going, to help them fill the gaps in their scripts, and to figure out whether what they say is *richtig oder falsch*. Make your guess.

What words of wisdom do the other language hackers have to offer? Which stories are real and which ones are *falsch*?

STEP 4: reflect on what you've learned

_____

_____

_____

HEY, LANGUAGE HACKER, SEE HOW THINGS HAVE CHANGED?

You've just learned how to talk about anything in the past. Now you can reminisce on the long-forgotten days when you couldn't speak German.

Next, you'll add even more detail to your conversations by describing the specific parts of your daily routine.

Dein Deutsch klingt schon super!

IT'S BEEN A WHILE!

Your mission

Imagine this – one of your German-speaking friends writes a blog about the daily routines of highly-productive people – like you – and you've been asked to contribute an article!

Your mission is to **prepare your best productivity advice** – in German – for the blog. Be prepared to **describe your daily routine** from your first morning beverage to your bedtime. Talk about **what works well** and **what you'd like to be different**.

This mission will broaden your ability to discuss your daily life and help you become comfortable with small talk in German.

Mission prep

- ⋯⟩ Talk about your hobbies, routines and daily life.
- ⋯⟩ Use versatile phrases to express your opinions and perceptions: *es ist wichtig zu, ich sehe, dass ...*
- ⋯⟩ Use phrases for seeing people you know again: *es ist lange her, ich freue mich, dich zu sehen.*
- ⋯⟩ Use expressions with *machen*, like *Sport machen.*
- ⋯⟩ Build upon modes of transport: *die U-Bahn nehmen, Fahrrad fahren.*
- ⋯⟩ Talk about what you would potentially do: *ich würde.*

BUILDING LANGUAGE FOR DESCRIBING YOUR DAILY LIFE

As a beginner German learner, it's difficult to be very detailed when you speak, so your energy is often best spent learning phrases that express a general idea of what you're trying to say.

But now you're quickly becoming an upper-beginner German learner! So it's time to learn some tricks for adding more detail to your conversations without a huge amount of new vocab. In this unit, we'll break a typical conversation into its component parts to develop a more complex strategy for helping each part flow well.

 #LANGUAGEHACK
the rephrasing technique for talking your way through complicated sentences

CONVERSATION 1

It's been a while!

You don't have to think it up on the spot - instead, prepare in advance with strategic phrases you can use to initiate, warm up, and extend any conversation.

When a conversation has passed the point of usual pleasantries, where should you go from there?

🔊 08.01 Ellen and Jakob are meeting for lunch at a café. Since they already know each other, they can't rely on the usual meet-and-greet expressions. What phrases do Jakob and Ellen use to 'warm up' the conversation?

Many expressions in German can be quite different to English, but *Bleib am Ball!* (Stay on the ball!) happens to be one that works in both!

Jakob: Hallo Ellen! Ich freue mich, dich zu sehen!

Ellen: Ja, es ist lange her!

Jakob: Und ich höre, dass dein Deutsch viel besser geworden ist. Also, erzähl mal, was gibt's Neues?

Ellen: Na ja, ich habe zurzeit viel zu tun. Vor kurzem habe ich angefangen, zu kochen. Ich mache einen Kochkurs!

Jakob: Echt? Und was hast du bisher gelernt?

Ellen: Letztes Mal haben wir gelernt, wie man einen Apfelkuchen macht. Im Kochkurs sieht alles so einfach aus, aber es klappt nie, wenn ich es zu Hause versuche.

Jakob: Komisch, das Problem habe ich nicht ... Meine Mikrowellen-Pizza schmeckt immer! Spaß beiseite, bleib am Ball! Es ist nur eine Frage der Zeit ... und der Übung! Es ist wichtig, zu üben.

Ellen: Ich weiß! Ich lerne schnell. Heute lerne ich, wie man einen Bienenstich macht!

CULTURE TIP:
Bienenstich
'Bee sting' cake consists of caramelized almonds on a sweet yeast dough and filled with a vanilla custard. They say that it's so tasty that the baker who invented it attracted a bee, who stung him, hence the name.

FIGURE IT OUT

1 Highlight the phrases in which Ellen says:

    a she's taking a cooking class.

    b what she and her class learned to make last time.

    c what she will learn to make today.

2 Use what you understood to fill in the missing details in English.

    a Jakob thinks that Ellen's German has gotten _____.

    b At her last class, Ellen learned to make _____.

    c Jakob jokes that his _____ is always good.

3 Use context to figure out how the speakers say 'It's good to see you!'.

    _____

4 Answer these questions, giving your answers in German.

    a *Was hat Ellen vor kurzem angefangen?*
       Sie _____

    b *Was macht Ellen heute?*
       Sie _____

5 Highlight the following German phrases in the conversation:

    a What's new?   b It's been a while.   c currently (at this time)

NOTICE

🔊 08.02 Listen to the audio and study the table. Pay special attention to the pronunciation of these phrases:

    Ich freue mich, dich zu sehen!   *vor kurzem*   *Spaß beiseite*

As well as 'to do', **machen** also means 'to make'. Wie praktisch!

Essential phrases for Conversation 1

German	Meaning
Ich freue mich, dich zu sehen!	I'm happy to see you!
Es ist lange her!	It's been a while!
ich höre, dass ...	I hear that ...
dein Deutsch viel besser geworden ist	your German has gotten a lot better (your German lots better become is)
Erzähl mal, was gibt's Neues?	Tell me, what's new? (Explain would-you, what is-there new?)
Ich habe zurzeit viel zu tun.	I'm very busy right now. (I have at-the-time a-lot to to-do.)
Vor kurzem habe ich angefangen ... zu kochen!	Recently I started ... cooking! (Ago shortly have I started to to-cook.)
Ich mache einen Kochkurs!	I'm taking a cooking class!
Und was hast du bisher gelernt?	And what have you learned so far?
letztes Mal ...	last time ...
wir haben gelernt, wie man ... macht	we learned how to make ... (we have learned, how one ... makes)
alles sieht so einfach aus	everything looks so easy (everything sees so easy out)
aber es klappt nie	but it never works
wenn ich es zu Hause versuche	when I try to make it at home (if I it to house try)
komisch	strange
Meine Mikrowellen-Pizza schmeckt immer.	My microwave pizza always tastes good. (tastes-nice always)
Spaß beiseite	joking aside
Bleib am Ball!	Keep trying! (Stay on ball!)
Es ist wichtig, zu üben.	It's important to practise.
Es ist nur eine Frage ...	It's just a matter ... (It is only a question)
der Zeit ... und der Übung!	of time ... and of practice!
Ich lerne schnell.	I learn quickly.
Heute lerne ich, wie man einen Bienenstich macht!	Today I'm learning how to make a bee-sting cake!

1 What two new phrases can you use to greet someone you haven't seen in a while?

_____   _____

2 Notice how German expresses these phrases. Write them out, using the literal translations in the phrase list to help you.

a currently _____

b I'm very busy _____

c recently _____

d I started to _____

e last time _____

f we learned how to _____

3 Use the phrase list to fill in the gaps in each expression.

a *Was hast du* _____ _____? (What have you **learned so far**?)

b *Ich werde es* _____ *lernen!* (I will learn it **quickly**!)

c *Zu Hause* _____ _____ _____ *!* (At home **it never works**!)

d _____ _____ _____ _____ _____ *der Zeit.* (**It's only a matter** of time.)

4 Determine which word is missing from each of the sentences.

a *Es ist wichtig, gut* _____ *essen.* (It's important to eat well.)

b *Meine Freundin hat angefangen, Architektur* _____ *studieren.*
   (My girlfriend has started studying architecture.)

c *Es ist gesünder, zu Hause* _____ *kochen.* (It's healthier to cook at home.)

5 *Viel zu tun* is a chunk you can combine with lots of other phrases. Given that, how do you think you'd say in German:

a There's still a lot do! _____

b My parents are very busy. _____

6 Notice the German phrase for 'We learned how to make' and 'Today I'm learning how to make'. Based on this, say the following in German.

a *Wie* _____ _____ *Apfelkuchen?* (How do you make apple cake?)

b *Wir* _____ _____, _____ _____ *Tango* _____.
   (We learned how to dance tango). (*tanzen* = to dance)

c _____ _____ _____ *ich* _____, _____ _____ *russische Buchstaben*
   _____. (Last year, I learned how to write Russian letters.)

GRAMMAR EXPLANATION: 'separable' (mix and match) German verbs

In Conversation 1, you met the phrase:

> *Alles sieht so einfach aus.*   (Everything looks so easy.)

which uses the verb *aussehen* (to look (like)), **separated into two parts**: *aus* (out) and *sehen* (to see). You can also see this in the phrase:

> *Ich wache um 7 Uhr auf.*   (I wake up at 7 a.m.)

Here you see the verb *aufwachen* (to wake up) 'separated' into the two parts: *auf* (up) and *wachen* (to wake). These are what we call **separable verbs**. When you see any of these prepositions attached to the head of a verb, it can change the verb's meaning:

> *an* (at), *auf* (up), *aus* (out), *mit* (with), *weg* (away), *zu* (to), *zurück* (back)

For example, *machen* (to make) can change to *aufmachen* (to open) or *zumachen* (to close). The usual German word order applies when you use these verbs: the verb head gets sent to the end of the sentence or phrase. (Unless it's in the dictionary form, and then it stays attached).

1 Try it! Can you guess the meaning of these separable verbs?

a *ausflippen* b *aufgeben* c *zurückgeben* d *ausgehen*

2 Now see if you can figure out how to say the following in German:
Example: (*anfangen*) When are you starting? → Wann fängst du an?

a (*ankommen*) I usually arrive at midday. (*am Mittag* = at midday)

_____

b (*ausgehen*) Every Friday I go out with Peter.

_____

c (*aufwachen*) I always wake up at 6 o'clock.

_____

d (*mitkommen*) Are you coming along today?

_____

e (*aufmachen*) Can you open the door? (*die Tür* = the door)

_____

And we have something similar in English! Think of the phrase 'tidy up'. In both English and German, the 'up' can move around in the sentence. Example: *aufräumen* (to tidy up) Ich *räume* mein Zimmer *auf*. (I'm tidying the room up.)

Because these words often have a meaning in their own right, you can use them to help you work out the meaning of new words. For instance, you might easily figure out that *mitarbeiten*, which combines *mit + arbeiten*, means 'to work with' or 'to co-operate'.

Past forms of separable verbs

So how would you use these mix-and-match verbs in the past tense? In the past, they get 'half' separated, and the letters **ge-** get added between the verb's head (preposition) and the rest of the word.

aufmachen (to open) → auf + *ge-* + (*macht*) = *aufgemacht* (**opened**)

(present form) → (preposition + *ge-*) + (rest of word) = (past form)

3 Try it yourself now. Review the table to fill in the missing forms.

Verb heads	Separable verbs	Meaning	Past forms	Meaning
an ('at', 'to')	anfangen	to start	a.	
	ankommen	to arrive	b.	
	anrufen	to call	c.	
auf ('up', 'on')	aufmachen	to open	aufgemacht	opened
	aufräumen	to tidy up	d.	
aus ('out')	ausgehen	to go out	e.	
	aussehen	to look (like)	f.	
mit ('with')	mitgehen	to go with (someone)	mitgegangen	went with
	mitkommen	to come along	mitgekommen	came along
	mitarbeiten	to cooperate	g.	
weg ('away')	wegbleiben	to stay away	h.	
	weglaufen	to run away	i.	
zu ('to')	zuhören	to listen to	j.	
zurück ('back')	zurückrufen	to call back	k.	
	zurückkommen	to come back	l.	

4 Based on what you see, how would you form the past of the phrases below?

Example: He came back three days ago. *(Er ist) (zurück + kommen) (vor drei Tagen)*

→ *Er ist vor drei Tagen zurückgekommen.*

a We went out on Friday with Hans. *(Wir sind) (aus + gehen) (am Freitag mit Hans)*

_____

b She opened the shop at eight. *(Sie hat) (auf + machen) (um acht Uhr den Laden)*

_____

c He called me back yesterday. *(Er hat) (an + rufen) (ihn gestern)*

_____

PRACTICE

1 Fill the gaps with the words given to make complete sentences.

    a *Wir haben* _____ _____ _____, *weil wir diese Woche* _____ *haben.*
       (We have **a lot to do**, because we **started** this week.)

    b ___ _____ *habe ich Maria* _____. *Sie* ___ _____, *in der Schule* _____ *arbeiten.*
       (I **recently** saw Maria. She **has started** to work at the school.)

    c _____ _____ *ist sie* _____. (**Last time** she **came along**.)

    d *Sie hat* _____ _____. ___ *sie krank?* (She **looked strange**. **Was** she sick?)

    e _____ *hat sie nicht* _____. (**So far** she hasn't **cooperated**.)

    f *Kannst du mich* _____? (Can you **call** me **back**?)

2 Describe two things you (or we!) have learned by combining your me-specific verbs with the phrase *haben + gelernt: haben + gelernt, wie man* + (any skill or activity)

Example: ich habe gelernt, wie man surft (*I learned how to surf*)

_____   _____

3 Study the example and rephrase the *German* sentences.

Example: *Ich spreche **seit** zwanzig Minuten mit Markus am Telefon. (anrufen)* (I've been talking with Markus on the phone **for** 20 minutes.) → Ich habe vor zwanzig Minuten Markus angerufen. (I called Markus 20 minutes **ago**.)

    a *Ich wohne seit einer Woche in Berlin. (ankommen)*
       Ich bin _____ einer Woche in Berlin _____.

    b *Ich lerne seit 2013 Deutsch. (anfangen)*
       Ich habe _____ _____ Jahren _____, Deutsch zu lernen.

    c *Er kennt mich seit einer Woche. (treffen)* Er hat mich _____ einer Woche _____.

    d *Das Restaurant ist seit einer Stunde offen. (aufmachen)*
       Er hat das Restaurant _____ _____ einer Stunde _____.

CONVERSATION STRATEGY: learn set phrases for each 'stage' of a conversation

A lot of people get nervous about what to say during a conversation. If you're meeting someone for the first time, it's easy – just introduce yourself. But if you've talked before, or you've finished your greetings, you'll need to keep the conversation going. When you understand the structure of a typical conversation, you can break it down into its component parts and prepare phrases to use at the different stages in a conversation. This way, you're never stuck wondering what to say next.

Warm up the conversation

During the first few seconds of a conversation use some longer pleasantries to give yourself time to collect your thoughts. For example:

⋯⟩ *Lange nicht gesehen!* (Long time no see (lit. long not seen)!)

⋯⟩ *Ich freue mich, dich zu sehen!* (I'm pleased to see you!)

Get the conversation started

Set a conversation topic into motion! Prepare phrases to get the other person talking for a few minutes:

⋯⟩ *Sag mal, was gibt's Neues?* (Tell me, what's new for you?)

⋯⟩ *Du siehst (gut / müde / glücklich / traurig) aus …* (You're looking (good / tired / happy / sad …)

⋯⟩ *Ich sehe, (du hast dich nicht verändert).* (I see that … you haven't changed).

Lead the conversation yourself

When it's again your turn to talk, think of some phrases you can use to lead the discussion on your own and introduce a new conversation topic.

⋯⟩ *Also, vor kurzem habe ich angefangen …* (Well, recently I started to …)

⋯⟩ *… als Sekretärin zu arbeiten, … einen Kochkurs zu machen,* etc.

⋯⟩ *In letzter Zeit habe ich …* (Lately I have been …)

Extend the conversation

Show your interest with filler words like *interessant!* or *echt?* But a slightly more detailed question, prepared in advance, will urge the other person to expand on the topic, and therefore extend the conversation. For example:

⋯⟩ *Und wie findest du es?* (And how do you find it?)

⋯⟩ *Und, macht es Spaß?* (So, is it fun?)

⋯⟩ *Und was denkst du?* (And what do you think?)

Add detail to your conversations

Remember that you can get more out of a conversation by expanding on a topic with details about when, where, or how something happened. For example, to describe recent travels, you could say *Ich reise zurzeit viel für meine Arbeit.* But why not go on to elaborate on this by adding descriptive details (when? what?):

⋯⟩ *Das letzte Mal* (when) *bin ich … acht Stunden geflogen* (what) …

⋯⟩ *Das war für eine Konferenz …* (why) *… in Kanada* (where?)

Study the table and see how a conversation can flow:

Language hacker A	Language hacker B
Conversational warmers Es ist lange her! Ich freue mich dich zu sehen!	**Conversational warmers** Vielen Dank für / Danke für …!
	Starting replies Nicht viel. Alles ist wie immer
Conversational starters Sag / Erzähl mal, was gibt's Neues? Ich sehe … (du hast dich nicht verändert/du hast jetzt eine Freundin …) Erzähl mir von dir!	**Conversation leads** Also, vor kurzem habe ich angefangen, … Im Moment mache ich … Als wir letztes Mal / das letzte Mal gesprochen haben, habe ich… Example: … als Sekretärin gearbeitet … / … einen Kochkurs gemacht … / etc.
Conversation extensions Und, gefällt es dir? Und wie findest du es? Wie interessant! Erzähl mir mehr!	**Conversation details** Letztes Mal (when?) … zu Hause (where?) habe ich … Apfelkuchen (what?) Heute (when?) … Bienenstich (what?)

1 In Conversation 1, Ellen describes her hobby, cooking, then elaborates by adding descriptive details. Look back at the conversation to identify the details Ellen gives.

a (when?) *Das letzte Mal* (what?) _____   c (when?) *Heute* (what?) _____

b (what?) *Ich mache*   (where?) _____

2 Can you find the other conversation components in Conversation 1? Highlight:

a two conversational warmers   c two conversational leads
b two conversation starters   d one conversation extension

3 Now create some conversation starters using the verbs *wissen*, *kennen* or *sehen* in their correct forms.

a I know that (you come from England) _____

b Do you know (Sarah's new boyfriend)? _____

c Have you already seen (this film)? _____

PUT IT TOGETHER

1 What is your hobby? Pick a hobby you'd like to be able to describe. Use the phrases *Vor kurzem habe ich angefangen …* or *Im Moment, …* along with vocab you look up to create two of your own conversation leads.

_____

_____

2 Now create a script in which you describe your hobby to a friend. Start with a conversational lead, but then go on to add details like:

⋯⋗ why / when you started it (*Vor kurzem, anfangen*)
⋯⋗ details of what you did last time (*Letztes Mal, wenn ich versuche …*)
⋯⋗ what you've learned or achieved so far (*Bisher*)
⋯⋗ use *Es ist … zu* or *Ich bin …, dass* (example: *interessant …*) somewhere in your description.

_____

_____

_____

_____

_____

_____

_____

CONVERSATION 2

Your daily routine

What do you normally do in a day? In a week?

🔊 **08.03** Ellen and Jakob are talking about their daily routines. How does Ellen say 'it was strange at first'? What helped her get into the swing of things?

Jakob: Mir scheint, alles läuft gut für dich in Berlin!

Ellen: Ja, danke. Zuerst war es komisch, aber jetzt habe ich Routine. Morgens, vor der Arbeit, gehe ich gemütlich in der Stadt spazieren.

Jakob: Ich auch. Normalerweise gehe ich nachmittags mit dem Hund im Park Gassi. Ab und zu fahre ich Fahrrad.

Ellen: Ich fahre überall Fahrrad! Ich nehme nicht die U-Bahn – ich brauche frische Luft.

Jakob: Ich nehme auch nur selten die U-Bahn, weil ich oft mit dem Auto zur Arbeit fahre.

Ellen: Und mittags esse ich immer im gleichen Restaurant – hier haben sie nämlich die beste Gulaschsuppe.

Jakob: Meistens koche ich zu Hause, aber manchmal experimentiere ich ein wenig und gehe in ein neues Restaurant. Hier bin ich zum ersten Mal.

Ellen: Du warst noch nie in meinem Lieblingsrestaurant hier? Du solltest unbedingt etwas essen! Ich lade dich ein!

This very German word, which roughly translates as 'leisurely', 'comfy' or 'unhurriedly' perfectly describes a warm and friendly environment, especially when socializing at places such as at a Biergarten.

Here we see another separable verb head: ein. It's the separable chunk equivalent of 'in' and has that meaning implied (here, to invite 'in'). Ex: *Ich lade dich ein* while meaning 'I invite you' in this context is a means of saying 'it's my treat'.

FIGURE IT OUT

1 Who does what? Tick the correct box.

	goes for a walk before work	rides a bicycle	takes the car	always has lunch at a restaurant	sometimes tries new restaurants	prepares lunch at home
Ellen						
Jakob						

2 Which phrase means 'It seems to me'? Write it out here in German.
How is it used in the conversation: as a starter, warmer, or extension?

_____   _____

3 Look at the language pairs. Can you figure out which phrases mean 'in the mornings', and 'in the afternoons'?

Abend	(evening)	⋯⟶ ___abends___	(in the evenings)
Montag	(Monday)	⋯⟶ ___montags___	(on Mondays)
a *Morgen*	(morning)	⋯⟶ _____	(in the mornings)
b *Nachmittag*	(afternoon)	⋯⟶ _____	(in the afternoons)

4 Answer the questions in German.

a *Was macht Ellen vor der Arbeit morgens?*

Sie _____

b *Wann geht Jakob normalerweise mit dem Hund Gassi?*

Er _____

c *Wo fährt Ellen Fahrrad?*

Sie _____

d *Wie oft nimmt Jakob die U-Bahn?*

Er _____

e *Warum nimmt Ellen die U-Bahn nicht?*

Weil sie _____

f *Wie fährt Jakob oft zur Arbeit?*

Er _____

NOTICE

🔊 08.04 Listen to the audio and study the table.

Essential phrases for Conversation 2

German	Meaning
Mir scheint ...	It seems to me ...
alles läuft gut für dich!	everything is going well for you!
Zuerst war es komisch,	At first it was strange
Morgens, vor der Arbeit	In the mornings, before work
gehe ich gemütlich in der Stadt spazieren	I go for a leisurely walk around the city (go I leisurely in the city to-walk)
normalerweise	normally
nachmittags	in the afternoon
gehe ich mit dem Hund im Park Gassi	I walk my dog in the park. (go I with the dog in-the park dog-walk)
ab und zu ...	now and again ... (from and to)
Ich fahre überall Fahrrad!	I ride my bike everywhere!
Ich nehme nicht die U-Bahn.	I don't take the metro.
Ich brauche frische Luft.	I need fresh air.
selten	rarely
Weil ich oft mit dem Auto zur Arbeit fahre.	Because I often drive to work. (Because I often with the car to-the work drive.)
Und mittags esse ich immer ...	And at lunchtime I always eat ...
im gleichen Restaurant	in the same restaurant
manchmal experimentiere ich ein wenig	sometimes I experiment a little
meistens koche ich zu Hause	I usually cook at home
Du warst noch nie in meinem Lieblingsrestaurant hier?	Have you never been here in my favourite restaurant before?
Ich lade dich ein!	It's my treat!

VOCAB: 'in the mornings'
As an alternative to *jeden Morgen* (every morning) you can simply say *morgens*. It literally means 'mornings', but when you're talking about your routine, it's clear that you mean 'every' morning.
This works with other words like *mittags* (lunchtimes), *montags* (Mondays), *dienstags* (Tuesdays) and so on.

VOCAB: how many times
You can also use any number + *mal* (times) to describe *Wie oft* ... (how often) you do something, e.g. *einmal*, *zweimal*, *dreimal*. If you've asked someone to do something 'lots of times', you can even use *zigmal* (umpteen times).

1 Rephrase the statement *(Mir scheint) alles läuft gut für dich!* into a question.

This could be used as a conversation starter.

_____

2 Use the conversation to fill in the table with 'detail phrases' you could use to answer the questions: When? How often? Why? / How? Where?

Conversation details

TIME		MANNER	PLACE
When?	How often?	Why? / How?	Where?
in the morning 1 _____	normally 5 normalerweise	by car 13 _____	in the park 15 im Park
in the afternoon 2 nachmittags	usually 6 _____	leisurely 14 _____	around the city 16 _____
at lunchtime/noon 3 _____	now and then 7 _____		everywhere 17 _____
before work 4 _____	rarely 8 _____		to work 18 _____
	often 9 _____		in the same (restaurant) 19 _____
	always 10 _____		at home 20 _____
	sometimes 11 _____		
	never 12 _____		

Word order: keep your TeMPo in German!

In German, the order of words in descriptive sentences follows a particular pattern (which has conveniently been outlined for you in the table!). German usually presents the **time** first (when / how often), followed by the **manner** (why / how) of the sentence, and finally, the **place** (where). If you think about keeping your **TeMPo** in German, you'll remember the Time–Manner–Place order!

CONVERSATION 2 ⊷⋯ 177

3 Use the details from the table to create the phrases Ellen and Jakob use. Be sure to use TeMPo word order.

Example: Jakob walks his dog. [where?] [when?] [how often?]

gehe / mit dem Hund / ich / Gassi

⋯⋗ _Normalerweise gehe ich nachmittags mit dem Hund im Park Gassi._

a. Ellen goes for a walk. [when?] [how?] / [where?] [when?]

spazieren / ich / gehe

_____

b. Jakob rides his bike. [how often?]   fahre / Fahrrad / ich

_____

c. Ellen rides her bike. [where?]   Fahrrad / fahre / ich

_____

d. Jakob goes to work. [how often?] [where?] [how?]   fahre / ich

_____

e. Ellen eats lunch. [when?] [where?] [how often?]   esse / ich

_____

f. Jakob cooks. [where?] [how often?]   ich / koche

_____

4 Now use the detail phrases given in the box to create sentences using TeMPo word order.

bei meinen Eltern (at my parents' house) _mein Spezialfrühstuck mit Eiern_ (my special breakfast with eggs) _mitten in der Nacht_ (in the middle of the night)	_mit dem Motorrad_ (by motorbike) _jedes Jahr_ (every year) _nach Hause_ ((to) home) _zum Laden_ (to the shop)

a I drove to the shop by motorbike in the middle of the night.

_____

b Every year I make my special breakfast with eggs at my parents house!

_____

VOCAB EXPLANATION: using *machen* to describe what you do

The verb *machen* means 'to do' or 'to make' in German. Because it's so versatile, you can use *machen* + noun to describe a lot of the activities you might do (which means fewer new verbs to learn)! So if you don't know a verb, try using *machen*! Here are some common expressions using *machen*:

Activities, hobbies, and getting around

German	Meaning	German	Meaning
Musik machen	to play music	*das Abendessen machen*	to make (cook) dinner
Sport machen	to exercise	*Kaffee machen*	to make coffee
ein Spiel machen	to play a game	*Übungen machen*	to exercise (do exercises)
einen Spaziergang machen	to take walks	*eine Reise machen*	to take a trip
ein Foto machen	to take photos	*einen Besuch machen*	to visit (someone)

PRACTICE

1 Fill in the gaps to complete the story in German.

a *Ich _____ gern _____ – _____ von der Couch zum Kühlschrank und _____.*
(I like to **take walks – usually** from the sofa to the fridge and **back**!)

b *_____, aber _____ lasse ich meinen Mann das _____.* (**Now and then I make coffee in the mornings**, but **normally** I make my husband **do** it!)

c *Ich liebe hausgemachten Kuchen … _____ den hausgemachten Kuchen aus dem Haus meiner Nachbarin!*
(I love homemade cake … **In the afternoon, I often eat** the homemade cake from my neighbour's house!)

d *Ich bin ein blitzschneller Athlet! _____, als ich _____, war ich schon _____ fertig.*
(I am a lightning-fast athlete. The **last time**, when I **exercised**, I was already finished **five minutes later**!)

e *_____ jedem Fußball_____ bin ich total ausgepowert. _____ meine Lieblingsmannschaft verliert!*
(**After** every football **game**, I'm completely exhausted. **Especially if** my favourite team loses!)

VOCAB: *more about machen!*
German uses *machen* for other phrases as well, as we would in English:
···❯ *das Bett machen* (to make the bed)
···❯ *einen Fehler machen* (to make a mistake)

Machen is also used in some phrases where we would use 'to take':
···❯ *mach's gut!* (take care!)

And there are other phrases that we'd express completely differently:
···❯ *(das) macht nichts!* (it doesn't matter)
···❯ *jemandem Mut machen* (to encourage someone / make someone encouraged)

2 Now create new sentences on your own describing your daily or weekly routines. Use at least three detail phrases from the table, and be sure to use the TeMPo word order.

_____

_____

_____

Do you build things? Do you jog every day? Do you sing ... dance ... code ... bodybuild? This is your chance to describe real parts of your life in German!

3 What are some of your hobbies? Look them up in your dictionary, then create two simple sentences that describe things you like to do. Example: Ich spiele Violine.

_____   _____

4 Next, practise adding detail to your basic phrases.

a _Was machst du gern?_ Choose one of your hobbies as a 'base' to add details to.

Example: Ich fahre Fahrrad, Ich spiele Klavier ...

_____

b Now use detail phrases to describe when, how, where, etc. you do that activity.

Example: Ich spiele Klavier am Wochenende bei meinen Eltern.

_____

c _Wie findest du das?_ Use the phrase _zuerst war es ..., aber jetzt ..._ to describe what you think of it.

Example: Zuerst war es schwierig, aber jetzt habe ich viel Spaß!

_____

5 _Wo ist dein Lieblingsort?_ Now think about one of your favourite places near you.

a Write a simple sentence about it in German.

Example: Ich gehe gern in die Bibliothek.

_____

b Then use the phrase *Ich gehe in ..., um ...* to say why you go there and how often.

Example: Ich gehe oft in die Bibliothek, um Bücher zu lesen!

_____

c *Warst du noch nicht in (Stadt)?* Now use *Ich war noch nie in ...* to say somewhere you've never been before, but would like to go one day.

Example: Ich war noch nie in Sydney!

_____

PUT IT TOGETHER

Write a script describing different parts of your normal routine, hobbies or interests, and make sure to add detail phrases. You might talk about:

···❖ how you get to work / school every day
···❖ your hobbies, interests, or other activities
···❖ details of how often, when, where, why, or how
    you do different things.

CONVERSATION 3

Going out at night

As your conversation comes to an end, you'll want to be ready to make plans for next time!

◀) 08.05 How does Jakob ask 'What are you doing after this?'

VOCAB: *heute Nachmittag*
To say 'this afternoon', German literally says *heute Nachmittag* (today afternoon). Also: *heute Morgen* (this morning) and *heute Abend* (this evening).

> **Jakob:** Was machst du danach? Ich möchte mit Freunden in den Park gehen, um Fußball zu spielen. Möchtest du mitkommen?
>
> **Ellen:** Ich würde schon gerne, aber leider habe ich schon vor, mit jemandem einkaufen zu gehen. Ich würde etwas später kommen, wenn ihr dann noch spielt.
>
> **Jakob:** Ich weiß nicht, wie lange wir spielen werden, aber ich mache heute Abend bei mir zu Hause eine kleine Party. Du solltest auch kommen!
>
> **Ellen:** Cool, das mache ich auf jeden Fall! Was sollte ich mitbringen? Und um wie viel Uhr?
>
> **Jakob:** Ich würde sagen um 20 Uhr. Ein Dessert wäre perfekt. Du machst doch heute Nachmittag einen Bienenstich, vielleicht könntest du den mitbringen?
>
> **Ellen:** Das ist eine clevere Idee! Und wo wohnst du?
>
> **Jakob:** Meine Wohnung ist in der Nähe vom Bahnhof, gegenüber vom Kaufhof.
>
> **Ellen:** Könntest du die Adresse aufschreiben?
>
> **Jakob:** Klar! Und wenn du dein Handy bei dir hast, kann ich es dir auf der Karte zeigen!

CULTURE TIP:
what to bring
If you're invited into someone's home, feel free to bring a gift to show your appreciation! If the event includes a meal or snacks, avoid bringing food yourself (unless requested) as it could clash with the hosts' plans. Chocolate, flowers, wine or a gift from home are always good ideas. Or you can ask your host what they might like you to bring, as Ellen does here.

FIGURE IT OUT

1 *Richtig oder falsch?* Select the correct answer.

   a After this, Jakob is going to have a drink with his brother.   *richtig / fals*
   b Jakob invites Ellen to go with him and then to a get-together. *richtig / fals*
   c Ellen has already planned to go to her cooking class.   *richtig / fals*

2 Can you guess the meaning of the phrases based on words you already know?

a *Möchtest du mitkommen?* _____

b *Was sollte ich mitbringen?* _____

c *Könntest du die Adresse aufschreiben?* _____

d *Ich würde gerne.* _____

NOTICE

🔊 **08.06** Listen to the audio and study the table.

Essential phrases for Conversation 3

German	Meaning
Was machst du danach?	What are you doing after this?
Möchtest du mitkommen?	Would you like to come along?
Ich würde schon gerne, aber leider …	I'd love to, but unfortunately …
… habe ich schon vor, mit jemandem einkaufen zu gehen.	… I've already planned to go shopping with someone.
Ich würde etwas später kommen, …	I would come a bit later, …
… wenn ihr dann noch spielt.	… if you're still playing then.
Ich mache heute Abend …. eine kleine Party.	I'm having a small party this evening …
bei mir zu Hause	at my house
Du solltest auch kommen!	You should come too!
Das mache ich auf jeden Fall!	I'll definitely do that!
Was sollte ich mitbringen?	What should I bring?
Um wie viel Uhr?	What time? (At how many hours?)
Ich würde sagen um 20 Uhr.	I would say at 8 p.m.
Ein Dessert wäre perfekt.	A dessert would be perfect.
Vielleicht könntest du den mitbringen?	Maybe you could bring that along?
Meine Wohnung ist in der Nähe vom Bahnhof.	My apartment is near the station. (in the vicinity of-the train-station)
Könntest du die Adresse aufschreiben?	Could you write down the address?
Wenn du dein Handy bei dir hast, …	If you have your mobile on you, …
… kann ich es dir auf der Karte zeigen!	… I can show it to you on the map!

VOCAB: *bei* as 'at the house of'
Bei in German works exactly like 'chez' in French: both can mean 'at the house of.' So *bei mir* means 'at my house', *bei dir* 'at your house', *bei Judith*, 'at Judith's house' and so on.
Zu Hause just means 'at home'. So in this conversation, though *bei mir* would work perfectly well on its own, *zu Hause* is just added for clarity.

VOCAB: *Karte*
Karte is a German word you'll see a lot. On its own it means 'card' or 'ticket', but it's often used in compound nouns, where the meaning is clear from context, so Germans don't always bother to say the whole word.
Karte is commonly used for *Speisekarte* ('menu', as you saw in Unit 6), *Geburtstagskarte* (birthday card), *SIM-Karte* (SIM card), *Spielkarte* (playing card) and *Kinokarte* (cinema ticket). The list is endless!
Here the word is used for *Landkarte* (map).

1 Can you identify the detail phrases the speakers use to expand on their thoughts? Look at the first line of the conversation and write out the detail phrases about Jakob in German:

    a Where is he going? Er geht _____

    b Why is he going? Um _____

    c Who is he going with? Mit _____

2 This conversation is all about making plans. Look at the phrase list and note the different phrases you could use to ...

    ⋯⟩ ... invite someone to a get-together or to do something with you. Say in German:

    a What are you doing ... ? _____   c Would you like to come? _____

    b I'm having a small party ... _____   d You should also come! _____

    ⋯⟩ ... accept (or decline) an invitation. Say in German:

    e I will definitely do that! _____   g ... but unfortunately ... _____

    f I would love to! _____   h I've already planned to ... _____

3 Find the following details in the phrase list and highlight them.

    a after this   d this evening   g near the station   j with someone

    b a bit later   e at 8 p.m.   h my apartment

    c then   f at my house   i to go shopping

4 Now find the German phrases for asking for and giving details.

    a What should I bring? _____

    b At what time? _____

    c Can you write down the address? _____

    d I can show it to you on the map. _____

5 This conversation uses a new verb form you can use to talk about potential plans – what you 'would' or 'could' do. Look at the table, and use the phrase list to complete the right and left columns. Notice which German verb form corresponds to the English translation and fill it in.

Verb	Example	Meaning
möchtest (would you like / want)	Möchtest du mitkommen?	Would you like to come?
(it would be)	Ein Dessert wäre perfekt.	
(I would)	Ich würde schon gerne. Ich würde kommen. Ich würde sagen, ...	
(you could)	Vielleicht könntest du den mitbringen? Könntest du ... aufschreiben?	

GRAMMAR EXPLANATION: forming the conditional with *würde* (would)

Talking about a possible future (what you would do) is done very similarly in German and English! You simply use *würde* (would) + the dictionary form of whatever verb you want to use. You can create the 'would' (conditional) form with almost any verb, and the endings for this form are almost the same as for the present tense.

ich würde, du würdest, er würde, wir würden, ihr würdet, sie würden.

The only exception is that the er/sie-forms end in -e rather than -t.

Examples: *Ich würde heute Abend ausgehen, aber ich bin zu müde.*
(**I would** go out tonight, but I'm too tired.)
Würdest du mitkommen? (**Would you** come with me?)

Though you use *würde* with most verbs in German, a few use an alternative (as in past tense forms you've seen). The three most important are: *hätte* (would have), *wäre* (would be), *könnte* (could / would be able to).

Conditional forms

haben (to have)	hätte (would have)	Ich hätte morgen Zeit.	I'd have time tomorrow.
sein (to be)	wäre (would be)	Das wäre toll!	That would be great!
können (to be able / can)	könnte (could)	Könntest du mir helfen?	Could you help me?

Try it! Fill in the gaps with the conditional ('would' forms).

a Ich _____ gern in Deutschland _____. (**I'd love to live** in Germany.)

b Ich _____ ein großes Haus in Berlin. (**I'd have** a big house in Berlin.)

c Leider _____ es zu weit weg von meinen Eltern. (Unfortunately it **would be** far from my parents.)

d Ich _____ sie nicht oft besuchen. (I **wouldn't be able to** visit them often.)

PRACTICE

1 Use different phrases for making plans in German.

   a What should I wear? (to wear = *anziehen*) _____

   b What time does it end? (to end = *aufhören*) _____

   c When should I arrive? _____

2 Practise using different phrases for inviting someone to do something. Select from the English suggestions to complete the original sentence in German in two different ways.

Example: *Essen wir* _____···_____ *im chinesischen Restaurant?*
(this afternoon) (Monday) (soon) (at 7 p.m.) (next week)

···▸ *Essen wir* **heute / Montag Nachmittag** *im chinesischen Restaurant?*

   a *Was machst du* _____···_____ (after this) (later) (at 5 p.m.) (tonight) (tomorrow)

     _____ _____

   b *Ich möchte* _____···_____ *Freizeit Sport machen. Kommst du mit?*
     (after this) (later) (at 5 p.m.) (tonight) (tomorrow)

     _____ _____

   c _____···_____ *du mitkommen?* (would like) (going) (can)

     _____ _____

   d _____···_____ *dir helfen?* (could) (will) (tomorrow morning)

     _____ _____

3 Mix and match phrases for accepting or turning down an invitation. Complete the original sentence in German in two different ways.

   a *Das wäre* _____···_____. (cool) (perfect) (amazing) (fun) (impossible) (too late)

     _____ _____

   b *Ich würde sehr gern, aber* _____···_____. (unfortunately …) (I already have plans) (I'm busy)

     _____ _____

4 Practise recognizing the meaning of conditional verbs by writing the English of these phrases.

   a *Du würdest vorbereiten* … _____   c *Ich würde … reisen.* _____

   b *Das wäre* … _____   d *Du könntest* … _____

5 Say in German:

   a Would you like to learn German with me? _____

   b Could you ask me next time? _____

   c I'd go out, but it's too late. ____ _____

#LANGUAGEHACK: the rephrasing technique for talking your way through complicated sentences

When you speak in your native language, you're used to expressing yourself with a lot of complexity and nuance. So how do you convey your more complex thoughts and feelings when you are still only working with the very basics of the language?

Expressing yourself with even limited language skills is largely a matter of skilful rephrasing. You'll need to simplify your sentences to use words and phrases you are more comfortable with. Here's how to break it down.

Figure out the core idea

⋯⋗ First, recognize that the rules of expressing yourself as an eloquent native do not (usually) apply to you as a beginner German learner. The nuanced language you search for in your head and the desire to know how to say what you want and how to convey the right tone and courtesy ... Sometimes, you have to just let that go.
  'I'm sorry ... I just overheard you speaking German ... do you mind if I practise a few phrases with you? ... I hope I'm not bothering you ...'

⋯⋗ Next, figure out the one core idea you're most trying to express then simplify it dramatically. So the initial idea may become:
  'You speak German? Me too! Let's talk.'

⋯⋗ Finally, translate this simpler concept or 'piggy-back' your idea off another expression that works just as well: *Sprichst du Deutsch? Ich auch! Sprechen wir!*

Divide and conquer

Sometimes you'll find that one way to express yourself involves a long sentence with many commas, verb forms and other issues to solve. When this happens, you can take a 'divide and conquer' approach to split the sentence up.

Example: *Er wohnt jetzt in Berlin, also in der Stadt, wo er seine Frau, die Anna heißt, getroffen hat.* (Now he lives in Berlin, the city where he met his wife, whose name is Anna.)

→ *Er wohnt jetzt in Berlin. Dort* (there) *hat er Anna getroffen. Sie ist seine Frau.*
  (He lives in Berlin now. He met Anna there. She's his wife.)

Use booster verbs to simplify a sentence

Let's consider another tricky sentence structure: *Es macht Spaß, Filme auf Deutsch anzusehen!*

When you come across complicated sentences using separable verbs or *zu*, you can use booster verbs to change the sentence into a simpler form. For instance: *Ich sollte Filme auf Deutsch ansehen. Das macht Spaß!*

> The easiest way to split up a long train of thought is to use reference words to break an idea into small sentences, but to make it clear that they expand on the same idea. You can also present them as a sequence of events. The easiest reference words to use are **dort**, **hier** and **dann** ('there', 'here' and 'then'), or **er**, **sie**, **es** and **sie** ('he', 'she', 'it' and 'them'). Don't be afraid to repeat keywords (like Anna) if you can't find an easier reference!

YOUR TURN: use the hack

Remember, this is a skill, which means that practice is the key to getting better.

1 Rephrase each of the lines given, with a shorter translation in German that conveys a similar meaning, but avoids complicated grammar.

Example: I'm probably not going to be up for a night out with you.

   → <u>Ich kann nicht mit dir ausgehen.</u> (I can't go out with you.)

   a I'm so happy that we were able to come to the restaurant together.

   _____

   b I would really love it if you would be willing to dance with me.

   _____

   c I'd rather we took that afternoon trip to the supermarket later.

   _____

2 In each of these sentences, the original English uses forms you haven't learned yet in German. A simpler German version has been started for you – fill in the blanks to complete the simpler phrases.

   a Because he speaks German very well, he got a new job in Germany that's very interesting.
   Er spricht _____. *Deshalb hat er jetzt* _____. _____
   sehr interessant.

   b After completing his studies he travelled to Valencia, where he began to learn Spanish.
   Zuerst hat er sein Studium abgeschlossen. Dann ist er _____.
   _____ *hat er angefangen* _____.

3 Use booster verbs to change each of the sentences into simpler forms.

   a *Es ist wichtig, sie morgen anzurufen (to phone). Du* _____ *sie anrufen. Das ist wichtig.*
   b *Es ist gesund, spät aufzustehen (to get up). Man* _____ *spät aufstehen. Das ist gesund!*
   c *Es ist unmöglich (impossible), neu anzufangen. Wir* _____ *nicht neu anfangen.*

PUT IT TOGETHER

1 A German friend has come to visit you in your home town. Give your local know-how for what your friend should do to get the best out of the visit. Describe:

···→ the first thing that he / she could or would do (*Zuerst könntest du ...*)

···→ the places you would visit and why (*Ich würde ... besuchen*)

···→ the activities you would do together (*Wir könnten ein Taxi nehmen, um ... zu ...*)

···→ other insider tips (*Ich glaube, das beste Museum wäre ...*).

2 Now imagine that someone has invited you to go on an exotic adventure – think kayaking down the Amazon River or climbing Mount Everest. You'd have a lot of questions! Create a script that uses phrases and questions to discuss an invitation like this in German. Use your dictionary as often as you need.

···→ Say when you'd have free time and when you could go. (*Ich konnte ... fahren ...*)

···→ Ask for details of trip – where it is, when it starts, when it ends. (*Wann beginnt die Reise?*)

···→ Ask about things you should bring. (*Sollte ich ... mitbringen?*)

···→ Talk about how you think it would be. (*Ich glaube, das wäre ...*)

COMPLETING UNIT 8

Check your understanding

1 🔊 08.07 Listen to the audio rehearsal, in which a German speaker, Carolina, describes her routine as well as things she wishes she could do. Feel free to take notes or listen to it again.

2 🔊 08.08 Now listen to questions about what you've just heard and answer them out loud in German.

_____

_____

_____

_____

Show what you know ...

Here's what you've just learned. Write or say an example for each item in the list. Then tick off the ones you know.

☐ Write a short phrase that describes one of your hobbies.
☐ Give three different details about your hobby.
☐ Use *machen* to talk about two different activities.
☐ Recognize the meaning of prepositions such as *auf*, *zu* and *aus*.
☐ Use separable verbs in the present and past tense (e.g. *anfangen / angefangen*)
☐ Give three phrases that describe your normal routine using:
    ☐ 'often' and 'usually'
    ☐ 'sometimes' and 'now and then'
    ☐ 'always' and 'never'.
☐ Say 'I would' and 'I could' in German.

COMPLETE YOUR MISSION

It's time to complete your mission: give your best productivity advice to be published on your friend's blog. To do this, think about the things you do regularly. You could even read some German blogs about productivity and mindfulness to help you.

Try searching online for *produktiver sein* or *effektiver arbeiten*.

STEP 1: build your script

Keep building your script by using the phrases you've learned in this unit combined with 'me-specific' vocabulary to answer common questions about yourself. Be sure to:

···⟩ talk about different parts of your life and weekly routine
···⟩ describe where you go, how you get there and what you do
···⟩ include details of how often, when, where, why or how
···⟩ describe something else you would love to do but haven't done yet
···⟩ describe what you like about your routines and what could be better.

To complete this mission, go online to the #LanguageHacking community for help!

STEP 2: learn from your mistakes, and others'... *online*

The key is that if you're making mistakes, you're learning. And if you speak, you can even notice them better and fix them yourself. Added bonus: you can learn from the mistakes of other language hackers too. So look at the corrections and comments people leave – you'll find that your common mistakes are most likely shared.

It's time to complete your mission. Share your productivity advice with the rest of the community! And in return, enjoy some free advice about how you can be more effective in your life. Go online to find your mission for Unit 8.

When learning a new language, mistakes are inevitable. Part of the charm of speaking a second language is realizing that people are much less critical than you imagine!

Use the community space to find out perhaps how you can make learning German part of your daily routine.

STEP 3: learn from other learners

What productivity tips can you gain from other language hackers? After you've uploaded your own clip, check out what the other people in the community have to say about their routines. **Your task is to tell at least three different people what was most useful about their routine**.

This time, incorporate conversation starters, leads or extensions to help get the conversation flowing, e.g. *Ich sehe, dass du …* (I see that you …).

STEP 4: reflect on what you've learned

_____

_____

_____

_____

HEY, LANGUAGE HACKER, YOU'RE ALMOST THERE!

In this unit we talked a lot about the strategy behind preparing for the kinds of conversations you are likely to have. All the scripts you've been building are preparing you for this ultimate goal.

With the strategies you'll learn next in Missions 9 and 10, you will be amazed at how well your first conversation goes …

Nur Mut!

9 DESCRIBE IT!

Your mission

Imagine this – you're applying to be a tour guide in a German-speaking city. You have to prove your ability to describe a place in detail and give recommendations for where to hang out and what to do.

Your mission is to pass for a local by describing a city you know well (or want to know well!). Be prepared to do your research and give a short description of the highlights of what to do and see. But here's the twist – don't say the name of the city. See if others can *guess*! **Describe the best places, explain their characteristics**, and say how it might suit **different personalities**.

This mission will enable you to communicate more creatively by explaining the characteristics of people, places and things in the world around you in more detail.

Mission prep

···⟩ Describe places, landscapes, and where you live: *Ich wohne auf dem Land.*
···⟩ Say what you miss using the verb *vermissen*.
···⟩ Describe the weather and environment: *es ist warm*.
···⟩ Describe people and their personalities: *abenteuerlustig, traditonell*.
···⟩ Learn phrases for shopping: *billiger, im Angebot, bar bezahlen*.

BUILDING LANGUAGE FOR DESCRIBING THE WORLD AROUND YOU!

You're getting closer to your first conversation with a native in German! You know how to say who the important people are in your life and what they do, but now you'll describe their personalities and characteristics as well. With this new vocab, you can express your thoughts more creatively in German – when you can't think of a word you need, just *describe* it instead!

 #LANGUAGEHACK
use your hidden moments to get German immersion for the long-term

CONVERSATION 1

Describing the city

CULTURE TIP: *the Spree*
A great way to see Berlin is on a cruise through the *Spree* river that runs through the city.

VOCAB: *an as 'at' or 'about'*

An (at) as in *an der Tür* (at the door) is also used for places your mind goes to, in phrases involving 'thinking' or 'remembering'. In this conversation *an* is used with *denken*, meaning to 'think about'.

CONVERSATION STRATEGY: *word order for emphasis*
German word order allows you to emphasize different words depending on how you arrange them in a sentence. For instance, the simple statement *Es gibt Kaufhäuser in jeder Stadt* (There are department stores in every city) is written here as *Kaufhäuser gibt es in jeder Stadt*, which emphasizes the ubiquitous nature of department stores: 'Department stores – they're everywhere' (they're nothing special). But if you said *In jeder Stadt gibt es Kaufhäuser*, it would imply 'Every city has department stores!' (it doesn't matter if you go in this city or another).

When you start talking to people from other countries, they are going to show interest in where you're from and how it's different from where they're from. Let's prepare you for these conversation topics now by building your script to describe different places.

🔊 09.01 Ellen is getting ready to fly back to England, and she's thinking about what she misses about home. She describes her home town to her friend Jakob as they hang out by the *Spree* on a sunny day. What word does Ellen use to say she's flying 'back' soon to the UK?

> **Ellen:** Ich fliege bald nach England zurück. Das ist meine letzte Woche in Berlin!
>
> **Jakob:** Wie schade! Hast du Heimweh?
>
> **Ellen:** Ich liebe Berlin, aber weißt du, dass ich eigentlich auf dem Land wohne? Ich vermisse das Meer und auch den Strand und die Wälder bei mir. Aber ich werde oft an Berlin und an die freundlichen Leute hier denken.
>
> **Jakob:** Ich weiß. Ich werde dich auch vermissen! Hmm, ich habe eine Idee … warum kaufst du nicht ein paar Geschenke für deine Familie, bevor du fliegst? Die werden dich auch an deine Zeit in Berlin erinnern.
>
> **Ellen:** Das ist eine sehr gute Idee! Ich liebe Shopping! Wo sollte ich die Geschenke kaufen?
>
> **Jakob:** Hmm … das kommt darauf an. Warst du schon im KaDeWe? Das ist ein riesiges historisches Kaufhaus. Es ist viel schöner als ein Einkaufszentrum.
>
> **Ellen:** Ich weiß nicht … Kaufhäuser gibt es in jeder Stadt. Heute scheint die Sonne und es ist warm, also möchte ich den Tag lieber draußen verbringen.
>
> **Jakob:** Aber das KaDeWe ist ein absolutes Highlight! Das gibt es nur in Berlin! Lass uns doch jetzt für eine Stunde ins KaDeWe gehen und danach können wir auf dem Ku'damm spazieren gehen.
>
> **Ellen:** … und wenn wir müde sind, setzen wir uns in ein nettes Café und essen ein Eis.
>
> **Jakob:** Perfekt! Los geht's!

FIGURE IT OUT

By now you have a great base of German vocabulary, so now it's even more important for you to actively fill in your gaps. It's a good idea to **highlight** any **new words you come across**, and make a note to add them to your script or study materials.

1 The following sentences are *falsch*. Highlight the word(s) that make them incorrect, and write the German words that are *richtig*.

   a It's Ellen's last day in Berlin.   _____

   b Ellen and Jakob are planning to go dancing.   _____

   c Ellen will often travel to Berlin.   _____

   d They're planning to take a walk on the Ku'damm
      before they go to KaDeWe.   _____

2 Use your understanding of the conversation to figure out the meaning of the phrases.

   a *Wie Schade!* _____

   b *Ich fliege bald nach England zurück.* _____

   c *Heute scheint die Sonne und es ist warm ...* _____

   d *... also möchte ich den Tag lieber draußen verbringen.*

   _____

3 Answer the questions in German.

   a *Wann fliegt Ellen nach England zurück?* _____

   b *Was vermisst Ellen?* _____

   c *Wie findet Ellen Jakobs Idee?* _____

   d *Was kauft Ellen für ihre Familie?* _____

   e *Möchte Ellen unbedingt ins Kaufhaus gehen? Warum / Warum nicht?*

   _____

   f *Was machen Ellen und Jakob, wenn sie müde sind?* _____

4 Using context along with words you already know, find the German phrases in the conversation and write them out.

   a in the countryside _____   d historic department store _____

   b outside _____   e the sea _____

   c the beach and the forests _____

NOTICE

🔊 09.02 Listen to the audio and study the table. Repeat out loud, trying to mimic the speakers.

You've seen cases where German uses haben (to have) when we would say 'to be' in English, like *ich habe Hunger* (I'm hungry) and *du hast recht* (you're right). Here, Jakob asks Ellen if she's homesick by asking, **Hast du Heimweh?** (literally: 'Have you homesickness?')

Word for word, this phrase is a little tricky, but best learn it as a chunk for the German way of saying 'it depends'.

Essential phrases for Conversation 1

German	Meaning
Ich fliege bald nach England zurück.	I am flying back to England soon.
Wie schade!	What a pity!
Hast du Heimweh?	Are you homesick?
auf dem Land	in the countryside
Ich vermisse das Meer	I miss the sea
und auch den Strand	as well as the beach
und die Wälder bei mir	and the forests close to my home
Aber ich werde oft an Berlin und an die freundlichen Leute hier denken.	But I'll often think about Berlin and the friendly people here!
Warum kaufst du nicht ein paar Geschenke für deine Familie, bevor du fliegst?	Why don't you buy a few gifts for your family before you fly?
Die werden dich auch an deine Zeit in Berlin erinnern!	Those will also remind you of your time in Berlin!
Wo soll ich die Geschenke kaufen?	Where should I buy the gifts?
das kommt darauf an	it depends
Es ist viel schöner als ...	It's much prettier than ...
Heute scheint die Sonne und es ist warm.	Today the sun is shining and it's warm.
also möchte ich den Tag lieber draußen verbringen	so I prefer to spend the day outside
Lass uns doch ... gehen	Let's go ...
und wenn wir müde sind, setzen wir uns in ein nettes Café	and when we're tired we'll sit down in a nice café
Los geht's!	Off we go!

1 For each item below, find the first phrase in the phrase list, then write it out in German. Next, use this to translate the second corresponding phrase.

a I miss _____

  I'll miss this city. _____

b I'm flying back _____

  Before I fly back home _____

c I'll think about _____

  When I think about my time here _____

d I'll remind you _____

  It reminds me of the beach. _____

e When we're tired, we can sit down. _____

  If you're tired, why don't you go sleep? _____

VOCAB: (sich) erinnern – 'to remember' / 'to remind'
In German, *erinnern* means 'to remind', but *sich erinnern* 'to remind oneself' is also a common way of saying 'to remember'! For example,
⋯⊱ *Ich erinnere mich nicht, was ihre Name ist* (I don't remember what her name is),
⋯⊱ *Kannst du mich an deine Adresse erinnern?* (Could you remind me what your address is?)

2 Refer back to the conversation and the phrase list. In the following phrases, what do the words in bold refer to?

Example: **Die** *werden dich auch an deine Zeit in Berlin erinnern....*
⋯⊱ Die Geschenke

a **Das** *ist eine sehr gute Idee!*

  _____

b **Es** *ist viel schöner als ein Einkaufszentrum.*

  _____

c **Das** *gibt es nur in Berlin!*

  _____

3 Match the German phrases with their correct English translations.

a *Lass uns doch*   1 It depends
b *Los geht's!*   2 Let's ...
c *Wie Schade!*   3 What a shame!
d *Das kommt darauf an*   4 Off we go!

4 A good memory technique is to learn vocab in 'clusters' – learning words of a similar theme together. Use your dictionary to fill in the numbered blanks in the vocab tables.

Landscape and nature vocab

German	Meaning	German	Meaning
1.	the country(side)	der Wald	the forest
die Berge	2.	die Bäume	4 .
der See	the lake	3.	the sun
die Stadt	the city		

City vocab

German	Meaning	German	Meaning
5.	the bank	6.	the police station
das Geschäft	the shop	7.	the church
das Einkaufszentrum	the shopping centre	das Rathaus	8.
die Apotheke	9.	10.	the stadium
die Bäckerei	the bakery	das Kaufhaus	the department store
die Straße	11.	der Park	the park
das Museum	the museum	12.	the library

PRACTICE

1 Look up new words you'd need to describe where you live and the landscape in your area. Do you live near the ocean? In the suburbs? In a third story walk-up? Add your 'me-specific' vocab to the Landscape and nature vocab list.

2 Use the vocab you've just looked up to practise describing where you live.

Example: I live in ...   Around the corner, there is / there are ...

_____

_____

3 Now do the same about a family member or friend.

Example: He / she lives near ...   On his / her street, there is / there are ...

_____

_____

VOCAB EXPLANATION: talking about the weather

Wie ist das Wetter? - What's the weather like? (lit. 'How is the weather?')
When you want to describe the weather, you'll use the expression _es ist_.
Most of the time, you'll simply need to say _Es ist_ + description.

Es ist ... schön (nice) / _schlecht_ (bad) / _heiß_ (hot) / _kalt_ (cold) / _kühl_ (cool) /
        warm (warm) / _wolkig_ (cloudy) / _sonnig_ (sunny) / _windig_ (windy)

Two important exceptions are:

    Es regnet (it's raining) and _Es schneit_ (it's snowing).

1 Practise creating new sentences in German to describe the weather.

  a It's nice out. _____

  b The weather is bad. What a pity! _____

2 Use _Es ist_ to give two sentences describing the weather where you are
   right now. _____ _____

PUT IT TOGETHER

Create a script in which you describe where you live, or a place that you
love to visit, in as much detail as possible. Be sure to include descriptive
words (adjectives and pronouns) and answer the questions:

···⟩ What is the landscape like?

···⟩ What is the weather usually like? Sometimes like?

···⟩ What would you miss most about it?

> You now have a greater ability to talk about your environment, so let's put that into action!

   Ich wohne ...

_____

_____

_____

CONVERSATION 2

Describing personalities

Now let's focus on a whole new set of descriptive words you can use to talk about people and their personalities.

🔊 09.03 Ellen and Jakob are now shopping, and discuss what gifts Ellen should get for her family, based on their personalities. What words does Ellen use to describe her sister, brother, and parents?

CULTURE TIP:
einkaufen (**shopping**)
While the *Ku'damm* or the *Friedrichstraße* are nice to visit, my favourite spots for shopping are actually the *Flohmärkte* (flea markets) at *Mauerpark* and at *Boxhagener Platz*, which take place every Sunday. I love to *feilschen* (haggle) to get a good deal. It's more fun than when you know the price is fixed, and excellent for practising your German numbers!

Ellen: Dieses Kaufhaus ist wirklich beeindruckend! Es gibt so viele Geschäfte!

Jakob: Weißt du schon, was du kaufen möchtest?

Ellen: Ich möchte für mich viele Sachen kaufen, aber ich weiß nicht, was ich für meine Familie kaufen soll!

Jakob: Na, kannst du sie beschreiben?

Ellen: Das ist schwierig – meine Schwester zum Beispiel ist abenteuerlustig und sie möchte wirklich eines Tages nach Deutschland kommen. Soll ich ihr ein typisches Souvenir von Berlin kaufen?

Jakob: Du könntest ihr einen bunten Buddy-Bären und Schokolade kaufen, oder? Und für uns auch eine Tafel Schokolade!

Ellen: Klar! Dann zu meinem Bruder. Ähm … er ist jung, deshalb glaube ich, dass ein Souvenir superlangweilig für ihn wäre. Was soll ich jemandem kaufen, der nur Videospiele toll findet?

Jakob: Du kannst ein Zubehör für seine Spiele finden! Elektronische Geräte sind oft billiger hier, weißt du?

Ellen: Ah ja, das erinnert mich daran – sein Kopfhörer ist alt … Er braucht einen neuen. Und zum Schluss, meine Eltern sind eher traditionell und sie haben mir schon gesagt, ich soll ihnen eine Tasche aus Berlin mitbringen.

Jakob: Das war klug von Ihnen! Vielleicht sollten wir ihnen zwei Taschen kaufen, in blau und schwarz!

FIGURE IT OUT

1 *Richtig oder falsch?* Select the correct answer.

    a   Ellen is shopping for her friends.   *richtig / falsch*

    b Jakob helps Ellen with ideas for presents.   *richtig / falsch*

    c Ellen knows exactly what to buy.   *richtig / falsch*

2 Answer these questions about the conversation.

    a *Was wird Ellen ihrer Schwester kaufen?*
       einen _____ *und* _____ .

    b *Warum? Was sagt Ellen über sie? Sie ist* _____ .

    c *Was würde Ellens Bruder über ein typisches Souvenir denken?*
       Dass ein Souvenir _____ .

    d *Was sagen Ellen und Jakob über Ellens Eltern?*
       Sie sind _____ , *und sie sind*
       _____ .

    e *Was sagt Jakob über elektronische Geräte in Deutschland?*
       Sie _____ .

3 Find the following phrases in the conversation and highlight them.
Then write out the word in bold in German.

    a that **reminds** me _____

    b she **really** wants _____

    c a souvenir **would be** _____

    d and **finally** _____

    e my parents are **rather** traditional _____

    f really **boring** _____

NOTICE

◄)) 09.04 Listen to the audio and study the table.

Essential phrases for Conversation 2

German	Meaning
Dieses Kaufhaus ist wirklich beeindruckend!	This department store is really impressive!
Es gibt so viele Geschäfte!	There are so many shops!
Kannst du sie beschreiben?	Can you describe them?
Das ist schwierig.	That's hard.
meine Schwester ist abenteuerlustig	my sister is adventurous
ein typisches Souvenir	a typical souvenir
einen bunten Buddy-Bären kaufen	to buy a coloured Buddy-Bear
eine Tafel Schokolade	a bar of chocolate
er ist jung	he is young
superlangweilig	really boring
Was soll ich jemandem kaufen, ...?	What should I buy someone ...?
sein Kopfhörer ist alt	his headphones are old
Elektronische Geräte sind oft billiger hier	electronic devices are often cheaper here
das erinnert mich daran	that reminds me
er braucht einen neuen	he needs a new one
und zum Schluss	and finally
meine Eltern sind eher traditionell	my parents are rather traditional
zwei Taschen, in blau und schwarz	two bags, in blue and black

1 Find the adjectives in the conversation and write them here.

a impressive _____
b adventurous_____
c typical _____
d coloured _____
e young _____
f boring _____
g old _____

h new _____
i traditional _____
j black _____
k wise _____
l hard _____
m blue _____
n cheap _____

2 Another effective memory technique is to learn new words in pairs with their opposites. Use the adjectives from the phrase list and a dictionary to complete the sentences.

a *Das ist nicht* _____, *das ist* _____.   (It's not **easy**, it's **hard**.)
b *Das ist nicht* _____, *das ist* _____.   (It's not **unique**, it's **typical**.)
c *Sie sind nicht* _____, *sie sind* _____.   (They aren't **stupid**, they are **intelligent** (wise).)
d *Sie sind nicht* _____, *sie sind* _____.   (They aren't **modern**, they are **traditional**.)
e *Sie ist nicht* _____, *sie ist* _____.   (She's not **adventurous**, she's **shy**.)
f *Er ist nicht* _____, *er ist* _____.   (He's not **old**, he's **young**.)

CONVERSATION STRATEGY: shortcut to using adjectives before nouns easily

Adjective endings tend to change depending on the noun that follows. Learning these rules can be very intimidating at first and won't enrich your conversation abilities much. Luckily, there are two handy tips to bear in mind!

Guess -e or -en: It turns out that *-e* and *-en* are the most frequent adjective endings, so if you're unsure, just pick one, and you will not only be fully understood, but will have pretty good odds at guessing right!

Reword your sentence: However, remember that if you change your sentence to make sure no noun follows the adjective, you don't have to apply any ending to it!

For example, instead of *Ich habe die* **neuen** *Bücher gekauft.* (I bought the new books.), you could say:

⋯▸ *Ich habe die Bücher gekauft, die* **neu** *sind.* (I bought the books that are new.), or
⋯▸ *Ich habe Bücher gekauft, und sie sind* **neu**. (I bought books, and they are new.)

Much easier!

1 How could you avoid using adjective endings in these German sentences?

Example: *Das ist ein gutes Buch.* → Ich finde, das Buch ist gut. (I find the book good!)

a *Hier gibt es keine schönen Gebäude.* →
(The buildings here are not beautiful.) _____

b *Der riesige Bahnhof ist neu.* → (The train station is huge and new.)

_____

c *Du hast eine nette Freundin.* → (Your friend is nice.) _____

d *Ich möchte die bunten Buddy-Bären kaufen.* →
(I want to buy the buddy-bears, which are colourful.) _____

PRACTICE

1 Complete the table with the the missing adjectives (in their base forms), based off the corresponding translation. Use your dictionary to look them up if you need to.

Describing people

German	Meaning	German	Meaning
1.	shy/timid	abenteuerlustig	2.
3.	ugly	4.	beautiful/pretty
alt	5.	6.	young
komisch	7.	8.	typical
9.	unpleasant	sympathisch	nice
pessimistisch	10.	11.	optimistic
12.	proud	bescheiden	13.
14.	funny	ernst	15.
dumm	16.	intelligent	17.
arrogant	18.	19.	wise/smart
normal	20.	21.	friendly

2 Create new sentences with adjectives that describe things in your life. Be sure to look up words in your dictionary if you need to!

a *Ich bin* _____

Meine Arbeit ist _____ _____

b *Mein Vater / Freund / Bruder ist* _____

Sein Haus ist _____

c *Meine Mutter / Schwester / Freundin ist* _____

PUT IT TOGETHER

Prepare for these questions now by creating a script in which you explain the personalities of at least two important people in your life. Make your script as 'me-specific' as possible by looking up any new descriptive words you'll need now, so you'll have them ready during your conversations.

···⟩ Describe two different people in your life.
···⟩ Use adjectives to describe their personalities.
···⟩ Include sentences that use different word orders.
···⟩ Use the conversation strategy to avoid adjectives when possible (but don't worry about adjective endings when you can't avoid them).

Example: <u>Meine Schwester ist komisch/meine komische Schwester.</u>

CONVERSATION 3

It looks like ...

You've learned to describe people and places – now let's build new vocab you can use to describe things.

🔊 **09.05** Ellen is looking for those headphones for her brother and asks Jakob for advice on which ones are best. How does Ellen ask, 'Is this one OK?'

Ellen: Dieses Geschäft verkauft anscheinend Kopfhörer.

Jakob: Für welche Art von Videospielen braucht dein Bruder Kopfhörer?

Ellen: Für Online-Games ... passt der hier?

Jakob: Nein – der rote ist zum Joggen. Mir scheint, der grüne wäre für deinen Bruder am besten. Der hat auch die beste Qualität.

Ellen: Woher weißt du das denn?

Jakob: Ich kenne die Marke – er sieht hochwertig aus. Dein Bruder wird ihn sicher toll finden. Normalerweise ist er teuer, aber heute ist er im Angebot und kostet er nur die Hälfte! Dein Bruder wird ihn sicher toll finden!

Ellen: Diesen Preis kann ich nicht bar zahlen – ich muss mit meiner Kreditkarte zahlen.

Jakob: Das ist kein Problem, sie akzeptieren Kreditkarten. Gehen wir zur Kasse? Dein Bruder wird sicher denken, du bist die coolste Schwester der Welt!

FIGURE IT OUT

1 The following statements about the conversation are *falsch*. Highlight
   the words that make each one incorrect, and write the correct phrase
   in German.

   a Ellen's brother needs new headphones for jogging.

   _____

   b The headphones are not expensive.

   _____

   c Ellen is going to pay in cash.

   _____

2 What are the two possible ways of paying mentioned in the conversation?

   _____

3 Use your understanding of the conversation to answer the questions.
   a Which headphones are better for jogging?   *der* _____
   b Which headphones are better for Ellen's brother?   *der* _____

4 Based on your understanding of context in the conversation, how do
   you think you'd say 'half' and 'on sale' in German?

   _____

NOTICE

◀)) 09.06 Listen to the audio and study the table.

Essential phrases for Conversation 3

German	Meaning
Dieses Geschäft verkauft anscheinend Kopfhörer.	This shop appears to sell headphones. (This shop sells apparently headphones.)
Für welche Art von Videospielen braucht dein Bruder Kopfhörer?	What kind of games does your brother need headphones for?
für Online-Games	for online games
Passt der hier?	Is this one OK? (Pass the (one) here?)
der rote ist zum Joggen	the red one is for jogging
Mir scheint, der grüne wäre für deinen Bruder am besten.	It seems to me, the best one for your brother would be the green one.
Der hat auch die beste Qualität.	It's the best quality. (It has also the best quality.)
Woher weißt du denn das?	How do you know? (From-where know you then that?)
Ich kenne die Marke.	I recognize the brand.
er sieht hochwertig aus	it looks like good quality
Normalerweise ist er teuer	Normally it's expensive
heute ist er im Angebot	today it's on sale
heute kostet er nur die Hälfte	today it's half price
Ich kann nicht bar bezahlen.	I can't pay in cash.
Ich muss mit meiner Kreditkarte zahlen.	I have to pay with credit card.
Sie akzeptieren Kreditkarten.	They accept credit cards.
Gehen wir zur Kasse?	Shall we go to the till?
Du bist die coolste Schwester der Welt!	You are the coolest sister in the world!

Whenever you want to say things like 'the big one', 'the blue one' or 'the small ones' in German, you don't need to translate 'one'. Simply use der/die/das, etc. before the adjective: *der rote* (the red one), or here *der grüne* for 'the green one'.

1 What words/phrases could you use to ...

⋯▷ ask or say what something looks like?

   a *Dein Bruder _____ wie ein Gamer _____!* (Your brother looks like a gamer!)

⋯▷ ask 'from where' (or 'how come')?

   b _____ *kennst du sie?*

     (Where do you know her from?)

⋯▷ say 'what kind'

   c _____ _____ *von Geschenk brauchst du?*

     (What kind of gift do you need?)

⋯▷ say what you need something for

   d *Ich brauche es _____ meine Schwester.*

     (I need it for my sister.)

2 If you needed to describe an item you wanted to a shopkeeper, you could use the following phrases from this conversation. Write them out in German.

a this one   _____

b the red one   _____

c the green one   _____

d the best one   _____

3 If you don't know the word for the item, you could also just say the name of *die Marke* (the brand). Which international brands could you use to ask these questions?

a *Verkaufen/Haben Sie* _____?   (shoe brand)

b *Ich möchte ein* _____.   (tissue brand)

c *Ich nehme eine* _____.   (cola brand)

d *Ich möchte einen* _____ kaufen.   (computer brand)

e *Kann ich mit deinem* _____ *zur Arbeit fahren?* (car brand)

You'll recognize a lot of familiar brands in Germany, and you can use this to your advantage when you're trying to describe what you want.

4 How would you say in German:

a a little expensive   _____

b pay in cash   _____

c pay with my credit card   _____

d the checkout   _____

PRACTICE

1 Practise creating new questions in German you could use to ask about things when shopping.

a How much does the black one (f) cost?   _____

b What is the quality like? (How is the quality?)   _____

c Can I take this now?   _____

d Do you accept credit cards?   _____

e I can only pay in cash.   _____

f What kind of cable do you have? (*Kabel*)   _____

g Is this on sale?   _____

h Where is the till?   _____

2 Fill in the blanks with the missing words in German.

a *Kann ich die* _____ *ansehen?* (Can I have a look at the **red one**?)

b *Ich kenne die* _____ *nicht.* (I don't know that **brand**.)

c *Ich werde an der* _____ *bezahlen.* (I'll pay at the **till**.)

d *Ich möchte die* _____ *links.* (I'd like the **big one** on the left.)

3 Fill in the missing translations in the table.

Describing things

Adjective	Meaning	Colour	Meaning
lang(e)	1.	gelb(e)	yellow
kurz(e)	short	rot(e)	red
breit(e)	wide	blau(e)	blue
leichte(e)	2.	weiß(e)	white
schwer(e)	3.	grün(e)	green
dick(e)	thick	schwarz(e)	black
dünn(e)	thin / slim	grau(e)	grey
		braun(e)	brown

CONVERSATION STRATEGY: 'the ... one!'

This is a set phrase you can adapt in countless ways to communicate what you're describing, without saying its name! Let's build on your ability to use this construction.

Fill in the gaps with the missing word to describe an object or objects you may be talking about.

'The ... one(s)!'

German	Meaning	German	Meaning
der hier	this one	der da	that one
der / die / das Schwarze hier	the black one	1. die	the white one
der / die / das Kleine hier	the small one	2. das	the big one
der / die / das Neue hier	the new one	3. die	the old one
der / die / das Billigere hier	the less expensive one	4. die	the more expensive one
der / die / das Linke hier	the left one	5. die	the right one
der / die / das Andere hier	the other one	6. der	the nice one

PUT IT TOGETHER

Was suchst du? (What are you looking for?)

Now it's time to build sentences you could use to describe something you are looking for, want to buy, or have lost. Think of one or two items to describe, and then be as creative as you can to describe the item without using the word for the item itself. You might include:

⋯⋗ what it looks like, what you need it for, or what type of person you're getting it for
⋯⋗ what brand it is or what colour it is
⋯⋗ a description using 'this' or 'that one' or 'the ... one'
⋯⋗ any other descriptive adjectives that you know!

Ich suche ...

_____

_____

_____

_____

#LANGUAGEHACK: use your hidden moments to get German immersion for the long-term

Don't overlook the value of these short periods of time. They really add up, and more importantly, they're a great way to consistently keep up momentum in your learning.

Rather than thinking about how many months or years it may take to learn German, an incredibly effective learning strategy is to focus instead on the *minutes* it takes.

The minutes you put into your language every day is what truly counts. Not everyone has a few hours every day to devote to German – but everyone has a few minutes. Even if you live a busy lifestyle, you can still find 'hidden moments' throughout your day for German practice.

Standing in the queue at the supermarket, waiting for the lift, sitting on a bus, train or taxi, waiting for a tardy friend ... all of these are wasted moments in our days. These moments are perfect for squeezing German practice into your daily life.

Instead of making a distinction between 'study blocks' of German, why not blend it into your life to make language learning a habit?

German immersion – from anywhere

As you've followed Ellen's story, perhaps you've thought how lucky she is to go to Germany to improve her German through immersion! But in fact, thanks to technology, you can create a German immersion environment from anywhere in the world, no matter where you live.

When you do have bigger windows of time to practise German, you can create an at-home immersion environment in loads of different ways:

LEARNING STRATEGY:

study on the go
When I'm learning a new language, I always use a vocab study app and other tools designed for use on the go and pull them out whenever I'm waiting around. Since my smartphone is with me anyway, I use it to learn what I can, when I can, even if it's just a word or two. See our Resources for some suggestions!

⋯⋗ You can connect with other learners (like you've been doing with our online community!) to get practice with them through regular video / audio calls.
⋯⋗ You can listen to live streaming radio or watch streaming video from Germany (or another German-speaking country) online.

···⟩ Do you play *Videospiele*? You can change the language settings on your games to German!

···⟩ You can also change the language of websites you use often and even your computer and smartphone operating system to German.

YOUR TURN: use the hack

1 Look at the apps and online Resources we recommend. Pick a few to start with, then add them to your computer or smartphone now so they are ready and waiting for you during your hidden moments.

2 Look at the websites, apps, games, browsers and even the operating system you use the most, and see if they have an option to change the language to German. Since you are already used to the interface and know where you'd normally click or tap, why not go ahead and change the language?

You'll see it's not that bad, and you can always change it back if you find it too hard. Usually, you'll just need to look for *Sprache* or *Spracheinstellung* under *Configuration* (sometimes called *Einstellungen* or *Optionen*).

COMPLETING UNIT 9

Check your understanding

1 ◀)) 09.07 Listen to this audio rehearsal, in which someone describes their environment and people around them. Feel free to take notes or listen to it multiple times.

2 ◀)) 09.08 Next, listen to the questions about the audio rehearsal you've just heard and answer the questions out loud in German.

Show what you know ...

Here's what you've just learned. Write or say an example for each item in the list. Then tick off the ones you know.

- ☐ Say something you miss using *vermissen*.
- ☐ Give two sentences describing where you live.
- ☐ Say 'it's hot', 'it's cold' and 'it's raining'.
- ☐ Give a sentence that uses an adjective to describe a family member's personality. Put the adjective in the right position in the sentence and use the correct gender.
- ☐ Use three different adjectives to describe your favourite clothes in German. Put the adjectives in the right word order and gender.
- ☐ Ask the questions, 'Can I pay in cash?' and 'Can I pay with a credit card?'

COMPLETE YOUR MISSION

It's time to complete your mission: pass for a local and use your descriptive language to point out the best places in town to a foreigner. To do this, you'll need to describe the details and characteristics of different places, people and things.

STEP 1: build your script

Think about your favourite city. What does it look like? How would you describe the buildings, the atmosphere and the people? Build a script you can use to give more detailed descriptions of places, people and things.

⋯⟩ describe what it's like in your favourite city
⋯⟩ say what type of landscape is nearby
⋯⟩ say what the weather is usually like
⋯⟩ explain what the houses, apartments or neighbourhoods look like
⋯⟩ describe the personalities of people living there
⋯⟩ incorporate new verbs you've learned (*vermissen, zurückfliegen, kaufen*)
⋯⟩ match adjectives to the gender and number of the objects they describe.

Write down your script, then repeat it until you feel confident.

Learn every day, even if it's just a little. You will learn more if you distribute your practice.

STEP 2: a little goes a long way ... *online*

This is your last dress rehearsal before you speak one-on-one with a native speaker! If you're feeling good about your script, go ahead and give it another go! Go online, find your Unit 9 mission, and share your recording with the community for feedback and encouragement.

STEP 3: learn from other learners

How did other language hackers describe their city? What city are they describing? Would you hire them as a tour guide? Ask them two more questions about the city.

STEP 4: reflect on what you've learned

Did you learn any new words or phrases in the community space? Did you find a new place to add to your bucket list? What did you learn about the gaps in your scripts?

HEY, LANGUAGE HACKER, ARE YOU READY?

You've just learned how to describe pretty much anything, as well as how to work around any gaps you may have in your German. I know you're ready for the ultimate mission – do you?

Bist du bereit? Los geht's!

10 HAVING YOUR FIRST CONVERSATION

More importantly, you know how to use clever #languagehacks and conversation strategies to make the German phrases you know stretch even further for you.

Your mission

You've worked hard. You've kept at it. And now, you're armed with a solid base in the German language.

Your mission is to have a one-on-one conversation – online with video activated – with a native German speaker.

This mission will set you up with the phrases, the confidence, and an insider look at how to have your first conversation in German – even if you don't think you're ready.

Mission prep

···⟩ Prepare the essential phrases you need to have a conversation.
···⟩ Develop the mindset: overcome nerves; don't worry about the grammar.
···⟩ Find a language partner, and schedule your first conversation!
···⟩ Apply what you've learned in the context of a first conversation.

BUILDING LANGUAGE FOR HAVING A CONVERSATION

Here's where all of the vocabulary – and just as importantly – all of the conversation strategies you've learned over the past nine units come into play. You're going to have your first 'face-to-face' conversation with another German speaker!

Face-to-face conversations with a native German speaker can be intimidating. That's why I like to 'cheat' by having my first few conversations in a new language with a partner online. This takes off the pressure, and you have the added luxury of being able to quickly search for words or phrases with online translators and dictionaries. Let's take a look at how you can strategize your own first conversations!

#LANGUAGEHACK
develop a cheat sheet and go into 'autopilot' during your first conversation

YOUR FIRST CONVERSATION

🔊 **10.01** Listen to this 'first' conversation between a language hacker (LH) and his German conversation partner. It will give you a good idea of how a typical first conversation in German might start. As you listen, highlight any words or phrases you'd like to use in your own first conversation with a native speaker.

HACK IT:
'Groundhog-Day' your way to fluency
Through the beauty of the internet, you can **have the same 'first conversation' over again** with different language partners until you feel comfortable with it. Then start speaking with the same people again and again to push yourself into new territories.

I suggest you use this phrase even if you already know the name of your language partner in advance. After all, the point of this conversation is to practise using the phrases you know!

Ingo: Hallo!

LH: Hallo, wie heißt du?

Ingo: Ich heiße Ingo. Und du?

LH: Ich heiße Benny.

Ingo: Freut mich, dich kennenzulernen, Benny. Sag mal, wo wohnst du?

LH: Ich bin Ire, aber jetzt wohne ich in New York.

Ingo: Ah, wie interessant! Irland. Ich war noch nie in Irland. Aber ich war einmal in New York, als ich 20 Jahre alt war. Warst du schon einmal in Deutschland?

LH: Nein, noch nicht. Eines Tages will ich wirklich nach Deutschland reisen ... Es tut mir leid – ich habe erst vor ein paar Wochen angefangen, Deutsch zu lernen. Kannst du ein bisschen langsamer sprechen?

Ingo: Na klar! Es tut mir wirklich leid.

LH: Du bist sehr geduldig! Danke, dass du mit mir sprichst. Also, seit wann unterrichtest du schon Deutsch?

PUT YOUR CONVERSATION STRATEGIES INTO ACTION

What should I say?

Every conversation has a certain 'formula' – phrases you can expect the conversation to include. We've talked a lot about this throughout this book. You can use the expected nature of conversations to your advantage.

Imagine that you are talking with our native German speaker, Ingo, for your own first conversation in German. In this case, the conversation will flow in a slightly different way. Use the prompts given to practise applying phrases you know, and fill in the gaps in the conversation.

Ingo: Guten Tag, freut mich, Sie kennenzulernen.

LH: (Greet your language partner.)

1 _____

Ingo: Ich heiße Ingo. Und Sie?

LH: (Give your name and ask if you can speak in the *du* form.)

2 _____

Ingo: Natürlich, wenn du möchtest!

LH: (Thank him for talking with you today.)

3 _____

Ingo: Kein Problem – es macht Spaß. Warum lernst du denn Deutsch?

LH: (Answer his question about why you're learning German.)

4 _____

Ingo: Sehr gut! Sprichst du noch andere Sprachen?

LH: (Say whether or not you speak any other languages.)

5 _____

Ingo: Mein kanadischer Schüler hat mir gesagt, dass die Sprache sehr schwer ist!

LH: (Say that you couldn't understand what he said. Ask him to write it out.)

6 _____

Ingo: Natürlich. Ich habe einen Schüler aus Kanada. Er findet die Sprache sehr schwer.

Now that you've seen two examples of a first conversation in action, let's start preparing you for the real thing.

#LANGUAGEHACK: develop a cheat sheet to go into 'autopilot' during your first conversation

Here's how I know you can handle this conversation, even if you think you're not ready: because you're going to 'cheat', so to speak.

I like to prepare for my conversations online by making up a cheat sheet of words and phrases I plan to use during the conversation – and I can have it right in front of me (on paper, another window, or another device) the whole time.

We'll do the same thing for you. You're going to have your own phrases ready, planned out, and written out in front of you, so you'll be able to glance at them while you're speaking German. This way, it doesn't matter if your mind goes blank. You'll just take a breath, and look at your cheat sheet.

Let's get to work preparing your cheat sheet. I like to separate mine into four parts:

1 Essential phrases

2 Survival phrases

3 Questions I plan to ask

4 'Me-specific' phrases

Essential phrases

My essential phrases are the words and phrases I know I'll need to use in every conversation. These are usually greetings and sign-off words, as well as questions I expect to be asked and my planned answers.

I've started you off with some suggestions. Write out the ones you plan to use in German, and then add some new ones of your own.

There is no shame in 'cheating' here. This isn't an exam. This is a conversation. Consider your cheat sheet as a crutch that helps you make the transition from studying German to speaking German. By using a cheat sheet now, you will get to the point where you don't need it a lot faster. It gives you momentum so that you become a lot more experienced at speaking over less time.

Essential phrases

(Refer to Units 1–3 for inspiration.)

Greetings	Sign-offs
Hallo! Wie geht's?	Bis zum nächsten Mal!
Hallo, schön, dich zu treffen!	Ich muss jetzt gehen.

(Refer to Units 1–6 for inspiration.)

Typical questions	Prepared answers
Wie heißt du?	
Woher kommst du?	
Wo wohnst du?	
Wo arbeitest du?	
Warum lernst du Deutsch?	
Sprichst du noch andere Sprachen?	

Don't worry about thinking up every possible word or phrase you might need. It's impossible and it's not a good use of your time! Instead, let the language tell you what you need to learn. Use the language you know now in natural conversation – however much or little it may be – and you'll quickly learn the 'me-specific' phrases that you haven't (yet!) added to your script.

Survival phrases

Don't be afraid of making mistakes in German. Instead, expect them. Prepare for them. Have a plan for dealing with difficult moments. Even if you forget every word you know or can't understand a single word the other person is saying, you can still have a conversation if you've prepared your survival phrases.

Here are some suggestions. Add some new ones of your own.

(Refer to Unit 3 for inspiration.)

In the heat of the moment there's a lot to think about. Don't worry about saying single words to get your point across. You can always add a *bitte* to the end to make sure your partner knows you don't mean to be impolite!

Full phrases	Or shorten them!
Kannst Du (bitte) einen Moment warten?	Moment bitte! Moment!
Kannst du das (bitte) aufschreiben?	Schreiben … bitte?
Kannst du das (bitte) wiederholen?	Wiederholen?
Kannst du (bitte) langsamer sprechen?	Langsamer …?
Ich verstehe nicht.	Wie bitte?
Kannst du das (bitte) noch einmal sagen?	Nochmal?

Questions I plan to ask

Speaking German with a new person gives you an opportunity to learn about that person's life, language and culture! I make sure I prepare in advance if there's anything in particular I'm curious to know.

Plan out a few questions that you can ask the other person. You can use them to take the pressure off you, while the other person talks for a while. And they are great to have ready for when there's a lull in the conversation. You might ask about:

···⫶ life in the other person's country (*Ist es jetzt kalt in Deutschland?*)
···⫶ the German language (*Das Wort 'dagegen' – was bedeutet das?*)
···⫶ the other person's life, work, or hobbies (*Was machst du gern am Wochenende?*).

I've already mentioned a few good options, but make sure you add some more of your own.

Prepared questions
(Refer to Units 2–9 for inspiration.)

Wie ist das Wetter in …?

Wie sagt man auf Deutsch …?

'Me-specific' phrases I want to practise

These are the conversation topics specific to me that I want to practise – my interests, what I've been doing lately, what my upcoming plans are, and the people in my life.

In your first conversation, if you've practised your essential phrases and your survival phrases, everything else is just a bonus! I like to create a goal of a few new phrases I want to practise during each conversation. But keep it to just a few – between two and five phrases – which is plenty to accomplish in your first conversation. You could prepare to talk about:

···⟩ what you're interested in (*Ich liebe Science-Fiction!*)

···⟩ what you've been doing today or lately (*Ich habe einen Artikel über deutsche Politik gelesen.*)

···⟩ what your upcoming plans are (*Ich möchte am Wochenende tanzen gehen.*)

···⟩ the people in your life (*Meine Freundin spricht ein bisschen Italienisch.*)

'Me-specific' phrases

Ich liebe …

Ich möchte …

Mein Freund / Meine Freundin …

GETTING READY FOR YOUR FIRST CONVERSATION

I highly suggest having your first few conversations online with video enabled. Technology really is your friend in this situation. In an online chat, you can easily refer to your notes, and you can even look up words on the spot or put phrases you need into an online translator – right in the middle of the conversation.

Know this: if all else fails, you can have an entire conversation in German even if you only know these three phrases: *Ich verstehe nicht. Schreib das bitte. Einen Moment.* Don't believe me? Envision it. Worst case scenario:

⋯⋗ Your conversation partner says *Hallo*, you say *Hallo* (success!). But then she says, @yego^3*8ham#3pt9ane1&? And your mind goes blank.
⋯⋗ You reply with **Ich verstehe nicht. Schreib das, bitte!**
⋯⋗ She types out what she said and sends it to you via chat. You select what she wrote, copy it and paste it and quickly find a translation. Ah, you think, I understand! But now it's your turn to respond, and your mind, again, goes blank.
⋯⋗ You say, **Einen Moment, bitte!** She waits patiently while you type what you want to say in English into your online translator. You hit enter and get a translation in German. You read out the words in your best German accent.
⋯⋗ Rinse and repeat.

I prefer to use automatic translation as a crutch, and never as a replacement for language learning.

In fact, you'd be surprised by how much you'd learn even in this worst case scenario. Even if you forgot every single phrase you learned in German except these three, you could have a conversation (of sorts) in German with another person. And you would learn loads of German by the end of it.

Is this scenario ideal? No. But is it better than not having a conversation at all? Absolutely.

Luckily, you've already been preparing for this moment for the past nine missions. So you're ready – even if you think you're not. Trust me on this.

Here's how I suggest you set yourself up for your conversation.

⋯⋗ Open up your cheat sheet and keep it within easy view.
⋯⋗ Have your translation tool ready (see our recommended Resources).
⋯⋗ Get ready to connect the call.
⋯⋗ Just before your conversation, practise listening to and repeating some German audio.

WHAT TO EXPECT

During this conversation, don't focus on saying things perfectly. Being understood is the main goal here. Don't stress about knowing all the grammar, using precisely the right word, or having a perfect accent.

> **CONVERSATION STRATEGY: *handling your nerves***
> It's typical for a beginner to expect to be judged by the other speaker. If you find yourself staring at the screen, afraid to push that Call button – and we've all been there – have a friend nearby to boost your confidence. Don't worry! The other person is probably just as nervous as you!
> A language exchange partner may be worried more about how their English sounds than how you sound speaking German! And a new teacher may be hoping to make a good first impression!

Let's review some of the skills you've learned throughout this book.

⋯⟩ **Rephrasing** – Take many of the phrases you ideally want to say, and simplify them. This is an essential skill for language hackers.

⋯⟩ **'Tarzan German'** – Don't be afraid to speak in 'Tarzan German'! If you know how to say something right, say it right. But if you know how to say something kind of wrong, then say it wrong! Your language partner will help you figure out the wording you need.

⋯⟩ **Learn from your gaps** – Despite rephrasing, you'll realize there's still a lot you don't yet know how to say. And as you talk, you'll realize you've been pronouncing some words wrong. Your partner may correct you. Good! This is valuable information. Take notes!

⋯⟩ **When in doubt, guess!** – Finally, if you're not sure what your conversation partner just said, guess! Use context to infer the meaning of the entire phrase.

Talking one-on-one with another person is the best language practice you can get. If there's one secret to #languagehacking, this is it. Enjoy your first conversation, and the many others to come after that!

Your purpose is to learn, practise, and gain confidence. If you remember this, you can't fail. You'll have plenty of time to improve and impress in later conversations.

Remember that perfectionism is your enemy in language learning. If you guess right, the conversation will advance, and if you guess wrong, you'll have had an opportunity to learn something new. And that's what this is all about!

Don't take corrections personally. Appreciate them as they help you improve.

COMPLETING UNIT 10

Check your understanding

CONVERSATION
STRATEGY: *warm
up before your first
conversation!*
Practising with audio
is one of the best
ways to prepare for
a conversation. It will
get your ears and your
tongue 'warmed up' for
the conversation. An
hour or two before your
German conversation
begins, come back to
these exercises and
replay them to help
you get into the flow of
German.

One mission left to go! Review the phrases and conversation strategies
from the unit one more time. When you're feeling confident, listen
to the audio rehearsal, which will help you practise your listening,
pronunciation and speaking skills.

1 Practise answering common questions.

🔊 **10.02** Listen to the audio rehearsal, which will ask questions in German.

⋯⟩ Practise answering the questions by giving spoken responses in German
that are true for you.
⋯⟩ Pause or replay the audio as often as you need.

2 Practise listening to someone describe herself.

🔊 **10.03** In this audio rehearsal, a German speaker talks casually about
herself. Listen to the audio, and after each clip, use what you understand
(or can infer) to answer questions about the speaker.

This is exactly
what you'll be
doing in your first
conversation -
listening to your
partner and using a
combination of your
new #languagehacking
skills and context to
help you through even
the tricky parts.

⋯⟩ What is her name? _____
⋯⟩ Where is she from? _____
⋯⟩ Where does she live now? _____
⋯⟩ How long has she been teaching German? _____
⋯⟩ Does she speak any other languages? If so, which ones? _____
⋯⟩ What are some of the things she is interested in? _____

Notes:

_____

_____

_____

_____

Show what you know ...

Before your final mission, make sure that you:

- ☐ Write up the essential phrases you'll need into your cheat sheet.
- ☐ Write up survival phrases and add them to your cheat sheet.
- ☐ Prepare 2–5 'me-specific' phrases you want to practise. Add them to your cheat sheet.
- ☐ Prepare at least three questions you plan to ask. Add them to your cheat sheet.

What are your goals?

Know what you want to accomplish or what phrases you'd like to practise. Be realistic, but ambitious! And be flexible – you never know where a conversation will take you, and that's a very good thing for language learners. Write out a few notes on what you want to practise during your first conversation, or create your own bingo sheet! Then, find your language partner.

Don't forget, whether it's learning new phrases, or improving your pronunciation, it's always OK to ask directly for the help you need!

My partner Lauren likes to set up 'conversation bingo' for herself when she's practising a language online. She writes out a few phrases she wants to practise during the call (either by speaking them or hearing them), and tries to cross off as many as she can.

Echt? Wirklich?		Als ich 20 Jahre alt war, ...	
ich ... gern	Mir scheint ...		um ehrlich zu sein – wie du vielleicht weißt – soweit ich weiß
gestern – heute – morgen	Habe ich dir schon erzählt, dass ...?	Was? Wer? Wo? Wie viele?	
ein bisschen	ab und zu		mit dem Auto – mit dem Bus

COMPLETE YOUR MISSION

It's time to complete your mission: having a one-on-one conversation with a native ... online. To do this, you'll need to prepare to:

- ⋯▷ say hello and use essential greeting vocabulary
- ⋯▷ ask at least three questions
- ⋯▷ give your answers to commonly asked questions
- ⋯▷ use survival phrases when you can't understand or need help
- ⋯▷ say goodbye or set up a time to talk again.

STEP 1: find your conversation partner and schedule your first conversation

Follow our Resources to find a conversation partner online and schedule your first chat with them now.

When you're setting up your first conversation online, the first thing to do is send out a few messages to the exchange partners or teachers who look like a good fit for you. Break the ice and send them a message (in German of course!) to set up your first chat. A good icebreaker tells the other person:

⋯⋗ your name and German level
⋯⋗ what you'd like to practise or discuss during the conversation.

Here's an example:

> Hallo! Ich heiße Ellen. Ich möchte mit Ihnen Deutsch sprechen. Können wir uns duzen? Ich möchte einfache Sätze üben. Ich möchte zum Beispiel meinen Namen und mein Land sagen. Ich bin Anfängerin. Können wir auch morgen sprechen? – Danke für die Geduld mit mir!

Be friendly, and give a short introduction to yourself and what you want to practise – but don't say too much! Save some phrases for the conversation. Write out your own icebreaker now.

STEP 2: go all the way ... *online*

The first time might be scary, but it will get easier! Go online and have your first conversation in German for an authentic experience and good time!

Here's what to do during your conversation:

⋯⋗ Practise rephrasing your thoughts into simple forms.
⋯⋗ Speak 'Tarzan German' if you have to – it's better than nothing!
⋯⋗ Take note of any gaps in your German vocabulary.
⋯⋗ Write down any phrases or words you want to say, but don't know yet.
⋯⋗ Write down new words or phrases you want to review later.

STEP 3: learn from other learners, and share your experience!

Tell the community how it went. (Or, if you're nervous, head over to see how other people's first conversations went.) **Your task is to ask or answer at least three questions from other learners:**

HACK IT: *time pressure is your friend*
Schedule it for tomorrow or the earliest possible slot. Don't give yourself a long window to get ready – overthinking this step can lead to procrastination later. Make a request for the next time slot, and don't look back!

Remember, your first conversation is just that – a first conversation. The only way to get to your 50th conversation is to get the first one out of the way, then keep going from there.

···⟩ Were you nervous? How did you handle your nerves?

···⟩ What was your teacher or exchange partner like?

···⟩ What went well? What didn't? What would you do differently next time?

STEP 4: reflect on what you've learned

After your first conversation, it's easy to focus on the words you didn't know or the things you couldn't say. But it's much more productive to focus on your successes instead. Were you 'only' able to give your name and your job, and say that you live with your cat? Those are huge wins! Don't overlook your achievements.

···⟩ What were your wins? What phrases were you able to say or understand?

···⟩ Review the notes you took during your conversation. What words did you need that you don't know yet? What new words did you learn?

As for the words you didn't know – that's one major benefit of having one-on-one conversations! You learn very quickly where the gaps are in your script, so you can work on filling them.

HEY, LANGUAGE HACKER, YOU JUST HAD A CONVERSATION IN GERMAN

Or at least you should have!

You just broke one of the biggest barriers in language learning! Now that you've crossed that threshold, you are on a fast track to fluency in German that most people only ever dream about. Enjoy this milestone.

And remember – your second conversation will be even better than your first. Your third will be even better than that. Schedule your next spoken lesson now – don't put it off – that ticking clock is a powerful motivator for language hackers.

Your next mission: *Weiter so!* Keep it up!

ANSWER KEY

UNIT 1

CONVERSATION 1

Figure it out **1** I am. **2** You. **3** a. Designerin b. England c. Berlin **4** a. Ich komme aus … b. Ich komme aus Amerika/Kanada. **5** Und du? (And you?)

Notice **1** a **2** a. Ich bin. b. Ich wohne in (Berlin). c. Ich komme aus Berlin. d. Ich komme aus Deutschland.

Grammar explanation: _-in_ female ending **1** Examples: Frankreich, Österreich, Brasilien (countries); Designer, Lehrerin, Ingenieur (professions); das Kino, das Fernsehen, die Reise (interests) **2** Examples: Ich bin Jack. Ich bin Engländer. Ich bin Student. **3** a. Ich bin Lehrer. Und du? b. Ich komme aus Kanada. Und du? c. Ich wohne in Berlin. Und du?

Put it together Examples: Ich bin Marta. Ich komme aus England. Ich wohne in Hamburg. Ich bin Architektin.

CONVERSATION 2

Figure it out **1** a. Was sind deine Hobbys? b. Pop, klassische Musik c. Gitarre/guitar, Gymnastik/gymnastics, Basketball/basketball **2** Gitarre, Basketball, Hobbys, aktiv, Musik, Gymnastik, singe, Pizza, Fan, super, Pop, ist, und, okay **3** a. but b. favourite **4** a. Ich höre gern b. Ich höre nicht gern c. Ich spiele d. Ich singe gern **5** nicht

Notice **1** a. Lieblingsbuch b. Lieblingssong **2** a. ist b. sehr **3** a. I listen-to not gladly pop. b. I play gladly basketball. **4** a. 2 b. 1 c. 6 d. 4 e. 3 f. 5 g. 8 h. 9 i. 7 **5** a. Ich trinke gern Kaffee. b. Ich esse gern Bratwurst. c. Ich fotografiere nicht gern. d. Ich spiele gern Tennis. e. Ich esse nicht gern Bananen. f. Ich spreche gern Deutsch. **6** a. Ich bin Tolkien-Fan. b. Ich bin ein Jazz-Fan. c. Ich bin ein Volleyball-Fan.

Your turn: use the hack **2** a. e-mail b. computer c. knee **3** Examples: video (Video), English (Englisch), summer (Sommer), winter (Winter), school (Schule)

Practice   2 Examples: a. Ich spiele (nicht) gern Tennis. b. Ich höre (nicht) gern Radio.
c. Ich esse (nicht) gern Pizza. d. Ich esse (nicht) gern Spaghetti. e. Ich trinke (nicht) gern Kaffee. f.
Ich trinke (nicht) gern Bier. g. tanze (nicht) gern Tango. h. Ich esse (nicht) gern Brokkoli.   3 Was sind
deine Interessen? Was sind deine Lieblingsalben? Was sind deine Lieblingsautoren? Was sind deine
Lieblingsfilme? Was sind deine Lieblingssongs?   4 Examples: a. Ich esse nicht gern Brokkoli, aber
Salat ist okay. b. Ich bin ein Madonna-Fan. Ich bin ein Fußball-Fan.

Put it together   1 Examples: Ich komme aus den USA. Ich wohne gern in Köln. Ich lerne gern
Deutsch. Ich bin ein Radler-Fan. Ich trinke nicht gern Kaffee. Ich reise gern.

2 Examples: a. Ich spiele gern Fußball. b. Ich esse gern Pizza. c. Ich trinke gern Bier. d. Ich esse
nicht gern Brokkoli. Ich lerne nicht gern Mathematik.

CONVERSATION 3

Figure it out   1 a. Ich möchte Land und Leute kennenlernen und vielleicht einen Job finden.
b. Dein Plan ist toll! c. Dein Deutsch ist sehr gut. Bravo!   2 a. I have family here b. Your plan is great!
c. maybe to find a job d. I find the language fascinating   3 warum; weil   4 Examples: Familie, hier,
lerne, finde(n), faszinierend, Job, Plan, gut

Notice   1 a. Warum lernst du Deutsch? (Why learn you German?) b. Ich möchte Land und Leute
kennenlernen. (I would like land and people get to know.) c. Ich möchte hier wohnen. (I would like
here to live.)   2 Danke schön!   3 a. wohnen b. kennenlernen c. finden   4 a. 2 b. 1 c. 4 d. 3

Conversation strategy: smooth out your sentences with connector words   1 a. und
b. weil ... na ja c. oder d. aber   2 a. Ich spiele gern Basketball und Tennis. b. Ich schwimme gern,
aber ich jogge nicht gern. c. Ich möchte Salat oder (ich möchte) Bratwurst essen. d. Ich lerne
Englisch, weil … na ja … ich möchte in Kanada wohnen.

Grammar explanation: combining two verbs   1 a. Ich möchte Pizza essen. b. Ich möchte
Deutsch sprechen. c. Ich möchte Ellen helfen. d. Ich möchte Berlin sehen.   2 a. Ich möchte in
Deutschland wohnen. b. Ich lerne gern Sprachen. c. Ich spreche gern Deutsch. d. Ich möchte Kaffee
trinken. e. Ich möchte singen. f. Ich möchte klassische Musik hören. g. Ich reise gern.   3 a. Ich finde
b. Ich möchte, wohnen. c. Ich lerne gern d. Ich reise e. Ich möchte, kennenlernen. f. Ich esse gern
g. Ich möchte, studieren h. Ich möchte, verstehen

Put it together   Examples: Ich möchte Australien besuchen. Ich möchte Portugiesisch lernen. Ich
möchte einen Job finden. Ich möchte Kartoffelsalat essen.

COMPLETE YOUR MISSION

Build your script   Example: Ich bin Tom und ich bin Architekt. Ich komme aus Australien, aber ich wohne in Frankfurt. Ich spiele gern Tennis und ich höre gerne Techno. Ich lerne Deutsch, weil … na ja, ich möchte gern in Deutschland arbeiten.

UNIT 2

CONVERSATION 1

Figure it out   1 a. two b. ja c. three   2 a. falsch b. richtig c. falsch d. falsch   3 Echt?

Notice   1 a. Ich spreche ein bisschen Russisch. Ich spreche ziemlich gut Italienisch. b. Ich lerne nur Deutsch.   2 a. Echt? b. Noch nicht. c. Vielleicht.   3 a. Ich spreche gut Englisch. b. Ich möchte gut Deutsch sprechen.   4 a. ich spreche, du sprichst b. ich lerne, du lernst c. ich finde, du findest   5 a. 7 b. 3 c. 4 d. 1 e. 5 f. 6 g. 2

Grammar explanation: asking questions 1 a. Sprichst du Deutsch? b. Lernst du viel Deutsch? c. Sprichst du auch andere Sprachen?   2 a. Lernst du b. Wie findest du   3 a. Wohnst du in New York? b. Lernst du gern Englisch? c. Bist du Designer(in)?

Practice   1 a. nur b. Ich lerne ein bisschen c. Echt, ein bisschen Italienisch d. Sprichst du gut e. viel, sprechen   2 a. A b. A c. F d. F e. F f. A   3 a. Wohnt Alex in Berlin? b. Sprichst du Italienisch? c. Lernt Mark Deutsch?

Put it together   1 a. Japanisch b. Französisch c. Chinesisch Examples: d. Portugiesisch e. Arabisch   2 a. Examples: Ja, ich spreche Italienisch und Französisch./Nein, ich spreche nur Englisch. b. Ja, ich möchte Portugiesisch lernen./Nein, ich möchte nur Deutsch lernen.

CONVERSATION 2

Figure it out   1 a. seit zwei Wochen (for two weeks) b. Besonders Japanisch! Ich finde die Sprache exotisch und die Kultur ist so faszinierend.   2 a. nur b. sehr gut c. Sprachen d. Du sprichst schon sehr gut Deutsch! e. aber f. (…) möchtest du (…) lernen?   3 a. Bitte! b. wie viele c. seit wann   4 Examples: Japanisch, Arabisch, Englisch, exotisch, Kultur, lerne, finde, faszinierend

Notice   **2** Seit wann, when   **3** a. Sag mal! b. schon c. besonders   **4** a. schon b. Besonders
c. Sag mal   **5** a. Wie viele b. seit zwei Wochen c. Ich lerne, Sprachen d. Seit wann, Ich spreche,
seit   **6** a. Not yet. b. Still/more

Pronunciation explanation: the 'hard *ch*' and 'soft *ch*' sounds   **1** Soft *ch*: ich, nicht,
sprechen, sprichst, vielleicht, leicht; Hard *ch*: auch, noch, Sprache, Wochen   **2** a. Seit fünf Tagen.
b. Seit drei Jahren. c. Seit acht Monaten. d. Seit vier Wochen.

Practice   **1** a. Ich wohne seit September in Deutschland. b. Ich lerne seit neun Wochen Deutsch.
c. Seit Oktober lerne ich zwei Sprachen, Deutsch und Italienisch.   **3** Example: 223 5587 943 – zwei
zwei drei fünf fünf acht sieben neun vier drei   **4** Example: 35 fünfunddreißig

Put it together   **1** Example: Ich lerne seit Oktober Deutsch.   **2** Examples: Ich habe zwei Hunde.
Ich spreche vier Sprachen.   **3** Example: a. Seit wann wohnst du in Deutschland? b. Seit wann
unterrichtest du Deutsch?   **4** Example: Ich lerne seit vier Monaten Deutsch.

CONVERSATION 3

Figure it out   **1** a. jeden Montag / (jede Woche) b. jeden Tag   **2** a. richtig b. falsch c. richtig
d. falsch   **3** du lernst   **4** a. That's also very effective. b. How do you learn German?   **5** Vokabeln,
Kurs, effektiv, finde, online, Internet, lernen, gute Idee, praktisch

Notice   **1** a. Ich finde … b. Ich gehe lieber … c. Das ist ganz leicht. d. Gute Idee! e. Das stimmt.
f. Du hast Recht.   **2** a. Ich lerne nicht.
b. Ich spiele nicht

3

ich		du	
lerne	denke	lernst	denkst
gehe	weiß	gehst	weißt
finde	wohne	findest	wohnst
habe		hast	
sollte		solltest	

Conversation strategy: filler words   **2** a. weil … na ja … b. Also, weil … na ja … c. nun d. weil
… na ja …, ähm

Practice

1

ich form	*du* form
ich schreibe	du schreibst
ich verstehe	du verstehst
ich denke	du denkst
ich gehe	du gehst
ich versuche	du versuchst
ich studiere	du studierst
ich beginne	du beginnst

2 a. Du wohnst b. Ich lerne c. Ich möchte d. Liest du   **3** a. denkst b. Ich schreibe c. Wohnst du lieber, oder d. Gehst du e. Versuchst du   **4** a. Ich spreche gern Italienisch, aber ich spreche lieber Deutsch. b. Ich denke, du solltest jeden Tag Vokabeln lernen. c. Das stimmt. Russisch ist nicht leicht. d. Ich finde Deutsch leicht.

Put it together   Examples: Ich möchte gut Deutsch sprechen. Ich spreche (gern) Spanisch. Ich sollte mehr Vokabeln lernen. Ich denke, Deutsch ist schön, aber schwierig.

COMPLETE YOUR MISSION

Build your script   Seit wann lernst du Russisch? Wie viele Sprachen sprichst du? Sprichst du Italienisch? Wohnst du auch in Köln? Ich lerne Deutsch seit zwei Monaten. Ich habe jeden Tag Unterricht online. Ich spreche drei Sprachen. Ich spreche Englisch und ganz gut Französisch und ein bisschen Deutsch. Ich möchte noch Russisch lernen.

UNIT 3

CONVERSATION 1

Figure it out   **1** b. **2** vielen Dank, kein Problem, bitte   **3** Wie heißt du? Ich heiße ...   **4** Nice to meet you.

Notice   **1** Langsamer, bitte.   **2** Wo? (where?), Wie? (how?)   **3** a. Nett (Schön) b. Mir geht c. jetzt/ gerade   **4** a. I am b. you are c. I help d. you help

Practice   1 a. Wo b. Wie c. Wo/Wie d. Wie/Wo e. Wie f. Wo/Wie   **2** a. 3 b. 5 c. 1 d. 2 e. 6 f. 4   **3** a. Dein, sehr b. langsamer c. Wo, jetzt/gerade d. mir hilfst

Grammar explanation: *mir* (to me) and *dir* (to you)   **2** a. dir b. mir   **3** a. sage dir b. Gibst, mir c. dir sagen   **4** a. Möchtest du mir schreiben? b. Kannst du mir sagen? c. Ich möchte dir danken.

Put it together   1 Examples: Ich heiße Alex. Mir geht's heute sehr gut. Ich bin jetzt in Köln. Ich lerne deutsche Vokabeln. Ich habe Unterricht online. Ich arbeite.   **2** Examples: Du hilfst mir und ich helfe dir jeden Tag. Ich gebe dir das Buch. Ich sage dir die Wahrheit. Kannst du mir eine SMS schreiben?

CONVERSATION 2

Figure it out   1 a. richtig b. falsch c. falsch   **2** a. Ich bin hier [in Berlin], um Deutsch zu lernen! b. Ich bin also in Deutschland.   **3** Wirklich? Echt?   **4** Example: kannst = can   **5** a. Do you live in another city? b. Can you repeat that, please? c. One moment, please … I can barely hear anything.

Notice   1 a. Warum, um Deutsch zu lernen. b. Warum lernst du Deutsch? c. Ich lerne Deutsch, um in Berlin zu studieren. d. Ich lerne Deutsch, um in Deutschland zu arbeiten.   **2** a. wohne, wohnst b. bin, bist c. kannst, sagst d. arbeite, verstehe e. hören

Practice

1   **Question words cheat sheet**

Meaning	German	Meaning	German
Why?	Warum?	Who?	Wer?
What?	Was?	How long?	Wie lange?
How?	Wie?	Since when?	Seit wann?
Where?	Wo?	How much?	Wie viel?
Which?	Welche?	How many?	Wie viele?
When?	Wann?		
Can you?	Kannst du?	Do you want?	Möchtest du?

2 a. Wann? b. Wie viele? c. Wer? d. Wo? e. Seit wann? 3 a. Wie viele b. Was c. Seit wann d. Wann e. Warum f. Wer g. Welche 4 a. Wo wohnst du? b. Was sagst du? c. Warum möchtest du in Berlin arbeiten? d. Was meinst du mit 'Ich bin Designerin'? e. Seit wann arbeitest du in Stuttgart?

Grammar explanation: 'Tell me!' – the 'command' form a. Lern mal die Sprache! b. Sprich Deutsch, bitte! c. Wiederhol mal bitte! d. Denk mal nach!

Put it together Examples: Ich komme aus England, aber ich bin jetzt in Deutschland. Ich wohne seit September hier. Ich arbeite seit Oktober in Köln.

CONVERSATION 3

Figure it out 1 Webcam, Problem, muss, Computer, WLAN, Idee, RAM, deaktivieren, neu starten, Dings, alt 2 deactivate, restart, wifi, thingy, old 3 a. The problem is with Ellen's webcam. 4 a. Schlecht b. mir leid c. Bis dann! Bis zum nächsten Mal! d. ich weiß nicht, ich weiß 5 my, your

Conversation strategy: 'Tarzan German' a. Langsamer, bitte. b. Wie viel? c. Supermarkt … wo?

Conversation strategy: memorize the power nouns: *Mann / Frau, Ort, Dings* 1 Ich weiß das Wort nicht mehr! Also, mein Internet-Dings! 2 a. Buch-Ort b. Restaurant-Frau c. Film-Mann

Notice 1 a. du hörst b. ich brauche, du brauchst c. ich denke, du denkst d. ich muss 2 a. Ich brauche ein Smartphone. b. Ich denke, du kannst kaum etwas hören. c. Ich muss Peter wieder anrufen. d. Können wir auf Deutsch sprechen? 3 a. Ist nicht schlimm! b. Das passt! 4 Wie sagt man auf Deutsch? Ich weiß das Wort nicht mehr!

Your turn: use the hack 1 Because they end in -keit (feminine ending) and -ismus (masculine ending), respectively. 2 a. der Journalismus b. der Computer c. die Wohnung d. die Schwierigkeit e. die Freundschaft f. die Energie g. die Meinung h. der Winter

Grammar explanation: noun genders 1 a. Ich denke, deine Webcam ist neu. b. Ich denke, meine Verbindung ist nicht gut. c. Denkst du, mein WLAN ist schnell? d. Denkst du, dein Computer ist langsam?

Practice 1 a. Ich habe kein WLAN-Passwort, weißt du? b. Ich brauche kein WLAN; Ich habe kein Smartphone. c. Ich habe keine Webcam, aber ich habe ein Mikrofon. d. Ich habe ein Smartphone und ich brauche keinen Computer. e. Hast du einen Computer oder ein Smartphone? 2 a. Kannst, Computer b. musst mir c. möchte, Samstag, anrufen d. Brauchst du

Put it together   Examples: Ich denke, das Handy ist echt toll! Ich habe jetzt ein iPhone 6. Ich brauche einen Computer.

COMPLETE YOUR MISSION

Build your script   Example: Ich lerne heute Deutsch. Ich bin gerade in Berlin. Aber ich wohne und arbeite in Glasgow. Ich lerne Deutsch seit einem Monat. Ich gehe jeden Tag in den Deutschkurs und ich lerne online. Ich habe ein Smartphone. Aber ich lerne lieber am Computer. Ich brauche einen neuen Laptop.

Example: Ein Mann ... Marco ... total nett ... Architekt ... Arbeit in Madrid ... sprechen kein Deutsch aber sprechen Englisch ... lieben Berlin ... lesen viele Bücher ... spielen gern Tennis und Basketball.

UNIT 4

CONVERSATION 1

Figure it out   1 a. Judith comes from Austria. b. to practise German   2 a. Ich komme aus Österreich. b. Stört es, wenn ich mit Ihnen ein bisschen Deutsch übe? c. Ich muss noch viel üben. d. Lass uns also anfangen!   3 Excuse me.   4 a. üben b. Geduld c. Anfänger(in)   5 a. Gerne. b. Warum nicht? c. Kein Problem! d. Super!

Notice   1 a. Entschuldigung, sprechen Sie Deutsch? Stört es, wenn ich mit Ihnen ein bisschen Deutsch übe? b. Entschuldigung, sprichst du Deutsch? Stört es, wenn ich mit dir ein bisschen Deutsch übe? 2 a. 3 b. 1 c. 2 d. 4   3 Können wir uns duzen?   4   wir können

Grammar explanation: verb forms for wir and Sie   1 a. Möchtest b. denken c. Verstehst d. wohnen e. sprichst   2 a. Können Sie das wiederholen, bitte? b. Was essen Sie gern? c. Was machen Sie in Berlin? d. Können Sie mich jetzt besser hören? e. Können Sie mir bitte helfen? f. Möchten Sie anfangen zu üben?

Practice   1 Examples: Wir sind im Supermarkt. Wir sind auf einer Reise. Wir sind zusammen. Wir arbeiten zusammen. Wir arbeiten die ganze Zeit. Wir arbeiten im Supermarkt. Wir gehen die ganze Zeit spazieren. Wir gehen zum Strand. Wir essen die ganze Zeit. Wir essen zusammen.   2 a. Ich wohne noch in Europa. b. Arbeitest du noch in der Bank? c. Ich gehe noch zum Unterricht. d. Können wir noch üben? e. Ich bin noch ziemlich müde.   3 a. kaufen schon, sieben b. Sie können, wenn Sie möchten c. Wissen Sie/Weißt du, was, auf Deutsch d. super, hier e. Ich muss, noch, üben f. Stört es, wenn

Put it together   **1** Examples: Stört es, wenn ich mit Ihnen spreche? Stört es, wenn ich hier sitze? Stört es Sie, wenn ich rauche? Stört es, wenn ich die Toilette benutze?   **2** Examples:

Situation 1: Ah, du sprichst Deutsch! Hallo, nett, dich kennenzulernen. Ich bin noch Anfänger. Ich lerne seit September Deutsch. Und du?

Situation 2: Ich lerne Deutsch, weil ich die Sprache wunderschön finde! Ich hoffe Deutschland bald besuchen zu können. Ich möchte auch das Essen probieren und Deutsche kennenlernen.

Situation 3: Entschuldigung, stört es, wenn ich eine Frage stelle? Wie viel Uhr ist es? Wissen Sie, wann der Bus kommt?

CONVERSATION 2

Figure it out   **1** Du meinst, du möchtest nach Italien fahren?   **2** a. Italy (Italien) b. Austria (Österreich)   **3** I would like to visit other cities in Germany.   **4** a. Seit wann bist du in Berlin? b. eigentlich nicht c. ein paar Monate   **5** Du solltest … besuchen.

Notice   **1** Ich meine …   **2** Meinst du …?   **3** a. Ich esse gern Obst wie Bananen und Äpfel. b. Wie machst du das? c. Wie viele Hunde hast du? d. Du bist wie mein Bruder.   **4** a. 3 b. 4 c. 1 d. 5 e. 6 f. 2   **5** a. since when b. never c. afterwards d. maybe e. so much f. more g. other

Grammar explanation: vowel changes   a. schläfst b. siehst c. hilfst d. sprichst

Practice   **1** a. Ich möchte … nehmen. b. Ich nehme c. Du nimmst d. Ich möchte fahren e. Ich fahre f. du fährst   **2** a. Ich nehme den Zug b. Du nimmst den Bus. c. Ich fahre mit dem Auto. d. Du fährst mit dem Zug.   **3** a. solltest, nehmen b. siehst, viel c. andere, besuchen, wie d. Du meinst, Auto, e. nie, Sommer

Put it together   Examples: a. Ich reise viel. b. Ich fahre nach Hamburg. c. Ich fahre für ein paar Tage. d. Ich fahre nächsten Monat. e. Ich nehme den Zug.

CONVERSATION 3

Figure it out   **1** a. falsch (SMS schicken) b. falsch (die ganze Zeit Deutsch üben) c. falsch (Kann ich mitkommen?) d. richtig   **2** a. 1 b. 3 c. 2   **3** a. Weil … na ja … sie möchte ein Stück Torte im Café Lebensart essen. b. Von dort hat man einen Blick über ganz Berlin.   **4** a. Was machst du am Wochenende? b. Kann ich mitkommen? c. Das ist ja toll!   **5** Wir werden zusammen die Stadt entdecken.   **6** 0151/4693287

Notice   1 a. 3 b. 5 c. 2 d. 6 e. 1 f. 4   2 a. zuerst b. dann c. danach   3 a. Wir werden Deutsch sprechen. b. Ich werde dir schreiben. c. Du wirst in München wohnen.

Grammar explanation: word order in German   1 vielleicht, heute, eines Tages, im Sommer   2 a. Zuerst werde ich ... b. Dann werde ich ... c. Danach möchte ich ...   3 a. Normalerweise nehme ich den Bus. b. Am Wochenende werde ich das Schloss Neuschwanstein sehen. c. Nächste Woche möchte ich ein Buch lesen.

'Slingshot words': dass, weil, wenn (that, because, if)   1 ich morgen Zeit habe. 2 a. Ich lerne Deutsch, weil ich Familie in Deutschland habe. b. Ich werde Englisch mit dir üben, wenn du Deutsch mit mir übst.

Your turn: use the hack: 1 a. Kannst du schwimmen? b. Kannst du, verlassen c. Ich muss, teilnehmen d. Du solltest, probieren e. werde ich, umziehen   2 a. Ich werde beschäftigt sein. b. Ich werde ein Taxi nehmen. c. Wirst du im Sommer nach Spanien reisen? d. Wirst du zum/ins Restaurant gehen? e. Ich werde nicht nach Frankfurt reisen.

Practice   1 a. ich werde, Telefonnummer b. Morgen, Zeit, kann ich, kommen c. werde ich da/dort d. Gern, freue, dass ich, habe   2 a. Dieses Wochenende tanze ich mit dir. b. Zuerst möchte ich eine SMS schicken. c. Diese Woche werde ich ein Stück Torte essen. d. Dann werde ich die Stadt entdecken. e. Nächste Woche muss ich München besuchen. f. Dann kann ich mitkommen. g. Morgen sollte ich Zeit finden. h. Danach werde ich nach Italien fahren.

Put it together   1 Example: Ich werde im Januar Australien besuchen. Zuerst werde ich Sydney sehen und dort ein paar Wochen bleiben. Danach werde ich nach Melbourne oder Canberra fahren. Ich werde vielleicht in einem Restaurant essen oder etwas billig kaufen. Ich möchte unbedingt auch die Wüste sehen.   2 Example: Kann ich dir meine E-Mail-Adresse oder meine Telefonnummer geben? Super! Meine E-Mail-Adresse ist alexsmith@beispiel.com und meine Nummer ist 0049 347946239. Kannst du morgen anrufen oder mir eine E-Mail schreiben, bitte?

COMPLETE YOUR MISSION

Build your script   Example: Am Wochenende reise ich nach Österreich. Zuerst fahre ich nach Wien. Die Stadt ist wundervoll. Dort besuche ich die Hofburg, den Stephansdom und den Prater. Dann esse ich Sacher Torte im Café Central. Danach möchte ich nach Innsbruck reisen. Ich liebe die Berge. Ich fahre mit dem Zug nach Österreich.

UNIT 5

CONVERSATION 1

Figure it out   **1** a. Wer ist sie? b. Wie heißt sie? c. Sie heißt d. Sie kommt aus e. Sie ist f. Sie möchte   **2** a. lawyer – falsch: Ingenieurin b. a month – falsch: eine Woche c. to a restaurant – falsch: auf den Fernsehturm d. this weekend – falsch: nächstes Wochenende   **3** a. diese Woche b. nächstes Wochenende c. morgen d. danach e. jeden Sommer   **4** a. favourite student (f) b. my husband is c. tomorrow we plan to

Notice   **1** a. ich unternehme etwas mit b. wir verbringen die Woche c. Was habt ihr vor? d. Wir planen … zu …   **2** a. Hotel zu finden b. Deutsch zu sprechen c. Irland besuchen   **3** a. er b. sie c. wir d. du e. Sie f. ihr   **4** a. Sie ist Ingenieurin. b. Sie kommt aus Deutschland. c. Sie möchte die Stadt besuchen. d. Sie heißt … e. Er wohnt mit einem Freund. f. Er fährt jeden Sommer nach Italien. g. Was möchte er unternehmen?   **5** a. Diese Woche nehme ich den Zug nach Hamburg. b. Nächstes Wochenende besuchen wir Fiona in Irland. c. Morgen plane ich, eine Party zu machen.

Grammar explanation: 'he', 'she', 'you – plural'

1

Dictionary form	ich form	du form	er/sie form	ihr form
lernen	ich lerne	du lernst	er lernt	ihr lernt
können	ich kann	du kannst	er kann	ihr könnt
helfen	ich helfe	du hilfst	er hilft	ihr helft
schlafen	ich schlafe	du schläfst	er schläft	ihr schlaft
planen	ich plane	du planst	er plant	ihr plant

2 a. besucht b. lernt c. liest d. tanzt

Practice   **2** Examples: a. Schwiegermutter (mother-in-law), b. Schwiegereltern (in-laws) c. Enkel(kinder) (grandchildren)   **3** a. Geschwister b. Er, Lieblingsneffe c. Freund, werden zusammen d. Mutter arbeitet e. mehr, Eltern f. Bruder g. arbeitet, Papa/Vater h. Meine Freundin, jeden Tag, Sie   **4** Examples: a. Ich kenne meine beste Freundin von der Universität. b. Sie heißt Kristin. c. Sie arbeitet als Architektin in einem Büro.   **5** Examples: a. verbringe, Zeit mit meinem Bruder b. planen, zu Hause zu bleiben und zusammen zu essen.

Put it together   **1** Examples: Ich wohne mit meinem Freund im Ausland. Mein Bruder wohnt noch mit meiner Familie. Er ist Mathematiker und spielt Basketball.   **2** Example: Mein Lieblingsmensch ist mein Vater. Er wohnt mit meiner Mutter und meinem Bruder in den USA. Er arbeitet für eine Bank und er schwimmt gerne, wenn er Zeit hat.

CONVERSATION 2

Figure it out 1 a. Ja. b. Er heißt Jan. c. Sie kennt ihn und seine Familie seit zwanzig Jahren. d. Nein, sie wohnt nicht allein. (Sie wohnt mit Anna). e. Sie heißt Anna f. Weil sie alles kaputt machen. 2 die

Notice 1 a. verheiratet b. single c. zwanzig d. ihn e. schon lange f. außerdem 2 a. Besuche mich doch b. Du meinst c. schau selbst d. Jans Hund 3 a. ihn b. Ellens Schwester wohnt c. macht, alles kaputt d. besucht, jeden Sommer e. Außerdem

Grammar explanation: me, you, him, her 1 a. dich b. mich c. sie d. ihn 2 a. ihn b. mir c. sie d. ihr e. dich f. ihm 3 a. mich b. dich c. dir d. sie e. sie f. mir g. ihn 4 a. Seit wann kennst du sie? b. Gehst du ohne mich? c. Ich sehe ihn jeden Montag.

Practice 1 a. kenne b. Weißt c. kennen d. Wissen 2 Examples: a. Ja, ich habe einen Bruder und eine Schwester. b. Ich habe eine Freundin. c. Nein, ich habe keine Kinder. d. Ich wohne mit meiner Freundin.

Put it together Examples: Ich kenne meinen Freund seit der Universität. Wir sind seit sechs Jahren zusammen und wohnen seit 2014 zusammen. Wir möchten bald heiraten und die Hochzeitsreise nach Australien machen. Er sagt mir immer, dass ich ein bisschen verrückt bin, aber er liebt mich trotzdem.

CONVERSATION 3

Figure it out 1 a. She has two children. (Ja, wir haben zwei wunderbare Kinder.) b. She is not sure. (Ich bin nicht so sicher. Vielleicht eines Tages.) 2 a. a charming German (man) b. I am not so sure. c. often d. You never know. 3 She uses other words to express the same general concept (nicht für mich?) and she asks for help/for a translation (Wie sagt man auf Deutsch?) 4 a. Sie heißen b. Ihre Namen sind sehr schön c. Oh, das ist toll!

Notice 1 a. Hast du Kinder? b. Sie heißen 2 a. Ich bin sicher. b. Alles ist möglich. 3 a. Man weiß nie! b. Wie sagt man 'bye' auf Deutsch? c. Man kann es machen. d. In Deutschland sagt man das nicht. 4 a. 4 b. 5 c. 6 d. 1 e. 3 f. 8 g. 7 h. 2

Grammar explanation: possessives 1 a. ihr Bruder b. ihre Kinder c. unser Hund d. Ihre Frau e. sein Neffe 2 a. Alexanders, b. seine, c. Ihr, d. Eure

Practice   1 a. er ist b. Sie heißt c. wir verstehen sie d. wir treffen sie   2 a. Mein, seinen b. Meine Freundin, wir reisen, oft c. meine Mutter d. mit seinem Freund e. kenne meinen, Freund, lange 3 a. Möchtet ihr irgendwann ins Kino gehen? b. Sind sie hier? c. Er hat zwei Hunde. d. Ihre Eltern kennen mich nicht.   4 Examples a. Ich treffe bald Markus. b. Sie sind meine Schwestern und meine Eltern. c. Ihre Namen sind sehr originell.

Your turn: use the hack   1 a. Something related to technology/IT/upgrading devices, etc. b. Something related to relationships/family, etc. c. Something related to travel/getting a flight, etc. d. Something related to language learning.   2 a. Deutsch zu lernen. b. das Wetter nicht gut ist. c. heute möchte ich zu Hause bleiben.

Put it together   Examples: Meine Eltern heißen Jack und Mary. Mein Vater ist 60 Jahre alt und meine Mutter ist 58. Sie wohnen in Washington, in den USA.

Meine Kinder heißen Emily und Mark. Sie sind noch sehr klein, sind erst ein Jahr alt. Sie sind Zwillinge.

Ich habe auch zwei Hunde. Sie sind sehr gut (lieb) und sie machen nichts kaputt.

COMPLETING UNIT 5

Check your understanding.   1 Wir wohnen erst seit einem Monat zusammen.   2 Meine Tochter heißt Anna.   3 Ja, mein Hund heißt Kai.   4 Anna ist meine Schwester.   5 Nein, ich besuche meine Eltern nächstes Wochenende nicht.   6 Ja, wir reisen jeden Sommer nach Polen.   7 Mein Cousin hat vier Kinder.   8 Lea kennt meine Familie seit fünf Jahren.

COMPLETE YOUR MISSION

Build your script   Example: Die wichtigste Person in meinem Leben ist meine Freundin. Sie ist sehr wichtig, weil sie mir jeden Tag hilft. Wir kennen uns seit 10 Jahren. Wir sind seit 9 Jahren zusammen und wir wohnen seit 7 Jahren zusammen. Meine Freundin ist Malerin und arbeitet jeden Tag im Atelier. Sie ist sehr kreativ und sehr intelligent. Sie hat viele Freunde. Meine Freundin ist eine ganz besondere Person.

UNIT 6

CONVERSATION 1

Figure it out   1 a. für mich ein Schnitzel bitte, b. ich nehme Salat mit Hähnchenbrust c. wir nehmen zuerst Mineralwasser d. für mich einen Weißwein bitte   2 white wine   3 a. Ein Tisch für zwei b. Und zu trinken? c. Ein Tisch für drei. d. Und zu essen?   4 a. day - Good evening b. eating - Are you drinking something? c. red - white wine d. your (formal) - Here is your table (formal)

Notice   1 in German they say 'I have hunger'.   2 Wir nehmen zuerst Mineralwasser. Ich möchte gern ein Pils. Für mich einen Weißwein bitte.   3 Möchten Sie bestellen? Was möchten Sie essen? Hier ist Ihr Tisch.   4 a. I already know … b. I'll have … c. We already know … d. We'll have … e. Do you know …? f. Will you have …? g. Would you like to order? h. Will you drink something?

Practice   1 a. Möchten, bestellen b. Für mich, Rotwein c. nehme, Mineralwasser/Wasser d. Ich finde, Speisekarte/Karte e. glaube/denke, ich nehme f. schon Hunger g. Wir wissen, wir nehmen h. Hier ist, Lieblings-   2 Examples: die Spätzle (spaetzle), das Pizzabrot (pizza bread), der Kartoffelsalat (potato salad), der Strudel (strudel) / Examples: Können Sie bitte kommen? Ich nehme noch einen Rotwein, bitte.

Grammar explanation: compound (combined) nouns   1 a. tomato juice b. language school c. ambulance   2 a. 4 b. 1 c. 6 d. 3 e. 2 f. 5

Put it together   1 Examples: a. Ja, bitte. Ich nehme zuerst einen Salat. b. Ich möchte die Spätzle mit Pilzen bitte. c. Stimmt, ich habe sehr viel Hunger! Zu trinken nehme ich Wasser mit Kohlensäure. Vielen Dank. d. Können Sie bitte kommen? e. Ja, bitte. Ich nehme noch eine Flasche Wasser. f. Ja, heute habe ich viel Hunger und viel Durst!   2 Examples: Normalerweise esse ich zu Hause. Zum Frühstück trinke ich gern Milchkaffee und esse Brot mit Marmelade. Zum Mittagessen koche ich oft Nudeln oder esse auch gerne Salat. Zum Abendessen koche ich Fleisch oder Eier mit Gemüse. Den ganzen Tag lang trinke ich gerne Kaffee oder Tee und esse auch sehr gerne Obst wie Äpfel, Orangen oder Bananen.

CONVERSATION 2

Figure it out   1 a. das Pergamon Museum, das Haus am Checkpoint Charlie b. das Haus am Checkpoint Charlie c. es ist nicht so interessant d. Na ja …, wir können einen Kompromiss schließen.   2 It's a real highlight!   3 a. am Montag b. wir müssen natürlich … besuchen c. wenn du das interessanter findest d. dort sind viele Touristen e. Das stimmt nicht.   4 a. there are b. it's an absolute c. I find it (the exhibition – die Ausstellung) d. fewer tourists e. I know that ...

Notice   1 a. die meisten b. weniger c. besser 2 interessanter als   3 a. aktiver als b. schöner als c. netter als   4 a. ich finde b. ich finde die Ausstellung c. ich finde das Museum besser d. du findest e. wenn du findest f. ich weiß, dass g. ich weiß, dass dort viele Touristen sind   5 a. 6 b. 4 c. 5 d. 1 e. 10 f. 8 g. 9 h. 2 i. 3 j. 7

Practice   1 a. Gibt es hier nur drei Hotels? b. Es gibt keinen Wein bei mir. c. Es gibt viele Schulen in Deutschland.   2 Examples: a. Das klingt gut! b. Das stimmt! c. Ich bin nicht einverstanden. d. Ich bin einverstanden! e. Das stimmt nicht!   3 Examples: a. Ich finde, dass es zu viele Menschen in der Stadt gibt. b. Ich denke, dass wir weniger Kaffee und mehr Wasser trinken sollten. c. Meiner Meinung nach sind Hunde freundlicher als Katzen. d. Ich weiß natürlich, dass die beste Eissorte Schokolade ist.

Grammar explanation: comparisons   1 a. kleiner, der/die/das kleinste b. charmanter, der/die/das charmanteste c. fauler, der/die/das faulste d. interessanter, der/die/das interessanteste e. schwieriger, der/die/das schwierigste f. leichter, der/die/das leichteste   2 a. mehr Bücher als b. die schönste Stadt c. weniger Leute als d. das beste Restaurant e. der schlechteste Film f. Es ist besser als ...   3 a. kleiner als b. die kleinste c. Ich finde, schöner als d. Aber, die schönste e. größer f. der interessanteste g. schlechter als h. das schlechteste

Put it together   Examples: Es gibt so viele Highlights in Köln und ich möchte die Stadt bald besuchen. Ein Highlight ist unbedingt der Dom. Das beste Getränk dort ist das Kölsch. Köln ist kleiner als Berlin und die Leute sind freundlicher als in München. Meiner Meinung nach ist Köln die beste Stadt in Deutschland.

CONVERSATION 3

Figure it out   1 music, books   2 a. die beste deutsche klassische Musik von Beethoven, Bach und Mozart b. Sie hört nicht gern moderne Musik. c. Ellen wird Judith ein Buch geben. 3 mir empfehlen (x2), gebe dir (x2), danke dir   4 a. Wo ist der Kellner? b. Die Rechnung bitte! 5 a. Meiner Meinung nach b. Ich höre... lieber als c. Was kannst du mir empfehlen?

Notice   1 a. Spaß haben b. dafür   2 a. 3 b. 4 c. 1 d. 5 e. 2   3   a. Sag mal b. Was kannst du mir empfehlen? c. Kannst du mir ... empfehlen?

Practice   1 a. Ich bestelle Wasser ohne Kohlensäure. Ich bestelle ein Taxi. Ich bestelle die Rechnung. Ich bestelle noch ein Getränk. b. Examples: Ich möchte Deutschlands Geschichte besser kennenlernen. Ich möchte dich besser kennenlernen. Ich möchte diese Frau besser kennenlernen.   2 a. Klassik lieber als b. ist, Meinung nach c. ich werde dir, geben

Your turn: use the hack   Examples: a. Um ehrlich zu sein, ist es unbeschreiblich lecker. b. Leider nicht in Berlin wie du! Ich wohne in einem kleinen Dorf in der Nähe von Köln. c. Soweit ich weiß, habe ich schon alles. Vielen Dank! d. Leider kann ich zurzeit keinen Kaffee trinken, nur Tee.

Put it together   Examples: Mein Lieblingsbuch auf Deutsch ist Freuds 'Traumdeutung'. Ich finde dieses Buch sehr interessant, weil es heute noch wichtig für die Psychologie ist. Ich möchte Freuds Leben und Studien besser kennenlernen. Ich denke, dass er wichtiger und besser als Jung ist.

COMPLETING UNIT 6

Check your understanding   a. falsch b. falsch c. richtig d. falsch e. richtig

COMPLETE YOUR MISSION

Build your script   Example: Morgen gehe ich in mein Lieblingsrestaurant in München-Schwabing. Es ist sehr typisch und hat deutsche und regionale Spezialitäten. Dort sind nicht viele Touristen. Meiner Meinung nach ist es das beste Restaurant in München. Das Essen ist viel besser und viel billiger als im Stadtzentrum. Du solltest es unbedingt kennenlernen! Ich bestelle immer Leberkäse mit Brezeln und Senf, aber die Spezialität ist Schweinshaxe mit Sauerkraut und Kartoffelpüree. Zu trinken gibt es bayerisches Bier. Unter uns gesagt ist alkoholfreies Hefeweizen das beste Bier.

UNIT 7

CONVERSATION 1

Figure it out   1 a. am letzten Wochenende b. wir haben zusammen zu Abend gegessen c. Gestern haben wir … gesehen d. Wie war es? e. einmal vor vier Jahren f. Es war okay. g. Dort habe ich eine leckere Torte gegessen. h. wir haben über unsere Pläne für das Wochenende gesprochen   2 b   3 a. falsch (wir haben auch viele andere Sehenswürdigkeiten fotografiert) b. richtig c. falsch (morgen) d. richtig   4 really well   5 a. gestern b. heute c. morgen

Notice   1 a. Was hast du am letzten Wochenende gemacht? b. Judith und ich haben zusammen zu Abend gegessen. c. Wir haben über unsere Pläne für das Wochenende gesprochen.   2 a. am letzten Wochenende b. zusammen c. über unserer Pläne für das Wochenende

3

Dictionary form	German – past tense phrase	Meaning
machen (to do/to make)	Was hast du gemacht?	What did you do?
	Wir haben (Pläne) gemacht.	We made ... (plans).
	Es hat mir Spaß gemacht.	I had (fun)!
zu Abend essen (to eat dinner)	Wir haben zu Abend gegessen.	We ate dinner.
essen (to eat)	Ich habe gegessen.	I ate.
sprechen (to talk)	Wir haben (über) … gesprochen.	We talked (about)
sehen (to see)	Wir haben ... gesehen.	We saw ...
treffen (to meet)	Du hast (sie) getroffen.	You met (her).
fotografieren (to photograph)	Wir haben ... fotografiert.	We photographed ...
besuchen (to visit)	Ich habe … besucht.	I visited ...
gefallen (to like)	Hat es dir gefallen?	Did you like (it)?
	Es hat mir gefallen!	I liked (it)!

4   They use a form of the verb haben plus a form of the main verb. Most of the verb forms have 'ge-' at the beginning. The verb form ends either in -t or -en.   5 a. vor drei Tagen b. vor vier Tagen c. vor zehn Minuten d. vor sechs Monaten e. vor zwei Jahren

Grammar explanation: forming the past, with *haben*
1 a. hat, gelernt b. Habt, gemacht c. Hast, geübt d. Haben, gelesen e. haben, gesehen f. hat, gegeben g. haben, fotografiert h. habe, besucht   2 a. haben, gegessen b. hat, getrunken c. hat, geholfen d. hat, gefunden e. hat, geschrieben f. Hat, getroffen g. habe, genommen, gesprochen h. hat gewusst i. habe, gedacht

Practice   1 a. Das Restaurant ist toll. Dort habe ich vor zwei Tagen zu Mittag gegessen. b. Ich habe mit Martin über Deutschland gesprochen. c. Sie hat ihren Bruder in Dublin besucht.   2 a. Hat es ihm gefallen? b. Hat es ihr gefallen? c. Es hat mir gefallen. d. Es hat uns nicht gefallen.

Put it together   Example: Bei mir alles gut, danke. Gestern habe ich am Morgen gearbeitet und um 13 Uhr habe ich Mittagspause gemacht und Kartoffelsalat gegessen. Um 17 Uhr haben meine Kollegen und ich Feierabend gemacht. Wir haben Zeit im Biergarten verbracht. Wir haben Bier getrunken und über ein Projekt gesprochen. Wir haben viel Spaß gehabt.

CONVERSATION 2

Figure it out **1** a. a lot of (ein bisschen) b. a few weeks ago (vor ein paar Monaten) c. Berlin (Düsseldorf) **2** a. She practised some phrases. b. I forgot! You told me that already! c. Habe ich … richtig gesagt? **3** a. difference b. I decided c. homework d. between **4** hast gelernt, habe gelernt (2x), habe geübt, hast gemacht, habe gesagt, hast gesagt, hast begonnen, habe begonnen, habe entschieden, habe gekauft, bin geflogen, bin gereist, habe vergessen, hast erzählt

Notice **1** a. Habe ich … richtig gesagt? b. Ich muss sagen, dass … c. Du hast mir das erzählt. **2** Hast du dazu Fragen? Do you have questions about it? **3** entschieden, vergessen **4** a. ich habe gelernt b. ich bin geflogen c. ich habe geübt d. ich habe gekauft e. ich bin gereist f. ich habe vergessen g. ich habe entschieden h. du hast gemacht i. du hast mir erzählt j. du hast gesagt k. du hast begonnen

Grammar explanation: using *sein* **for movement** **1** a. ich bin gefahren **2** a. bin b. hat c. bist d. sind e. seid **3** a. bin ich, gereist b. Ich habe, gefunden c. bin ich, gefahren

4

1. Regular verbs	Past form	2. Irregular verbs	Past form
I talked	ich habe gesprochen	I went	ich bin gegangen
I said	ich habe gesagt	I thought	ich habe gedacht
I made	ich habe gemacht	I flew	ich bin geflogen
I bought	ich habe gekauft	I forgot	ich habe vergessen
I practised	ich habe geübt	I began	ich habe begonnen
I learned/studied	ich habe gelernt	I decided	ich habe entschieden
		I knew	ich habe gewusst
		I ate	ich habe gegessen

Put it together **1** Example: Ich bin vor drei Jahren nach Wien gefahren. Ich habe entschieden, nach Wien zu fahren, weil ein Freund dort wohnt. Wien hat mir sehr gut gefallen. Die Stadt war sehr schön und ich habe dort sehr viel Spaß gehabt. **2** Example: Ich habe Deutsch in einer Schule in Berlin gelernt. Einmal bin ich in die Bibliothek der Schule gegangen, aber es war Samstag. Um 16 Uhr bin ich zum Ausgang gegangen, und leider habe ich den Alarm ausgelöst! Sie haben mich dort vergessen und in der Schule eingeschlossen!

CONVERSATION 3

Figure it out **1** a. richtig b. falsch c. falsch **2** a. nervös b. Akzent c. Grammatik **3** a. Habe ich dir schon erzählt, dass …? b. Ich habe alles vergessen. c. Warum hast du … ? d. Ich wollte keine Fehler machen. e. Man muss so viel wie möglich sprechen. f. Ich war zu nervös, um zu sprechen. g. Als ich 13 Jahre alt war. **4** pronunciation

Notice **1** a. Habe ich dir schon erzählt b. Ich habe geglaubt, dass c. Ich habe vergessen d. Ich hatte e. als ich 13 Jahre alt war. **2** a. nichts b. alles c. nur d. nie e. schon f. wirklich g. so viel h. zu (viel) i. in j. von **3** a. Ich habe geglaubt/gedacht b. Ich habe vergessen, was c. Ich habe geglaubt/gedacht, dass d. Habe ich dir erzählt, was **4** a. alles b. nichts c. Alles

Practice **2** a. Er musste b. Ich hatte **3** a. Er war 31 Jahre alt, als er seine Frau kennengelernt hat. b. Ich wollte mit dir über Deutschland sprechen. c. Ich wollte Deutsch in Hamburg lernen. **4** Examples: a. Als ich noch in Brasilien wohnte, hatte ich kein Interesse an der Sonne. Aber jetzt möchte ich nur an den Strand gehen. b. Als ich auf dem Weg zum Theater war, habe ich Julian getroffen. c. Als ich 18 Jahre alt war, habe ich in England gewohnt und immer Tee getrunken. d. Als ich Manager bei der Firma Zamenhof war, habe ich meine Frau kennengelernt. **5** Examples: Habe ich dir schon erzählt, dass ich für zwei Jahre in Deutschland gewohnt habe? Habe ich dir schon erzählt, wie ich angefangen habe, neue Sprachen zu lernen? Habe ich dir schon erzählt, dass ich meinen Mann vor fünf Jahren kennengelernt habe? **6** a. Unterschied zwischen, Wörter b. Wir haben, Grammatik, Schule gelernt c. Wie, Aussprache, Habe ich, starken Akzent **7** a. Hast, verstanden, habe gesagt, dass b. so viel gegessen, als, letzte Woche c. Sie hat, gesprochen. Es war d. Ich habe, vergessen. Nächstes Mal e. Du hast mir, geholfen, Ich habe, benannt

Your turn: use the hack **1** a. Ich sehe jetzt/gerade den Film. b. Ich werde morgen den Film sehen. c. Ich habe letzte Woche den Film gesehen. **2** Also, vor drei Tagen bin ich da - nehme ich den Zug und sofrt sehe ich einen Wolf! **3** Examples: a. Ich bin vor einer Woche nach Deutschland gereist. b. Ich bin am letzten Samstag mit meinem Freund ins Kino gegangen. c. Vor zwei Jahren habe ich begonnen, Deutsch zu lernen. d. Gestern habe ich den ganzen Tag gearbeitet. e. Nächsten Mittwoch werde ich mit einer Freundin in einem Restaurant zu Mittag essen. f. In einem Jahr werde ich nach Australien reisen.

Put it together Example: Letztes Jahr war mein Deutsch viel schlechter und ich war sehr nervös. Ich habe nur mit meiner Lehrerin gesprochen. Und ich habe gedacht, dass Deutsch zu schwer ist. Aber ich habe entschieden, langsam zu sprechen und habe vergessen nervös zu sein. Seit damals habe ich viel mehr Deutsch gelernt.

COMPLETING UNIT 7

Check your understanding   2 a. Er hat Berlin vor einem Monat besucht. b. Sie haben viel gesprochen und auch Schokolade gegessen. c. Er ist mit dem Zug nach Hamburg gefahren.

COMPLETE YOUR MISSION

Build your script   Example: Einmal bin ich für meinen Job nach Frankfurt geflogen, aber ich habe nur ein bisschen Deutsch gesprochen. Für die Arbeit war es kein Problem, weil alle Englisch gesprochen haben. Aber danach bin ich in die Stadt gegangen, um ein Geschenk für meine Frau zu kaufen. Ich habe ein schönes Kleid gefunden. Aber die Frau in dem Geschäft hat kein Englisch gesprochen. Ich war zu nervös, um Deutsch zu sprechen. Ich habe alles vergessen, was ich gelernt hatte. Ich habe gedacht, wie sagt man 'How much does that cost?' auf Deutsch? Dann habe ich einfach gesagt: 'Preis?' und die Frau hat mich verstanden.

UNIT 8

Figure it out   1 a. Ich mache einen Kochkurs! b. Letztes Mal haben wir gelernt, wie man einen Apfelkuchen macht. c. Heute lerne ich, wie man einen Bienenstich macht!   2 a. better b. apple pie c. microwaved pizza   3 Ich freue mich, dich zu sehen!   4 a. Sie hat vor kurzem angefangen, zu kochen. b. Sie lernt, wie man einen Bienenstich macht!   5 a. Was gibt's Neues? b. Es ist lange her! c. zurzeit

Notice   1 Ich freue mich, dich zu sehen! Es ist lange her!   2 a. zurzeit b. Ich habe viel zu tun. c. vor kurzem d. Ich habe angefangen … zu … e. letztes Mal f. Wir haben gelernt, wie …   3 a. bisher gelernt b. schnell c. klappt es nie d. Es ist nur eine Frage   4 a. zu b. zu c. zu.   5 a. Es gibt noch viel zu tun. b. Meine Eltern haben viel zu tun.   6 a. machst du b. haben gelernt, wie man, tanzt c. Letztes Jahr habe, gelernt, wie man, schreibt

Grammar explanation: 'separable' (mix and match!) German verbs   1 a. flip out b. give up c. give back d. go out   2 a. Ich komme normalerweise am Mittag an. b. Jeden Freitag gehe ich mit Peter aus. c. Ich wache immer um 6 Uhr auf. d. Kommst du heute mit? e. Kannst du die Tür aufmachen?   3 a. angefangen (started) b. angekommen (arrived) c. angerufen (called) d. aufgeräumt (tidied up) e. ausgegangen (went out) f. ausgesehen (looked like) g. mitgearbeitet (cooperated) h. weggeblieben (stayed away) i. weggelaufen (ran away) j. zugehört (listened to) k. zurückgerufen (called back) l. zurückgekommen (came back)   4 a. Wir sind am Freitag mit Hans ausgegangen. b. Sie hat um acht Uhr den Laden aufgemacht. c. Er hat ihn gestern angerufen.

Practice   1 a. viel zu tun, angefangen b. Vor kurzem, gesehen, hat angefangen, zu c. Letztes Mal, mitgekommen d. komisch ausgesehen, war e. Bisher, mitgearbeitet f. zurückrufen   2 Examples: Ich habe gelernt, wie man Paella macht. Ich habe gelernt, wie man Tennis spielt. Ich habe gelernt, wie man auf Deutsch im Restaurant bestellt.   **3** a. vor, angekommen b. vor (drei), angefangen c. vor, getroffen d. hat vor, aufgemacht

Conversation strategy: learn set phrases for each 'stage' of a conversation
1 a. haben wir gelernt, wie man einen Apfelkuchen macht. b. es zu Hause zu machen, klappt es nie. c. lerne ich, wie man einen Bienenstich macht!   **2** a. Ich freue mich, dich zu sehen! Es ist lange her! b. Erzähl mal, was gibt's Neues? Ich sehe … c. Vor kurzem habe ich angefangen, … Letztes Mal haben wir gelernt, … d. Und was hast du bisher gelernt?   **3** a. Ich weiß, dass (du aus England kommst). b. Kennst du (Sarahs neuen Freund)? c. Hast du schon (diesen Film gesehen)?

Put it together   **1** Examples: Vor kurzem habe ich angefangen, ins Fitness-Studio zu gehen. Im Moment gehe ich zweimal pro Woche ins Fitness-Studio, aber ich sollte eigentlich mehr Sport treiben.   **2** Examples: Vor kurzem habe ich angefangen, Deutsch zu sprechen. Das letzte Mal, als ich versucht habe, einen Film auf Deutsch zu sehen, war es zu schwierig. Aber bisher habe ich viel mit Bennys Buch gelernt und jetzt schaffe ich es. Es ist sehr schön, dass ich jetzt so viel Deutsch verstehen kann.

CONVERSATION 2

Figure it out
1

	goes for a walk before work	rides a bicycle	takes the car	always has lunch at a restaurant	sometimes tries new restaurants	prepares lunch at home
Ellen	✓	✓		✓		
Jakob	✓	✓	✓		✓	✓

2 Mir scheint, … (a conversation starter)   **3** a. morgens b. nachmittags **4** a. Sie geht morgens vor der Arbeit in der Stadt spazieren. b. Er geht normalerweise nachmittags mit dem Hund im Park Gassi. c. Sie fährt überall Fahrrad! d. Er nimmt nur selten die U-Bahn. e. "Weil sie frische Luft braucht." f. Er fährt oft mit dem Auto zur Arbeit.

Notice   **1** Läuft alles gut für dich?   **2** 1 morgens 2 nachmittags 3 mittags 4 vor der Arbeit 5 normalerweise 6 meistens 7 ab und zu 8 selten 9 oft 10 immer 11 manchmal 12 nie 13 mit dem Auto 14 gemütlich 15 im Park 16 in der Stadt 17 überall 18 zur Arbeit 19 im gleichen Restaurant 20 zu Hause   **3** a. Morgens vor der Arbeit gehe ich in der Stadt spazieren. b. Ab und zu fahre ich Fahrrad. c. Ich fahre überall Fahrrad. d. Ich fahre oft mit dem Auto zur Arbeit. e. Mittags esse ich immer im gleichen Restaurant. f. Meistens koche ich zu Hause.   **4** Examples: a. Ich bin mitten in der Nacht mit dem Motorrad zum Laden gefahren. b. Jedes Jahr mache ich mein Spezialfrühstuck mit Eiern bei meinen Eltern.

Practice   1 a. mache, einen Spaziergang, meistens, zurück b. Ab und zu mache ich morgens Kaffee, normalerweise, machen c. Nachmittags esse ich oft d. Das letzte Mal, Sport gemacht habe, fünf Minuten später e. Nach, spiel, Besonders, wenn   2 Examples: Morgens fahre ich oft mit dem Auto zu meinem Lieblingscafé. Abends gehe ich dreimal pro Woche ins Fitness-Studio. Nachmittags treffe ich mich fast immer mit meinen Freunden.   3 Examples: Ich höre Musik. Ich gehe spazieren. Ich gehe ins Kino.   4 Examples: a. Ich spiele gern Gitarre. b. Ich spiele Gitarre gern am Wochenende mit meinen Freunden. c. Zuerst war es langweilig, weil ich nicht gut war, aber jetzt macht es Spaß.   5 Examples: a. Ich spaziere gern im Park. b. Ich gehe oft in den Park, um zu joggen. c. Ich war noch nie in Sydney, aber ich möchte gerne dahin fliegen.

Put it together   Example: Jeden Tag fahre ich um 8 Uhr mit dem Bus zur Arbeit. Wenn ich um 5 Uhr Feierabend mache, treffe ich mich mit einer Freundin und wir fahren zusammen ins Fitness-Studio. Da machen wir normalerweise eine Stunde Yoga.

CONVERSATION 3

Figure it out   1 a. falsch b. richtig c. richtig   2 a. Would you like to come along? b. What should I bring? c. Could you write down the address? d. I would love to

Notice   1 a. in den Park b. Fußball zu spielen c. Freunden   2 a. Was machst du …? b. Ich mache eine kleine Party. c. Möchtest du mitkommen? d. Du solltest auch kommen! e. Das mache ich auf jeden Fall! f. Ich würde schon gerne. g. aber leider h. Ich habe schon vor   3 a. danach b. etwas später c. dann d. heute Abend e. um 20 Uhr f. bei mir zu Hause g. in der Nähe vom Bahnhof h. meine Wohnung i. einkaufen gehen j. mit jemandem   4 a. Was sollte ich mitbringen? b. Um wie viel Uhr? c. Könntest du die Adresse aufschreiben? d. Ich kann es dir auf der Karte zeigen.

5

Verb	Example	Meaning
möchtest (would you like/want)	Möchtest du mitkommen?	Would you like to come?
wäre (it would be)	Ein Dessert wäre perfekt.	A dessert would be perfect.
würde (I would)	Ich würde schon gerne. Ich würde kommen. Ich würde sagen …	I would love to. I would come. I would say.
könntest (you could)	Vielleicht könntest du den mitbringen? Könntest du … aufschreiben?	Maybe you could bring that? Could you write down …?

Grammar explanation: forming the conditional with *würde* (would)   a. würde, wohnen
b. hätte c. wäre d. könnte

Practice   1 a. Was sollte ich anziehen? b. Um wie viel Uhr hört es auf? c. Wann sollte ich
ankommen?   2 a. Examples: danach b. um 5 Uhr c. Möchtest du d. Kann ich   3 Examples:
a. toll b. leider bin ich beschäftigt   4 a. You would prepare b. It would be c. I would travel d. You
could   5 a. Möchtest du Deutsch mit mir lernen? b. Könntest du mich nächstes Mal fragen? c. Ich
würde ausgehen, aber es ist zu spät.

Your turn: use the hack   1 Examples: a. Schön, mit dir im Restaurant zu essen. b. Möchtest du mit mir
tanzen? c. Ich gehe (lieber) später in den Supermarkt.   2 a. sehr gut Deutsch, einen Job in Deutschland,
Der Job ist b. nach Valencia gereist. Dort, zu lernen.   3 a. musst. b. sollte c. können.

Put it together   1 Example: Zuerst könntest du das Zentrum besuchen. Ich glaube, das
beste Museum wäre das Kunstmuseum. Ich würde danach auf jeden Fall den Dom besuchen.
Am Abend können wir ein Taxi nehmen, um in einem schönem Dorf in der Nähe zusammen zu
essen.   2 Example: Ich würde sehr gerne nach Afrika reisen und mit dir auf den Kilimanjaro gehen.
Ich könnte im Sommer reisen. Wann beginnt die Reise und wie lange würde sie dauern? Sollte ich
meine Freundin mitbringen? Ich glaube, das wäre eine unglaubliche Erfahrung.

COMPLETING UNIT 8

Check your understanding   2 a. lesen b. Scifi-Romane und Autobiographien c. Normalerweise
jeden Tag d. (Manchmal abends nach der Arbeit, aber) normalerweise nachts e. die ganze Zeit lesen

COMPLETE YOUR MISSION

Build your script   Example: Ich gehe jeden Tag morgens, vor der Arbeit, am Strand spazieren
und mache Sport. Ich gehe oft mit meiner Freundin schwimmen. Abends nach dem Abendessen
plaudern wir meistens ein bisschen. Und wir lesen gern jeden Abend vor dem Schlafen. Am
Wochenende gehen wir zusammen ins Kino oder in ein Restaurant im Stadtzentrum. Dahin fahren wir
mit dem Bus oder mit dem Auto. Manchmal kochen wir auch für Freunde bei uns zu Hause. Ich würde
gern öfter für meine Freunde kochen. Vor kurzem habe ich angefangen, Spanisch zu lernen. Ich habe
vor, jeden Tag ein bisschen zu üben, aber es ist schwieriger als gedacht. Ich würde auch gern einen
Fotografiekurs machen, aber ich weiß nicht wann.

UNIT 9

CONVERSATION 1

Figure it out   1 a. falsch (day, letzte Woche) b. falsch (dancing, Shopping) c. falsch (travel to, wird oft an Berlin denken) d. falsch (before, danach)   2 a. What a shame! b. I fly back to England soon c. The sun shines today and it's warm. d. I would rather spend the day outside.   3 a. Ellen fliegt nächste Woche/in einer Woche nach England zurück. b. Ellen vermisst England, das Meer und auch den Strand und die Wälder bei ihr. c. Sie glaubt/denkt, dass das eine sehr gute Idee ist. d. Geschenke e. Nein, Ellen möchte nicht ins Kaufhaus gehen, weil sie den Tag lieber draußen verbringen möchte. f. Wenn sie müde sind, setzen sie sich in ein nettes Café und essen ein Eis.   4 a. auf dem Land b. draußen c. der Strand und die Wälder d. historisches Kaufhaus e. das Meer

Notice   1 a. Ich vermisse; Ich werde die Stadt vermissen b. Ich fliege zurück; Bevor ich nach Hause fliege c. Ich werde an … denken; Wenn ich an meine Zeit hier denke d. Ich werde dich erinnern; Das erinnert mich an den Strand e. Wenn wir müde sind, können wir uns setzen; Wenn du müde bist, warum gehst du nicht schlafen?   2 a. Geschenke für ihre Familie zu kaufen b. KaDeWe c. KaDeWe   3 a. 2 b. 4 c. 3 d. 1   4 1. das Land 2. mountains 3. die Sonne 4. trees 5. die Bank 6. die Polizei 7. die Kirche 8. the city hall 9. pharmacy 10. das Stadion 11. the street 12. die Bibliothek

Practice   2 Examples: Ich wohne in England in Bristol. Meine Stadt ist in Meeresnähe und neben meinem Haus gibt es einen sehr schönen Park. Da gibt es auch viele Tiere.   3 Examples: Meine Schwester wohnt mit ihrem Freund in Deutschland. Bei ihnen gibt es einen wunderschönen Garten und sie haben einen Hund. In der Nähe von ihrem Haus gibt es auch einen tollen weißen Strand.

Vocab explanation: talking about the weather   1 a. Es ist schön draußen b. Das Wetter ist schlecht. Wie schade!   2 Examples: Das Wetter ist sehr schlecht draußen. Es ist kalt und windig.

Put it together   Example: Ich wohne in Valencia. Es gibt sandige Strände dort und das Wetter ist meistens sonnig und warm. Deswegen kann man auch im Winter die Sonne genießen! Es regnet selten und es schneit absolut nie. Wenn ich im Winter nicht in Valencia bin, vermisse ich das tolle Klima.

CONVERSATION 2

Figure it out   1 a. falsch b. richtig c. falsch   2 a. bunten Buddy-Bären, Schokolade b. abenteuerlustig c. superlangweilig wäre d. normal, klug e. sind oft billiger in Deutschland.   3 a. erinnert b. wirklich c. wäre d. zum Schluss e. eher f. langweilig

Notice   **1** a. beeindruckend b. abenteuerlustig c. typisch d. bunt e. jung f. langweilig g. alt h. neu i. traditionell j. schwarz k. klug l. schwierig m. blau n. billig   **2** a. leicht, schwierig b. einzigartig, typisch c. dumm, klug d. modern, traditionell e. abenteuerlustig, schüchtern f. alt, jung

Conversation strategy: shortcut to using adjectives before nouns easily   **1** a. Diese Gebäude sind nicht schön. b. Der Bahnhof ist riesig und neu. c. Deine Freundin ist nett. d. Ich möchte Buddy-Bären kaufen, die bunt sind.

Practice   **1** 1. schüchtern 2. adventurous 3. hässlich 4. schön 5. old 6. jung 7. strange 8. typisch 9. unerfreulich 10. pessimistic 11. optimistisch 12. stolz 13. modest 14. lustig 15. serious 16. stupid 17. intelligent 18. arrogant 19. klug 20. normal 21. freundlich   **2** Examples: a. eine optimistische Person. ein wunderbares Hobby für mich. b. der wichtigste Mensch meines Lebens. ein sehr altes Gebäude c. eine sehr lustige Person

Put it together   Example: Meine jüngere Schwester und mein älterer Bruder sind sehr verschieden. Sie ist eine sehr optimistische und freundliche Person. Er ist ein sehr kluger und ruhiger Mensch. Meine Schwester ist sehr klein, aber mein Bruder ist sehr groß. Sie sehen gar nicht ähnlich aus.

CONVERSATION 3

Figure it out   **1** a. jogging, für Online-Games b. not, ein bisschen c. in cash, (mit ihrer) Kreditkarte   **2** bar zahlen, Kreditkarte   **3** a. rote b. grüne   **4** die Hälfte kosten, im Angebot sein

Notice   **1** a. sieht, aus b. Woher c. Welche Art d. für   **2** a. der hier b. der rote c. der grüne d. die beste   **3** Examples: a. Nike b. Kleenex c. Pepsi d. Mac e. Audi   **4** a. ein bisschen teurer b. bar zahlen c. mit meiner Kreditkarte zahlen d. Kasse

Practice   **1** a. Wie viel kostet die schwarze? b. Wie ist die Qualität? c. Kann ich das jetzt nehmen? d. Akzeptieren Sie Kreditkarten? e. Ich kann nur bar zahlen. f. Welcher Art von Kabel haben Sie? g. Ist das im Angebot? h. Wo ist die Kasse?   **2** a. roten b. Marke c. Kasse d. große   **3** 1 long 2 easy 3 difficult

Conversation strategy: 'the ... one!'   **1** 1. weiße 2. große 3. alte 4. teurere 5. rechte 6. nette

Put it together   Example: Ich suche etwas. Es ist so groß wie eine Hand. Es ist grau und weiß. Das graue Teil ist hinten und das weiße vorne. Vorne ist ein schwarzer Bildschirm. Man benutzt es, um zu kommunizieren. Es ist sehr schön und teuer. Die Marke heißt 'Apfel' auf Deutsch.

Check your understanding   **2** a. Nein. b. Ein Freund von ihr c. wundervoll d. Es regnet e. Nein

COMPLETE YOUR MISSION

Build your script   Example: In meiner Lieblingsstadt scheint fast immer die Sonne. Es regnet nur manchmal. Die Stadt ist zwischen dem Meer und den Bergen. Im Meer kann man im Sommer schwimmen und in den Bergen kann man im Winter Ski fahren. Die Stadt ist groß aber sehr grün. Es gibt viele schöne Parks und viele breite Straßen mit Bäumen. Die Menschen fahren mit der U-Bahn oder mit dem Fahrrad. Sie sind optimistisch, nett und hilfsbereit. Es gibt viele alte Häuser, aber auch ein paar neue Hochhäuser aus Glas. Die sind modern und beeindruckend! Dort gibt es viele besondere Dinge zu kaufen. Ich möchte bald in meine Lieblingsstadt zurückfliegen. Ich vermisse sie sehr!

ACKNOWLEDGEMENTS

Though my name and face may be on the cover, there are many people whose voices and ideas are in these pages.

I was fortunate to meet many native German speakers who encouraged me when I was a struggling beginner, from my first true conversations in German with my flatmate **Stefanie** to the Berliners I met at language exchange events on a boat on the *Spree*. My German-learning experience has been filled with friends who made the language come alive and gave me the passion to inspire others.

There aren't enough praises I can sing about my editor **Sarah Cole**, who first reached out to me with the exciting prospect of collaborating with *Teach Yourself*. She worked with me over two years with unwavering support and passion for my vision of a modern language course. I cannot imagine that any other publisher could have brought so much life to these courses.

I am grateful to the rest of the *Teach Yourself* team in both the UK and US, who showed incredible enthusiasm in creating a totally new kind of language course. **Eleni Yiannoulidou** worked with me over many months to make large and small improvements to each chapter, and gave extremely helpful feedback all the way. **Melissa Baker** worked behind the scenes to juggle timetables and perform more than a few miracles to ensure all the pieces of this publishing puzzle came together.

This course would not exist without the tireless efforts of Ingo Treunowski and Judith Meyer. Ingo's vast experience as a language learner and keen eye for detail, as well as Judith's immense expertise in teaching German, helped ensure that the content of the course genuinely meets the needs of a modern language learner. **Jan, Clare** and **Alessandra** further helped bring my ideas to life.

I owe a huge thank you to the brilliant people at Team FI3M: **Bálint, David, Kittichai, Dávid, Joe, Ingo, Joseph, Adam, Holly and LC,** who kept my website and community, *Fluent in 3 Months*, running while I was busy writing these courses.

Finally, my partner **Lauren**, without whom this course never could have come to light. She is the Pepper Potts to my Tony Stark – she makes sure my crazy ideas run smoothly and professionally, and she came up with many of the cleverest concepts that you see in these pages. Her perfectionism and academic background turned my ideas for a good course, into a truly great one.